CARGO THEFT, LOSS PREVENTION, AND SUPPLY CHAIN SECURITY

CARGO THEFT, LOSS PREVENTION, AND SUPPLY CHAIN SECURITY

BY DAN BURGES

AMSTERDAM • BOSTON • HEIDELBERG • LONDON • NEW YORK • OXFORD
PARIS • SAN DIEGO • SAN FRANCISCO • SINGAPORE • SYDNEY • TOKYO

Butterworth-Heinemann is an imprint of Elsevier

Butterworth-Heinemann is an imprint of Elsevier
225 Wyman Street, Waltham, MA 02451, USA
The Boulevard, Langford Lane, Kidlington, Oxford, OX5 1GB, UK

Notices

Knowledge and best practice in this field are constantly changing. As new research and experience broaden
our understanding, changes in research methods, professional practices, or medical treatment may become
necessary.

Practitioners and researchers must always rely on their own experience and knowledge in evaluating and
using any information, methods, compounds, or experiments described herein. In using such information or
methods they should be mindful of their own safety and the safety of others, including parties for whom
they have a professional responsibility.

To the fullest extent of the law, neither the Publisher nor the authors, contributors, or editors, assume any
liability for any injury and/or damage to persons or property as a matter of products liability, negligence or
otherwise, or from any use or operation of any methods, products, instructions, or ideas contained in the
material herein.

Library of Congress Cataloging-in-Publication Data
Burges, Dan.
Cargo theft, loss prevention, and supply chain security / by Dan Burges.
p. cm.
Includes index.
ISBN 978-0-12-416007-1
1. Cargo theft-Prevention. 2. Cargo theft. 3. Business logistics. I. Title.
HV6652.B87 2012
658.4'73–dc23
                    2012007344

For information on all Butterworth-Heinemann
publications visit our website at www.elsevierdirect.com

Printed in the United States of America
12 13 14 15 10 9 8 7 6 5 4 3 2 1

Working together to grow
libraries in developing countries

www.elsevier.com | www.bookaid.org | www.sabre.org

ELSEVIER   BOOK AID
            International   Sabre Foundation

DEDICATION

To my wife and children, whose love and affection are the light of my life.

Team Burges

CONTENTS

PREFACE

Why Is This Book Needed?

In early May 2009, an organized crime group specializing in cargo theft was observed by police in Plainfield, Indiana. On an almost daily basis in the United States gangs are seen staking out logistics hubs across the country in such places as Plainfield, Memphis, Louisville, Atlanta, Miami, and Dallas-Fort Worth. This group was observed driving a late-model green sedan, conducting surveillance throughout several industrial park areas in and around the Indianapolis international airport.

The gang members were from Hialeah, Florida, the epicenter for cargo theft activity in the United States, and quite a distance from Plainfield.

A call to the Miami Tactical Operations Multi-Agency Cargo Anti-Theft Squad (TOMCATS), the nation's most well-known anticargo theft task force, confirmed the group's identity and their status as persons of interest in a number of ongoing investigations. At the TOMCATS' request, the Plainfield Police Department began surveillance of the group.

Eventually the gang left their hotel in Plainfield on Tuesday, May 5, and traveled east on Interstate 70 toward Ohio in a sedan and a "bobtail" (a tractor–trailer without a trailer attached). As the suspects left the jurisdiction of Plainfield, the police surveillance ceased.

At the same time, another big rig departed Plainfield, Indiana, also heading east on Interstate 70 toward Ohio, but this one was pulling a trailer loaded with high-value prescription drugs from a major pharmaceutical company.

Less than 12 hours later, the truck driver of the pharmaceutical shipment stopped at a truck stop along the Pennsylvania Turnpike for fuel and a quick break from the long drive. While the driver was paying for fuel inside the station, his load of pharmaceuticals jolted into motion, this time with a South Florida resident behind the wheel, and in an instant, $37 million in prescription medication was gone.

While it is not every day that loads of this extreme value are stolen on our nation's highways, cargo theft is, however, occurring multiple times every single day. In 2010 there was an average of two and a half tractor–trailers loaded with cargo being stolen daily in the United States with an average loss of $471,000 per incident.

Scope and Organization

The purposes of this book are to detail one of the most underreported and misunderstood crimes of our time and to provide a comprehensive methodology for establishing supply chain security and loss prevention programs that will assist in reducing theft and keeping cargo secure.

This book is presented in two parts. Part 1 covers the problem of cargo theft in detail. While the history of cargo theft goes back to the first time goods were moved from one point to another, this book focuses on the cargo theft problem in the 21st century.

Part 1 provides an in-depth analysis of the methods by which cargo theft occurs, who is committing these crimes, why cargo theft is so lucrative, and why most of the public has never heard of it.

Often people ask me "what do cargo criminals steal?" to which I simply reply, "walk into your house, turn around in a full circle, and everything you see a cargo criminal will steal." Cargo theft is a true market-driven crime. Loads of product are worth nothing to a theft gang unless they can sell them. Buyers of stolen goods have gangs target only items they know they can sell (or have already sold) on the black market. Consumer electronics, food, apparel, computers, building materials, furniture, appliances, liquor, perfume, metals, and pharmaceuticals—the list goes on and on—all of these products are at constant risk of being targeted by criminal elements throughout the year.

This part also discusses cargo theft through multiple modes of transportation, focusing on over the road trucking, but also includes cargo theft via air, ocean, rail, and pipeline. The first half of this book ends with a detailed look at the downstream costs incurred due to cargo theft, which can increase by multiple times over the initial loss value.

Part 2 proposes a methodology for mitigating the risk of cargo theft for both facility (manufacturing, warehousing, and distribution) and in-transit operations. Part 2 also covers the roles of personnel at every level in the supply chain and policies designed to not only secure cargo from origin to destination, but also assist in creating increased supply chain efficiencies beyond simply preventing thefts, as well as technologies available today and methods for employing these technologies into an overall strategy of risk mitigation and cargo recovery in the event of a theft.

Part 2 begins by analyzing methods of determining risk, a critical component to creating a logistics and security plan. Factors such as product type, geography (cities and states where cargo is shipped, transits through, stopped, or stored), existing security and in-transit security policies, and the ways supply chain channel and transportation partners are selected and audited to ensure compliance all have an impact on the potential for loss.

The goal of this book is to provide a clear understanding of the threat cargo theft poses to the national economy, along with the impact to individual supply chain stakeholders from the manufacturer all the way to the consumer. Additionally, the book provides a variety of methods and concepts for ensuring that cargo remains secure from origin to destination.

Once risk is determined, a methodology and level of security can be established using a layered approach including personnel, policies, and technology to ensure that the supply chain security plan is not reliant on a single person or device but rather an interwoven system that incorporates redundancies, thus casting a true net of security around cargo. Unfortunately, there is no silver bullet in cargo theft prevention; therefore, creating a combination (and at times even overlapping) of physical and procedural controls is a shipper's best bet. Chapter 13: Physical Security and Chapter 14: In-Transit Security discuss the multiple components necessary for a complete supply chain security and cargo theft prevention program, as well as providing a template for policy creation in both of these critical areas.

One of the most advanced methods of ensuring in-transit cargo security today is the concept of active monitoring. Active monitoring provides a combination of all three layers of a supply chain security program (people, policies, and technology) by which a shipper can establish in-transit security protocols for transportation providers. These policies are agreed to and provided to a third-party monitoring (command and control) center. This monitoring center is responsible for tracking shipments en route, sending location and other relevant data through covert, usually embedded, tracking devices. Covered extensively in Chapter 15: Active Monitoring, this concept has proven over time to be a most efficient and effective risk-mitigating tool; it can also be used by shippers for ancillary, yet important, purposes such as confirming transportation provider compliance with preshipment instructions such as routing, stopping points, and the like. Moreover, in the event that a theft occurs, response time is virtually immediate with the monitoring center able to contact local law enforcement and provide them with an accurate location of the stolen truck and cargo. If you read only one chapter in Part 2 of this book, I strongly encourage you to spend your time on Chapter 15: Active Monitoring, as it provides a step-by-step methodology for creating, implementing, and maintaining a program that will provide monitored in-transit cargo security.

At the end of each chapter in this book is a short summary of the primary or key points that the reader should take away. As industry professionals, educators, students, and crime enthusiasts, we all have busy lives and taking the hours to read every page is not always a luxury we have. If this applies to you and a summation is what you need, simply go to the end of each chapter and read these key points to ensure that you capture the primary elements of each chapter.

Additional resources are provided at the end of this book as well, including companies and organizations where additional information, products, and services can be found for supply chain security and theft prevention programs.

There are a variety of industry associations dedicated to spreading the word about cargo theft, sharing security best practices, and assisting members in discerning emerging threats and methods that thieves are using to victimize shippers, transportation providers, and other supply chain interests. Many of these organizations are discussed in this book, with contact details provided in the Resource section at the back of the book.

FOREWORD

One of the most thought-provoking books I read at the beginning of the new millennium was Thomas Friedman's "The World Is Flat." He was one of the first I remember having called out the way in which traditional boundaries, geographical and historical, that defined our world up to that time were collapsing around us as the economic advantages of globalization were pursued.

While I don't recall the more subtle points of all of the "flatteners" described by Friedman, those he made in the area of supply chains left impressions that have stuck with me. Although I was not at Dell at the time, I particularly remember what's referred to as his "Dell Theory of Conflict Prevention" or the notion that no two countries that are both part of the same global supply chain, like Dell's, will ever fight a war against each other. I guess only time will tell whether that proposition proves true. The title also alludes to the perceptual shift required of countries, companies, and individuals who wish to remain competitive in a global market where historical and geographical divisions are becoming increasingly irrelevant

In addition to perceptual shifts, real-world tactical shifts are also required as we grapple with the challenges of this new world. To help us avoid the pitfalls that would otherwise undermine the realization of the advantages of a globalized supply chain, experts like Dan Burges help us understand the risks of this new attenuated terrain. Dan particularly provides a clear understanding of the threat cargo theft poses in that world not only to the individual supply chain stake-holders—from the manufacturer all the way to the consumer—but to the national economy generally. To that understanding he adds a practical mix of methods and concepts for ensuring that cargo remains secure from origin to destination in a well-reasoned manner that prudently assesses risk and an entity's tolerance of it.

Many of us may lament the passing of a world in which discrete boundaries of interests could be rigidly defined. Out of the ensuing obscurity comes an opportunity—a necessity—to collaborate with critical partners in a way that will assure our interests will continue to be protected against unacceptable risks.

The cogent taxonomy Dan provides here should prove a valuable tool in the hands of security practitioners charged with that responsibility.

John E. McClurg
Austin, Texas, Winter 2011

ACKNOWLEDGMENTS

I thank Barry Conlon, CEO of FreightWatch, without whom I would have never entered the world of cargo security.

To Barry Tarnef, who has mentored me from my first day in the cargo security community—and without whom this book would not exist—never once asking for anything in return and being my sounding board before my frequent attempts to dive off the deep end. Barry, you're a consummate professional and valued mentor.

To John McClurg for not only writing the foreword to this book, but for being what I aspire to be.

Thank you to my parents who always knew those countless essays would pay off.

This acknowledgement would not be complete without thanking Ed Petow, Chuck Forsaith, Fred Burton, Dennis Stabile, Graciela Martinez, all the great people at FreightWatch, John Tabor, Kevin Johnson, Rich Widup, Alan Spear, John Monetta, Brandon Stroud, Victor Garcia, Joey Reed (Go Devils), Willie Morales, Mike McDonnell, Allen Gear, Tom Stimach, and the Microsoft Supply Chain Security team.

A very special thank you to the Starbucks Coffee Company, without whom civilization would be far less civilized.

To Fred Burton, whose mentorship, guidance, and inspiration have touched countless people and have meant the world to me. I'm truly blessed to have worked for you and with you.

A special thanks to Rick Adams, David Bevans, Amber Hodge, and the wonderful people at Butterworth-Heinemann for all their assistance, coaching, and faith in me on this project.

Finally, this acknowledgment would not be complete without the most sincere of thanks to two gentlemen—Tony Jeary and JB Glossinger. In early 2010 I spent a half day with Tony and it turned my life upside down, propelling me toward my goals and dreams in ways I could never have imagined. The wisdom and guidance Tony provided to me, taking time from his day-to-day coaching of the world's top CEOs, left an unmistakable mark on my consciousness and the clarity and focus I need to execute at the highest levels. And to JB Glossinger—I would not have written this book without JB's daily inspiration, giving me the drive to make it through the hard times and excel in the good times, improving by 1% every day.

ABOUT THE AUTHOR

Dan Burges CPP

Dan is the senior director of intelligence at FreightWatch International, where he specializes in supply chain intelligence and risk analysis. He is responsible for FreightWatch's global intelligence division, as well as the company's security assessment program. Dan started with the company as a business analyst, growing the intelligence division from the ground up. Previously, he was a security analyst with Strategic Forecasting's security division.

Dan has been featured providing supply chain security analysis for numerous media outlets, including the *Wall Street Journal*, CBS News, Fox News, *BusinessWeek*, *Newsweek*, the *International Herald Tribune*, and the *Financial Times*. He also writes for a variety of industry and trade publications and is a columnist for *Cargo Security International*.

Before joining FreightWatch, Dan served in the U.S. Army as a military police and antiterrorism officer. In 2003 he was deployed to Baghdad, Iraq, where he was awarded the Bronze Star for 18 months of service in the Middle East, overseeing security and antiterrorism operations at a forward operating base. Dan also served as duty officer at the U.S. detention center in Guantanamo Bay, Cuba, in 2002.

Dan is a graduate of the U.S. Military Academy at West Point where he received a degree in Political Science and Nuclear Engineering. He also holds a Master's degree in Criminology and the Certified Protection Professional designation. Dan lives in the Dallas/Fort Worth metroplex with his wife and two children.

UNDERSTANDING THE PROBLEM

CARGO THEFT 101

INFORMATION IN THIS CHAPTER:

- Overview of cargo theft in the United States
- What criminals target and how they steal in-transit cargo
- Summary of downstream costs from cargo theft
- Overview of industry efforts to combat theft gangs
- Discussion of government supply chain initiatives and their relation to theft prevention

Known as the "silent" or victimless crime, cargo theft ultimately costs the U.S. economy several billion dollars annually. At this point we are only able to give an estimated magnitude of the crime. Across the country, trailers loaded with hundreds of thousands of dollars in electronics, pharmaceuticals, clothing, tobacco, and other high-value goods are being stolen at an alarming rate right out from under the noses of those who make, store, and ship the goods that fuel our stream of commerce. And while the cargo theft gangs turn huge profits for crimes that carry very little risk, their victims are left scrambling to pick up the pieces.

Truck stops, parking lots, and other unsecured locations are becoming a veritable battleground between cargo criminals and those tasked with moving and securing goods in transit. What's more, the downstream costs incurred by our nation's manufacturers and shippers as a result of cargo theft exacerbate the direct monetary losses due to hidden and typically unbudgeted charges.

These are the costs that inflate the total value of theft incidents exponentially—costs that manufacturers bear in the short term as they remake, replace, and reship goods to their originally intended destinations, but costs that are partially borne by them but ultimately paid for by all of us at the cash register.

According to FreightWatch International, 899 cargo theft incidents occurred in 2010, a record high since FreightWatch began tracking cargo theft in 2006 (Burges, 2010, p. 2). Other organizations such as CargoNet, Chubb Insurance, and the Supply Chain Information Sharing and Analysis Center (SC-ISAC) all report comparable numbers using a variety of methods of collecting statistics and incident data.

While definitions of cargo theft vary and estimates of product loss values range from $8 to $30 billion per year, it is clear that this problem is having a devastating impact on the bottom lines of companies. Understanding the full impact of cargo theft on supply chain operations—and creating cutting-edge technologies and solutions to stay ahead of the gangs—is the imperative of all professionals in and around the industry, not just the ones whose companies are currently suffering losses.

In 2009, more than $188 million in pharmaceuticals alone were stolen off America's highways. The following year that sector suffered another $185 million in cargo losses. This is despite the fact that the drug industry has been securing its supply chains and fighting cargo crime on a national level since 2005, the year it became apparent to industry professionals that large-scale pharmaceutical theft had moved well beyond the discrete and seemingly random.

The forerunner in developing cargo theft prevention standards, however, was the high-tech industry, which has been tangling with theft gangs for well over a decade. Facing full-truckload losses of computers, cellular phones, televisions, gaming consoles, accessories, and more since the late 1990s, industry logistics and security professionals began sharing information. This led to the formation in October 1997 of the Technology Asset Protection Association, now the Transported Asset Protection Association (TAPA). As the number of thefts continued to rise into the 21st century, however, industry professionals became keenly aware that it was no longer a question of "if" a company was going to suffer a loss, but rather "when."

With this dose of reality as the motivating factor and information-sharing groups such as TAPA the means, in-transit security policies and procedures and formalized warehouse security standards for the manufacturing and distribution network came into existence.

And sure enough, these protective measures worked. Companies that began hardening the supply chain by implementing security protocols saw a marked decrease in cargo theft. However, the cargo thieves did what they do best: they adapted. With the vast U.S. supply chain providing virtually unlimited opportunities, the criminals simply adjusted their operations to target the weakest links—focusing on trailers left unattended in unsecured parking areas, facilities with minimal security systems, and transportation providers and intermediaries not following standard security practices. By ratcheting up defenses at fixed sites such as manufacturing plants, warehouses, and distribution centers and in transit, these early adopters essentially made themselves less vulnerable than others and, in effect, just redirected cargo thieves to seek out facilities and mobile assets lacking adequate protection.

The lack of formal theft reporting results in wild variations in estimates of total annual losses. In 2006, as part of the PATRIOT ACT renewal, cargo theft was added to the list of crimes that must be reported to the Uniform Crime Report (UCR). Despite this 6-year-old mandate, data have yet to be collected and entered by the Federal Bureau of Investigation (FBI), the law enforcement agency responsible for the UCR.

Organizations and private companies that track cargo theft and share data within the supply chain industry are able to capture the majority of high-value cargo thefts through company records, informal networks, law enforcement sources, open source documents, and other means. However, it is the unknown quantity of unreported lower-value thefts that makes estimating the total value of cargo theft such an exercise in futility.

No one can say for sure the true impact of cargo theft because it is one of the most underreported and underinvestigated crimes in the nation—hence its "silent crime" label. Yet it is one of if not *the* property crime with the highest payoff in the United States. According to Jared Palmer, general counsel at AFN, a third-party logistics provider (3PL), if all types of thefts were combined, including identity theft, bank robberies, jewelry theft, and others, their total loss would not equal the amount of losses suffered at the hands of cargo thieves.

Even in those cases where cargo theft incidents are reported to police, investigations can be more basic and involve fewer details as police forces and their resources are pulled into other, more pressing criminal matters, such as violent crimes, and if a culprit is apprehended and convicted, sentencing is light, with prison time rarely served. Cargo thieves take full advantage of the justice system, as arrested suspects released on minimal bail immediately return to their lucrative activities.

With cargo theft up 144% from 2006 through 2010 and no indication that thieves are becoming less active, the onus is on the logistics and supply chain security professionals to be forward-thinking, creative, and proactive in instituting effective in-transit and physical security procedures.

Evolution of Cargo Theft

And the problem is growing. Cargo theft increased annually by 5 to 15% from 2005 through 2010. Additionally, the average loss per incident increased dramatically, by more than 60% over the same time period. Single thefts resulting in seven-figure losses have become commonplace as thieves target specific, high-end products that can be fenced and sold easily on the black market. Prolific cargo theft gangs travel across the country, from south to north and east to west, seeking goods they have been tasked to steal and then transporting them, often to major cities on the East Coast or Los Angeles for sale on the black market, or to maritime ports for export principally to Latin America and Europe. From there, the stolen products are sold through a variety of methods, sometimes being reshipped to the United States for reintroduction into our domestic supply chain. This presents a twofold loss for the owner of the goods—not only do they not reap the benefit from the sale but an end consumer acquires their product at a significantly lower price.

The impact of a cargo theft goes well beyond the monetary loss that results from the stolen load or a warehouse burglary. Effects can be in the form of increased cost of goods to higher insurance premiums to decreased market share. Companies hit repeatedly by cargo thieves are compromised in their ability to deliver safe and reliable products on time and intact to the marketplace, resulting in loss of consumer confidence. Looking further downstream, additional costs resulting from cargo theft include manufacturing replacement goods, lost time and efficiency, potential product recalls, increased consumer prices, and the loss of intellectual property rights. All of these have direct impacts on the victimized company, the industry as a whole, and the U.S. consumer market, all of which pay for cargo theft.

Because of this, corporations are losing their tolerance for cargo losses, with many adapting more aggressive strategies to prevent theft. Using internal resources, external supply chain security consultants along with mandating security procedures to 3PLs and others who have the cargo in their care, custody, and control at some point, corporations are leading the way in cargo theft prevention and innovation. At the same time, they are growing more and more determined to see thieves prosecuted.

Unfortunately for the corporate security manager, it is an uphill battle, as well-organized, internationally connected and highly motivated cargo theft gangs continue to adapt their methods and redouble their efforts, meting every prevention strategy/tactic with another way to get at high-value, theft-attractive products. Furthermore, criminals who are arrested, even ones charged with thefts of goods worth millions of dollars, face notoriously low bail and shockingly light prison sentences— if they even bother to appear for trial. By avoiding violence in the commission of their crimes, unlike armed robbers, cargo thieves fly largely under the radar of most law enforcement, as well as the media whose coverage of these crimes could begin to shed some light on the serious scope of the problem.

Despite the significant toll cargo theft can have on a company's bottom line and a nation's productive output, surprisingly little is known about the gangs that repeatedly manage to steal full truckloads of multimillion-dollar product, make six-figure profits for a few days' work, and then vanish without a trace. The most prolific of these are the Cuban cargo theft gangs. Based in south Florida, primarily the Hialeah area, they have applied their knowledge and skills to a more lucrative trade, stealing cargo for brokers who have already made arrangements for their sale in bulk on the black market or to foreign companies that specialize in repackaging and reselling products to legitimate companies.

South Florida is not the only base of operation for cargo theft gangs. Los Angeles, Dallas/Fort Worth, and the New York/North Jersey areas are also known hubs of cargo theft activity, where cell members, while connected by ethnicity, work under a loose structure, different from traditional organized crime groups.

Targeting

There's a reason why cargo thieves target high-value, easily moveable, and "marketed" items. Cargo theft is a market-driven crime, and thieves simply steal what consumers want to buy by simply understanding our purchasing patterns. There's a method by which cargo theft gangs operate. With hundreds of thousands of tractor–trailers crisscrossing the United States on a daily basis, thieves generally do not simply pick a truck at random and see what they get nor do they decide one day to go out and steal a load of televisions or pharmaceuticals. For structure and direction in this seemingly endless sea of available cargo, they look for guidance from the broker.

Brokers, individuals who make their living buying and selling stolen merchandise on the U.S. black market, as well as through international firms (both legitimate and illegitimate), drive the market for stolen goods. These are the people placing the orders with professional cargo theft gangs for certain products, especially name-brand high-value commodities. But these are not purchase orders per se. They are orders to steal, and the broker pays the thieves pennies on the dollar, knowing he will make between 20 and 40% of the load's retail value.

To determine which products to target, the broker first asks the question that ultimately powers the nation's economy: What will the consumer buy? Televisions, computers, cell phones, bottled drinks, clothing, and pharmaceuticals—these are all products that can be found in households across America. And if the consumer will buy it, the cargo thief will steal it.

The purchasing of illicit products is not as foreign as one may think. "Who purchases stolen product?" is a common question. The answer is we do or, more accurately, consumers do. Indeed, brokers are incredibly skillful at reintroducing stolen product into the legitimate supply chain through shell companies, often based in Latin America. By offering discounted rates on high volumes of products, they easily sell to low-margin retailers who are unaware of the illicit nature of their purchase. Then the consumer becomes the final purchaser, fanning the flames of cargo theft, while manufacturers and distributors are left to bear the loss, of course, ultimately passing it down to consumers in the form of higher prices.

In the theft-to-order scenario, cargo thieves receive an order from a broker, or other purchaser, for a particular product or type of product. The theft gang commences research, finding where its targeted goods are manufactured, distributed, and shipped. The gang, generally three to six members, then travels to the location of the targeted product. Traveling economically, the gang will rent an economical car (usually having a girlfriend or someone without any direct connection to the gang handle the transaction), stay in a budget motel, and commence surveillance on the targeted facility.

While some theft gangs specialize in burglarizing warehouses and distribution centers, the vast majority of large-scale cargo thefts occur while loads are in transit. The gang will use surveillance to gather intelligence on transportation patterns; what time trailers are picked up; what companies are providing transportation services; routing; and if any stops are made near the point of departure.

In the most typical of cargo theft scenarios, the cargo theft gang identifies a loaded trailer at its point of departure and then follows the trailer from a safe distance until the driver stops and leaves the load unattended. The gang then moves in, stealing the tractor—trailer and its entire load in the blink of an eye.

Traditionally, the area at highest risk for in-transit theft is within 200 miles of the point of departure. Known as the "red zone," this stretch of road continues to be the area in which drivers must remain most aware of their surroundings and ensure they stop only in the event of an emergency. However, cargo theft gangs are now willing to travel incredible distances, with thefts occurring well over 500 miles from the point of origin.

Downstream Costs

America's manufacturers, distributors, and logistics/transportation companies suffer billions of dollars in direct losses annually. Unfortunately, these losses are only the tip of the iceberg, with a slew of associated costs inflating the total impact of the base amount.

Unplanned replacement manufacturing and assembly, expedited shipping, loss of competitive advantage, future sales and market share, increased marketing efforts to, inter alia, deal with concerned customers, insurance costs (deductibles and potential future premium increases), administrative time to report the claim, complete the requisite paperwork, and conduct preliminary investigation, and, in some instances, product liability issues and recall expenses all contribute to the total extent of loss that can be incredibly hard to quantify. These losses are not all absorbed by the companies that suffer the losses, rather some of the expense is ultimately passed down to the consumer.

The pharmaceutical and food industries face added complications when their products are stolen. When mishandled, products made to be ingested, injected, or eaten present consumer safety issues, and thus substantial corporate reputational (brand) concerns. In addition to protecting consumers from stolen product that might be tainted, companies have no choice but to spend millions more to recall and destroy perfectly good product that reached the shelves legitimately but happened to share the same lot number with a stolen product.

Cargo Theft Prevention

Where does the burden of responsibility lie when it comes to cargo theft prevention? When considering violent crimes such as murder, robbery, assault, and so on, many look to law enforcement agencies for crime prevention. While police (and punishments for convicted criminals) may serve a role in deterrence, Americans quite commonly take small steps to ensure their personal safety, such as locking the front door when leaving for the day, not walking down a dark alley at night, or parking in a well-lighted area. Similarly, each participant in the supply chain must take steps to deter cargo crime. From corporate security managers at manufacturing sites down to the transportation provider's driver, each member of the supply chain bears some of the responsibility for securing goods. But this will not happen on its own. It must be mandated from the top down with compliance checked to ensure that each provider is following prescribed procedures.

The use of private security in the supply chain is not new, although most of us think about manguarding at static facilities such as warehouses and distribution centers. What has been growing steadily over the past decade is the use of private security for over the road (in-transit) shipments. This role most assuredly does not duplicate that of law enforcement, as private security is focused primarily on theft prevention, whereas law enforcement's job is to attempt to recover cargo after it is stolen. However, some private security firms also are becoming deeply involved in the recovery process as well, using electronic cargo tracking to learn in real time when a load is off course and then notifying police and assisting them in locating the stolen cargo.

One particular electronic-tracking methodology is the use of embedded, covert tracking devices coupled with active monitoring that allows for shippers to "see" where their cargo is at all times, regardless of its location. This method of tracking has significantly increased the security of in-transit cargo and led to a spike in the recovery of stolen goods and the prosecution of numerous cargo thieves. It has also launched a new era in which private security and law enforcement now work hand in hand tracking down criminals and bringing them to justice.

Cargo theft affects a broad spectrum of stakeholders, most notably the product owner, often a manufacturer or a distributor that purchased the product. Others include freight forwarders and 3PLs, carriers, private security firms, insurance companies, police agencies, and the U.S. government (Departments of Justice, Commerce and Agriculture, and the Food and Drug Administration, to name a few). Each of these entities has a direct interest in cargo theft in the United States, largely because they regulate product being shipped, are responsible to protect cargo from loss, investigate cargo theft, and provide financial support for the losses. Also, each plays a significantly different role in keeping cargo secure.

The product owner is primarily responsible for loss prevention, using either in-house staff or independent supply chain/logistics security firms to assist. Freight forwarders and 3PLs share the task of product security, often complying with security measures directed by the product owner. The U.S. government regulates interstate shipping and ships product itself.

Insurance companies assist with loss prevention (best practices), loss mitigation, and subrogation tools to fairly allocate losses, as well as providing financial restitution to victims. And the police respond when losses occur, investigate and attempt to recover the product, and arrest the culprits. Cargo theft task forces exist in several states where theft is the most severe; these local, state, and/or federal agency units investigate cargo theft gangs actively, building cases against their members and assisting in recovering stolen goods.

Lack of In-Transit Security

it is not surprising that corporations pour millions of dollars into their physical and information technology security programs. Fences, cameras, alarms, motion detectors, and security officers are all considered by many as critical to the security of their company and product. An amazing truth in supply chain security, however, is that these same companies put multimillion-dollar loads into a trailer driven by someone they do not know, whose identification they did not check, who may or may not actually work for the transportation provider they claim to represent, and may not think twice about whether the load will arrive at its destination safely—or at all. From a virtual fortress to a trailer that doesn't even have a padlock on the door, this disparity is never realized until a company suffers its first full-truckload theft, and sometimes not even then.

A frequent question regarding cargo theft and its prevention is "What are the police doing about it?" While it is understandable to look to law enforcement for answers, the simple truth is that law enforcement cannot and does not serve in a theft prevention role, particularly in the supply chain. With hundreds of thousands of loads on the nation's roads at a given time, it is simply not practical to think police alone can make a dent in in-transit theft.

A good comparison is home security. As much as regular police patrols offer some comfort, the average homeowner does not rely solely on the police to prevent his home from being burglarized. Instead, he locks the doors and windows, perhaps has an alarm system installed, or opts for monitoring by a third-party security provider. All of these are personal steps taken by the owner to prevent a theft from occurring, none of which is reliant on law enforcement.

While it is incumbent upon every person that touches cargo to keep it secure and mitigate the risk of theft, the true responsibility lies with the shipper. Supply chain security policies and procedures, contractual agreements, visibility of every leg of the cargo's journey, and the ability to audit compliance with every supplier are crucial to a safe and sound supply chain. These steps, however, are often seen as too overbearing on suppliers or too costly or burdensome on the shipper.

Cargo theft is nothing new. Going back centuries, criminals attacked merchant ships, pilfered from loading docks, held up trains, and robbed stagecoaches on horseback. As transportation has evolved with new technology—superfreighters replacing wooden ships and tractor–trailers replacing horse-drawn wagons—so too have cargo criminals. Today's road pirates are organized at the international level, stealing, storing, and moving goods throughout the world while reaping profits measured in the billions of dollars.

Cargo Theft and Customs–Trade Partnership Against Terrorism (Theft Prevention vs Supply Chain Security)

After the attacks of September 11, 2001, fighting terrorism became the focus of virtually every law enforcement agency in the United States, especially at the federal level. Agents from the FBI, customs, and other organizations were moved from their daily assignments to work leads on terrorism plots aimed at the American public. During this transition, the U.S. supply chain was identified as a significant gap in the nation's security. The fear was that the supply chain could be exploited for purposes beyond the usual smuggling of stolen products, people, and narcotics—that it could be used by nefarious groups to smuggle a weapon of mass destruction into the country.

One solution to this problem was the establishment of the Customs–Trade Partnership Against Terrorism (C-TPAT) program. A voluntary initiative between the U.S. government and businesses, C-TPAT was established as a means of enticing businesses to adopt minimum security standards throughout their supply chains in return for fewer inspections and faster clearance at our ports of entry. The program's ultimate goal is to prevent the supply chain from being used by terrorist organizations for illicit purposes. Due to the massive volume of freight being imported on a daily basis, however, customs and border protection (CBP) simply does not have the manpower or equipment to screen every piece of cargo entering the country; therefore, one of the pillars of C-TPAT was to have U.S. importers assist CBP by vetting their overseas suppliers and their shipping practices so there would be end-to-end visibility of shipments.

Because of this, CBP has reached out to businesses, providing a set of security guidelines and a system of rewards for complying with them. So, a company that meets or exceeds these guidelines not only gains increased security, it also gets fewer CBP inspections, expedited processing for inspections, eligibility for the CBP Importer Self-Assessment program (ISA), and other benefits. Customs' goal is that by providing preferential treatment to their trusted trade partners, more companies will enter the program and remain compliant (Mento, 2004, p. 10).

In 2001, approximately 2% of all cargo coming into the United States was inspected (Tirschwell, 2003, p. 6). U.S. Customs (and later Homeland Security) quickly realized that this presented a significant threat to national security, which could not be mitigated through government action alone. The sheer volume of goods entering the domestic stream of commerce, coupled with the massive delays that a 100% inspection policy would cause, made such an action Draconian.

Based on their level of compliance and validation status with CPB, an importer is assigned a tier level. Each tier has specific requirements to meet, with more advanced levels requiring increased security and compliance efforts. Accordingly, however, no matter an importer's status, the aforementioned incentives are there.

Tier 1: In this, the basic level of C-TPAT certification, importers must show that they have met the minimum standards established by CBP. Tier 1 importers are subjected to fewer inspections during the import process compared to non-C-TPAT importers. They are also eligible for expedited cargo processing at the border ("FAST" lanes), receive "front of line" inspection privileges at ports should an inspection be required, and are eligible for ISA programs, as well as being able to attend C-TPAT training seminars. Of course another benefit that no one really wanted to contemplate was the fact that if a U.S. port did experience a major disruption, C-TPAT importers would be first to be processed when operations resumed.

Tier 2: Additional commitment demonstrated by an importer as a result of having undergone validation by CBP can make them eligible for Tier 2 status. A Tier 2 importer receives all the same advantages as a Tier 1 importer, but has significantly fewer security-related inspections of cargo.

Tier 3: For importers proven to exceed the minimum security criteria and having adopted what CBP considers security best practices can be granted Tier 3 status. A Tier 3 importer enjoys all the benefits of Tier 1 and Tier 2 and is subject to infrequent, at port, inspections. Tier 3 status is also a precursor to CBPs "Green Lane," a zero inspection program (except for occasional random inspections) for importers meeting established criteria, including shipment through a Container Security Initiative port and the use of prescribed (e.g., security seals that meet ISO PAS 17712 physical and mechanical specifications) container security devices.

The overall impact of C-TPAT has been an increased awareness on the part of importers and their supply chain partners with regards to basic security in preventing unauthorized product from being inserted into a container or trailer for transit into the United States. While this represents a clear improvement in overall supply chain security, there is a clear distinction between the goals of C-TPAT and those of companies looking to reduce their in-transit cargo losses. In a very basic sense, attaining C-TPAT status at the minimum allows a U.S. importer to get a holistic view of its supply chain and then can discover any security gaps along the path.

C-TPAT's primary end game is preventing weapons of mass destruction from being introduced into the U.S. supply chain. Because of this, container/trailer integrity is paramount, with seven-point inspection loading procedures and proper use of high-security seals being major focal points. The seven-point inspection consists of:

1. Front wall
2. Left side
3. Right side
4. Floor
5. Ceiling/roof
6. Inside/outside doors
7. Outside/undercarriage

While this clearly increases overall security, such efforts have little impact on theft prevention when viewed through the cargo theft lens. These security best practices do not prevent a thief from stealing an entire tractor–trailer while it is stopped or from opening container doors with a pair of bolt cutters and unloading the product from the back. In C-TPAT terms, the quick identification of a broken seal, which occurs when a container's doors are opened, would evidence load tampering. While vital for homeland security, this is not truly a theft-prevention measure.

However, any measure that would raise supply chain security awareness helps.

This distinction between antiterrorism security and theft prevention is critical. While they both serve vital roles in a company's secure and efficient supply chain, they are vastly different from one another, with only some overlap in basic practices. As such, a company that is C-TPAT compliant may be at extreme risk for cargo theft due to in-transit practices. Understanding and being able to recognize these differences are vital to a successful cargo security and theft prevention program.

Key Points

- Cargo theft has a serious financial impact on the U.S. economy that is not fully understood.
- What started with the high-tech sector in the late 1990s, the modern era of cargo theft now affects virtually every manner of consumer good.
- Cargo theft is committed by gangs that specialize in tractor–trailer theft and facility burglaries. The three most prolific gangs in the United States operate out of south Florida, New York/North Jersey, and the Los Angeles area.
- Cargo theft is known as the "silent crime" because these crimes are generally not prioritized by law enforcement and the judicial system. This is in large part due to the lack of violence associated with cargo theft, with less than 2% of cargo theft involving confrontation or force.
- It is the responsibility of every supply chain constituent to ensure cargo security.
- C-TPAT compliance does not necessarily equate to a secure supply chain. C-TPAT is aimed at preventing terrorist attacks, not cargo theft. Therefore, meeting minimum standards may not necessarily translate into less cargo theft. However, it is a start or a component to any existing security program.

CARGO THEFT DEFINED

INFORMATION IN THIS CHAPTER:

* Cargo theft defined
* Discussion of full truckload thefts—the preferred targets of cargo criminals
* Analysis of how, when, and where thefts occur
* Discussion of facility burglaries and other forms of cargo theft

> *Distrust and caution are the parents of security.*
>
> **Benjamin Franklin**

What Is Cargo Theft?

Cargo theft presents a unique and difficult challenge to manufacturers, distributors, terminal operators, third-party logistics providers, and transportation providers. While they create programs to secure facilities and product as they pass through a truly global supply chain at the same time being exposed to exploitation by creative and highly motivated theft gangs. FreightWatch International defines cargo as "partial or entire shipments, containers, or cartons of property which are contained in or on a trailer, motor truck, aircraft, vessel, rail, warehouse, freight station, freight consolidation facility, or air navigation facility." While cargo can be stolen at any point in the supply chain, the majority of large-scale losses in the United States involve the theft of loaded tractor–trailers. Warehouse burglaries are also a significant concern due to the likelihood of huge losses in a single incident, but the rate of warehouse burglaries is substantially lower than that of in-transit theft. Other forms of cargo theft involve smaller but more insidious pilferage events that result in fewer dollar losses for the victim, but occur at higher frequencies to make them of interest.

In the United States, cargo thieves are most commonly nonconfrontational and nonviolent. There are two primary methods of in-transit cargo theft. The first is the "potluck" method in which cargo thieves prowl truck stops and other locations seeking unsecured tractor–trailers they can steal, hoping for a load they can sell on the black market. In the second, more prevalent, method, cargo theft gangs actively seek out and track preselected loads of known high-value goods they can sell easily. The thieves then wait patiently to steal the loads when the driver stops and leaves the bounty unattended. Gangs using this method continually target the origin: manufacturers, distribution centers, and other nodes within the supply chain known to house and move the most lucrative goods.

Domestic cargo crime operates within loosely organized, transnational structures, without the strict hierarchy normally associated with traditional crime groups. These teams work independently of each other; moreover, each member has a specific duty, working to fulfill orders for cargo given to them by brokers who sell stolen goods on the black market. Latin American gangs have been the most effective in cargo crime across the nation. They can be neatly categorized into three distinct groups:

- Cuban gangs operating from the Miami, Florida, area
- Ecuadorian gangs operating out of the New York/North Jersey area
- Mexican/Central American gangs based in the Los Angeles Basin (Burges, 2009b)

Cargo theft groups exist in other areas, composed of criminal elements, such as the more traditional "mafia" groups operating in such metropolitan areas as Chicago, Dallas/Fort Worth, Atlanta, and Memphis. These locations suffer from the proliferation of these major cargo theft gangs in addition to their own indigenous players. Also, law enforcement agencies in Columbus, Ohio, have reported new groups of cargo thieves becoming active, made up primarily of members of the local Somali community.

Some street gangs, particularly those in the Los Angeles region, are getting into cargo theft because of its high payoff. While professional cargo theft gangs understand the value of remaining nonviolent in the commission of their crimes, street gangs often resort to such measures because they are inexperienced in cargo theft; for example, they will opt to attack a rig that is already running—and that is hijacking.

Theft of a Trailer

Cargo thieves prefer to target full "over the road" trailers because not only do they get a large quantity of product but it also comes ready for immediate movement to a controlled location where it can be safely off-loaded, stored, and ultimately distributed. Theft of a mixed, or less-than-truckload (LTL), shipment is not as favored because, even though the thieves may acquire their desired product, they also could end up with a majority of goods that have less street cachet. LTL shipments are more commonly involved in smaller, pilferage-type losses.

The saying "cargo at rest is cargo at risk" is well known throughout the supply chain industry. This is because the common denominator in 99% of all recorded full-truckload thefts is the freight was not moving at the time it was stolen. High-value loads left unattended at truck stops, parking lots, terminals, off streets, and other unsecured locations are ideal targets. Even criminals that conduct active surveillance and follow high-value loads for hundreds of miles will wait until the load is stopped and left unattended before they attempt the theft. This isn't necessarily the case in Latin America, the Asia-Pacific region, and some countries in Europe where cargo thieves will use weapons to force a truck driver to stop. This modus operandi (MO) is rarely seen in the United States where hijacking is a more severe crime, carrying tougher sentencing, and apparently simply not worth the risk for cargo thieves.

Cargo theft gangs are extremely proficient at breaking into tractors, starting the vehicles through a variety of methods, and leaving with the stolen product in a manner of minutes. In an interview after he was arrested by the Los Angeles County Sheriff's Department, one cargo thief revealed the ease by which thieves steal tractor—trailers. He also named the make and model of tractors known to be easier to break into and hot-wire.

Gangs will also target preloaded trailers parked at distribution centers and other shipping points for pick up. Certainly there are operational advantages for this practice as it saves time and money because the loaded trailers or containers can be moved away from dock doors, allowing continued activity from them and drivers just have to get in the truck and drive. However, the vulnerability is also present as the loads are highly mobile. The criminals will conduct surveillance on facilities to determine whether loaded trailers are staged and the level of security in place, especially during the time when there is no activity (night and weekends).

If they determine that minimal security is used and the trailers are not being checked they know they may have as much as a 60-hour window (even more if the theft takes place over a holiday weekend) to steal a load from the terminal lot and transport it before the cargo is reported stolen. This allows the criminal to transport the load significant distances without fear of being detected or apprehended. In such cases, there have been occurrences in which a stolen tractor—trailer was pulled over by police for a traffic infraction, a citation issued, and the vehicle released, all because the theft occurred over a weekend and the tractor–trailer had not been discovered missing and reported stolen.

Once the theft has occurred, removing markings such as trailer numbers and logos is often a priority. The gang members accomplish this by stopping in a secluded area and painting over any identifying features that would be noticeable to someone looking for that particular load. They will also remove or change numbers or lettering to make the trailer appear legitimate so it will not be identified as stolen if examined by law enforcement. This technique is being used less often by professional cargo thieves as they have realized that detection by trailer number is remote, as their stolen trailer is simply one of hundreds of thousands on the road at any given time. Additionally, they risk being observed in the act of painting over the numbers on a trailer, and this suspicious behavior could draw a law enforcement response.

Because a very large number of trailers are left unattended with the tractor still attached, the criminals commonly steal the entire rig. When this occurs, the thieves move the stolen tractor–trailer a short distance and then unhook the trailer, abandoning the stolen tractor. This is done for a couple of reasons: first, the tractor likely has a global positioning system (GPS) unit, which the thieves can disable but often will not out of fear that this action will trigger an alert. Second, because tractor markings are often more difficult and time-consuming to disguise, driving around in one "as is" could draw attention from law enforcement, increasing the likelihood of capture.

Instead, the gang will bring a tractor with them, generally one they have stolen in the past and have taken the time to remove tracking devices and distinguishing markings.

After the thieves have hooked up their tractor to the trailer, they will proceed to their destination. This is frequently the South Florida area for loads stolen east of the Rocky Mountains and Los Angeles for those stolen in the West. Using their own form of a supply chain, the criminals will transport, store, and eventually ship the stolen cargo to their buyer. This often involves the use of a warehouse for an extended period of time as the thieves store product that may contain serial numbers or be sought after by police. Then, once the heat dies down and the thieves feel more secure in fencing the stolen product it is moved to a seaport for shipment to Latin America (and sometimes Europe) or to the buyer's warehouse for further distribution and sale on the black market or re-entry into the legitimate market within the United States.

In another method of stealing cargo, albeit one of the more complicated ones, thieves pretending to work for a legitimate carrier pick up loads that freight brokers have posted on the Internet. This MO, which has surfaced more frequently since 2008, is common in the western United States, specifically California. Individuals using this method pose as an existing trucking company and make an online bid to transport a load. The thieves even send falsified paperwork to the freight broker, including copies of their operating authority.

The driver will arrive on site, present a driver's license (which is fake), and will then be given the load never to be seen again. According to the Los Angeles County Sheriff's Department and the California Highway Patrol, use of this MO shows no sign of slowing down. There are other variations on this fraud theme. In the most basic, a cargo thief simply presents himself to a plant, warehouse, or distribution center and either provides documentation or has information that would be consistent with a driver picking up a shipment. The cargo is loaded on the truck and, within a short period of time, the legitimate driver turns up only to be informed that the shipment has already been picked up. One would have to think that the imposter would need to have access to relevant information to pull this off successfully.

The other option, which is far more elaborate and therefore more difficult to ferret out, is when thieves decide to set up their own trucking company, going so far as to obtain operating authority from the Department of Transportation and even purchasing cargo legal liability and other insurance coverage. So in essence there is nothing obviously different about these trucking companies. Of course that is until a shipper tenders a load to them never to be seen or heard from again. Here you have a small initial investment resulting in a large future payoff.

When

Cargo thieves, while operating in a manner unique to their specific "trade," still follow many of the tactics used in the criminal world. For instance, like other thieves, the cargo variety generally prefers to carry out their crimes during periods when they are most likely not to get caught. In the supply chain, this means loads frequently are stolen over weekends, when warehouses and distribution centers are closed, and drivers have left their loads sitting in parking lots, truck stops, and anywhere else they can so they can take the time off. From 2006 to 2010, approximately 68% of all cargo theft incidents occurred between Friday evening and Monday morning. This time frame provides a significant window for thieves to steal the load and transport it long distances without risk of detection (Figure 2.1).

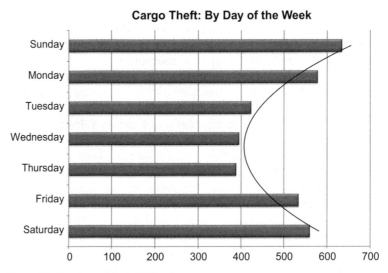

Figure 2.1 Courtesy of FreightWatch.

Again, as said previously, good transit security starts with the shipper, and while it is believed that the most critical component of any cargo-related program is carrier selection and security program compliance, we would be remiss if we made no mention that shippers or their customers (consignees) can make a demonstrable difference when it comes to weekend cargo theft. Many companies have well-defined receiving times at their facilities whether they be plants, warehouses, or distribution centers. These windows are sacrosanct, if not immutable, so all logistical decisions revolve around them.

Case in point, a company is importing containerized goods and wants them delivered to them between 8 and 10 a.m. on a Monday morning. This scenario seems rather innocuous unless you understand the realities of port/marine terminal operations. Many, actually most, terminals do not open until 7 or 8 a.m. so a trucking company has two options:

1. Get in the truck queue first thing Monday morning and hope they can get their "box" in time to make it to their destination at the required time.
2. Pick up the container Friday afternoon, in which case they have plenty of time.

The question is where does the trucker park the loaded container over the weekend? Unfortunately, there is no consistent answer for this as locations chosen by drivers are as diverse as the drivers themselves. Ultimately, and most critically though, is that the most likely location chosen by a driver will not be a secured environment for the cargo, but rather the most convenient location for their chosen activity while biding time.

A similar scene involving the domestic move of a full trailer load can also be made. A shipper gives a shipment to a trucking company on a Thursday or Friday and tells the driver the cargo does not have to be delivered until the following Monday or Tuesday.

If the load is lost in either of these instances, the first impulse is to blame the trucking company and/or driver. When you drill down into the particulars of the loss, perhaps you find other culpable parties.

Nighttime is another period of heightened cargo theft activity, as criminals by their very nature prefer to conduct their activities in the dark, out of eyesight and away from other people. John Tabor, national investigations manager for National Retail Systems, has said if he had to put his entire security budget into one thing, it would be lights. Well-lighted areas deter crime more than any other security feature, as criminals seek darkened areas in order to avoid detection. Additionally, when facilities do not have adequate lighting, surveillance cameras are less effective; the images captured by them are less clear at night, reducing the chances that the criminal will be identified should their activities be recorded.

Locations

More cargo thefts occur at truck stops than at any other place. Of all tractor–trailer cargo theft incidents in the United States, 68% occur in unsecured locations. From these thefts from unsecured locations, the most popular (intuitively) is from truck stops, with 82% of loads from an unsecured location. The reason for this is that unattended loaded tractor–trailers are there. Moreover, the speed at which cargo thieves operate makes every trailer sitting at a truck stop a potential target, regardless of whether the driver spends as little as 5 minutes inside the facility using the restroom and paying for fuel or a few hours showering, eating, and resting.

Of course, thefts occur anywhere tractor–trailers are left unattended. Drop lots (secured and unsecured), distribution centers, big box stores, other retailers, restaurant parking lots, and roadsides along with transportation provider yards are other target-rich environments.

In May 2009 a cargo thief driving a stolen tractor followed a company driver into a secure drop lot and hooked his tractor to a loaded trailer. Then, claiming he was from a different region of the United States and had forgotten the access code, the thief was able to convince the company driver to open the gate. The thief then drove off the lot with more than $200,000 in stolen product, thanks to the unwitting help of the very company he victimized. This incident highlights the risk inherent in leaving loads unattended as well as the creativity (and audacity) thieves will employ to steal them.

As stated previously, cargo theft gangs operate throughout the United States, actively seeking high-value products that can be fenced and sold easily on the black market or to foreign entities. While these gangs travel to wherever the cargo is located, cargo theft is centered primarily in areas with high numbers of manufacturing or distribution centers. Miami, Dallas/Fort Worth, Los Angeles, Atlanta, Memphis, Louisville, New Jersey, and Philadelphia are all known for their high rates of cargo theft. In some of these areas the thieves target a variety of product types. Memphis, for example, has high rates of pharmaceutical theft due to the presence of major drug company and wholesaler distribution centers; New Jersey also experiences a higher rate of stolen pharmaceutical loads due to the fact that there are a number of companies in the area, whereas Dallas/Fort Worth, an electronics manufacturing hub, sees significant amounts of thefts in this category, including cell phones and televisions.

Warehouse Burglaries

Although the primary MO of cargo thieves is to follow a loaded trailer and steal it at the first opportunity, gangs sometimes seek to increase their profits by filling multiple trailers worth of high-end goods in one fell swoop. Hence, warehouse break-ins are a developing trend in the United States. Moreover, less sophisticated "smash-and-grab" thefts are becoming a thing of the past as cargo thieves' techniques become more technologically advanced.

To carry out a successful warehouse/distribution center burglary today, cargo thieves conduct extensive intelligence-gathering and intensive surveillance. The gangs use a variety of techniques to gain information, ranging from the sublime (embedding gang members within intended targets, normally as temporary workers) to the simplistic (Internet searches, observing distribution routines, or simply asking questions). Factors cargo criminals consider in their surveillance mode include watching security officers on site, camera and alarm systems, and lighting.

This is why it is recommended that facility owners and operators deploy their security guards a bit unconventionally. In addition to their normal duties and external threat mindset (concerns with someone entering the premises and/or building), they also need to engage in countersurveillance—watching people who are watching them. Ultimately the thieves will decide whether they have enough data to disable alarm and camera systems without drawing a response from law enforcement.

To make a definitive determination, a common technique is to test a facility's response protocols associated with the alarm system. Gangs will intentionally set off the alarm by shaking or jarring a dock door or window without causing any noticeable damage. They then will retreat to a safe place to observe the response by the company and/or law enforcement. The idea is that after being called to the facility for two or three "false" alarms, management will assume the system is malfunctioning and turn it off. This of course gives the criminals free rein to break into the facility and steal as much product as they can while the facility remains closed. If a security guard from the alarm company or a manager is posted inside the facility while the alarm system is disabled, the gang will either move on to another facility or return another time to try a different MO.

In lieu of setting off the alarm system repeatedly in hopes it will be turned off, gangs also will cut the phone lines to disable the system. However, in case the facility has a redundant transmittal method in place, such as a cellular backup, the thieves will nonetheless try to avoid setting off the alarm. This is often done by cutting a hole in a dock door so that the alarm sensors protecting this access point won't be triggered or by gaining entry through a skylight (again, many facility owners do not factor in attack from above when designing their alarm systems; thieves are now using this way to entry a building so sensors need to be arrayed accordingly). Some gangs have attempted to gain entry by pointing hidden video cameras at a facility's keypad and then summoning a keycard holder to the location by pretending to represent the alarm company.

In one example, a cargo theft gang placed an ashtray/trash can combination by an employee entrance. Attempting to determine what the entry code for the employee door was, the gang hid a camera inside the trash can. The camera was pointed at the keypad in an attempt to record employees entering their entry code. The trash can was eventually discovered by a staff member as being out of place and, upon moving the can, the camera was found (Figure 2.2).

Once inside, the gang seeks out and disables any backup communication devices and closed circuit television (CCTV) systems. Some gangs will also spray paint camera lenses in order

Figure 2.2 Trash can with a camera hidden inside recording employee access codes. Courtesy of FreightWatch.

to reduce footage obtained before the CCTV system can be disabled. Inside information is always extremely beneficial in this process. During a March 2009 burglary in Olive Branch, Mississippi, the gang was captured on video sprinting directly to the alarm and CCTV systems to disable them, clearly they knew exactly where the systems were located.

In the now infamous March 2010 burglary in Enfield, Connecticut, criminals disabled the entire alarm system after lowering themselves through a hole in the roof directly over the room that housed the security communications equipment. These are both clear examples of criminals having extensive knowledge of a facility's layout, the locations of key security components, and the most effective means of disabling them without detection.

After all security and camera systems are disabled or bypassed, the gang will proceed to steal as much product as possible, often using the facility's own forklifts to move large amounts of product to the loading docks and into trailers. Cargo theft gangs are extremely efficient in this process. After viewing footage of a theft gang moving pallets through a warehouse, one manager said he wished his employees were as good forklift drivers as the criminals. As with in-transit cargo theft, gangs will often bring previously stolen tractors with them to a targeted facility and then use on-site trailers for transporting the stolen load. If no trailers are available at the facility, the thieves will have discovered the fact during their preop surveillance and will simply steal them as well.

Warehouse burglaries can be extremely lucrative. While the value of a single full truckload of cellular telephones averages $2.3 million, the net loss from a January 2010 warehouse burglary in Orlando, Florida, broke the $10 million mark.

As with in-transit thefts, the locations of warehouses can also play a major role in a criminal group's decision-making process. A facility located on a well-lighted, heavily trafficked street may present far too much risk for a gang to burglarize and they may opt to try to steal a load that in is transit after departing the facility. In the aforementioned Enfield, Connecticut, burglary, the facility was located in a secluded area and barely visible from the street unfortunately, there was a nice area aerial shot accessible via Google Earth; another facet of cargo criminality that must be considered. The thieves have computers and can look up the same type of information we all do. For example, they can surf the net looking for physical addresses of manufacturers, warehouses, and distributors of certain goods. Additionally, the thieves ensured themselves even more cover from detection because they hit on a night when the weather cooperated, bringing heavy rain and winds, causing substantial damage throughout the community. As of publication of this book, the Enfield warehouse burglary at $76 million is the largest on record.

CASE STUDY: BIG MONEY FOR CREATIVE CRIMINALS

Numerous factors must be considered when a company chooses a facility or warehouse to store and ship their cargo from. Often the size of the facility, costs, and accessibility by tractor–trailers play the most major roles. Because of this, the type of buildings used throughout the United States supply chain varies in almost every way imaginable—from standalone, state-of-the-art facilities, with perimeter fencing, single entry and exit points, all the way to a small warehouse sandwiched between other tenants in a larger industrial or even retail center, with no fencing, and multiple points of access.

Two of the most common methods for gaining entry into a warehouse are through the roof and through the shared wall of a neighboring business.

As gaining entry through a warehouse's skylight became increasing popular for criminals, it became more common for companies to install security countermeasures, such as steel bars and motion detection at points of roof entry (sky lights, access portals, etc.). To combat this, criminals began to cut holes in roofs, away from the points of entry, knowing that security coverage was less likely—sometimes knowing full well that security in a certain location did not exist due to inside information.

This method has been used in multiple cases over the past decade, most notably in the $76 million Enfield, Connecticut, heist, in another pharmaceutical warehouse burglary in Richmond, Virginia, in August of 2009, and in a $4 million cell phone heist outside of Chicago's O'Hare International Airport in 2008.

By attacking facilities in this manner, criminals are able to bypass the most common points of intrusion detection—doors, windows, roof access points—and gain entry to the facility interior.

Another increasingly popular method is to gain access to facilities that have a shared wall with other businesses by breaking into the neighboring business—presumably because the neighboring business has less (or no) security infrastructure in place and then cutting a hole through the shared wall, again bypassing the common points of intrusion detection.

On October 23, 2011, in Norcross, Georgia, an unknown number of suspects gained access into a cell phone distribution warehouse by cutting a hole through the concrete wall from an adjoining business that had a minimal security infrastructure in place. Once inside the facility, the criminals were able to deactivate the security system and proceeded to steal approximately $1.8 million in mobile phones. Cameras showed several of the suspects upon entry to the facility, but they were disguised, eventually pushing the cameras up to face the ceiling.

Within a year of that incident, two other facility burglaries had occurred, both within the Norcross, Georgia, area, and both through similar methods as the October 23 burglary.

While facility burglaries only comprise 4 to 5% of cargo theft incidents year after year, the average take can be 10 times that of a full truckload theft, as criminals will load multiple trailers as full as they can before departing.

On November 4, 2007, a distribution center in Grapevine, Texas, was hit for $8 million in TomTom GPS devices. A similar heist in Richmond Hills, Ontario, Canada, netted a crew over $10 million in printer cartridges, while another theft crew also obtained $10 million in goods from a warehouse burglary, this time stealing cell phones from a facility in Orlando, Florida, in January 2011.

As with over-the-road cargo theft, gangs that target warehouses and distribution centers are extremely creative; in fact, they are considered to be more creative and knowledgeable due to the increased level of security and risk of being detected and apprehended by entering a facility in lieu of stealing an unattended trailer. But with that risk comes significantly higher payouts, and while not every theft gang is quick to attempt a warehouse burglary, the right crew, with the right motivation, can certainly land big bucks if they do it right.

Other Forms and Modes of Cargo Theft

While over the road, full-truckload thefts and warehouse burglaries are the most common methods of stealing cargo in large quantities, other forms of theft certainly exist. While the majority result in the loss of trailers/containers or large-scale theft of a facility, smaller incidents occur with far more regularity, resulting in countless thefts at the single product or box level, undetected and seemingly impossible to quantify.

A few of the common forms of supply chain theft that cost the industry billions of dollars annually are given here.

Pilferage

One type of pilferage or attritional loss, also known as "leakage," within the supply chain, occurs when the perpetrator goes by another name—"your employee." Generally started with some sense of entitlement or "they owe me" mentality, a warehouse employee quickly opens a carton, pulls out the product, puts it in his car, and drives home. The next day he is anxious to return to work and try it again, regaining from the company what he feels is rightfully his.

While full-truckload thefts are generally conducted by those considered to be professional cargo thieves, pilferage often takes place from within, generally one piece at a time, far below any insurance deductible, done on a daily basis from the very people responsible for their care.

Pilferage, which shrinks the U.S. economy by millions, if not billions, of dollars each year, can be a gateway crime for other, larger forms of cargo theft as the theft of one piece grows to a box, then a case, then a pallet. As this new form of income becomes a way of life for the employee, movement to larger targets is often the next logical step. While this clearly is not the case with every employee who has ever walked out of a warehouse with product hidden in his lunch pail, it does hold true for uncountable others.

In 2009, a warehouse supervisor in Ohio was arrested and convicted on charges of cargo theft and conspiracy to commit cargo theft after he colluded with a truck driver to steal more than $200,000 worth of infant formula. The supervisor, who oversaw the entire staff and millions of dollars in product during his shift, very likely did not start off stealing on this grand scale.

Fictitious Pickup

A growing trend that started to flourish around 2005, fictitious pickup involves criminals posing as legitimate truck drivers, sometimes going so far as to create fake transportation companies, in order to secure and steal loads directly from shippers. In order to deceive companies into willingly, albeit unwittingly, giving up high-value loads, criminals have used online load brokering sites and other means of winning transportation bids or have simply shown up at facilities as drivers, claiming to be assigned a scheduled load.

A variation of this MO involves a driver for a transportation provider arriving at the pickup site ahead of his company's assigned driver and then simply disappearing with the fully loaded tractor–trailer. This MO has also been used by recently terminated drivers. Often after one of these thefts is discovered, a comment such as "Everyone knows Mike. He picks up every day" is heard from the red-faced shipper.

Driver Theft

Although similar to the fictitious pickup, driver theft occurs when the actual driver assigned by the transportation provider or contracted directly by the shipper, operating in a legitimate business, decides to steal the load. In its most common form, driver theft involves stealing part of a load while in transit or selling the product from the back of the trailer. On occasions, however, drivers will disappear with the entire load, never to be heard from again and the product long gone unless it turns up sold through the black market. These incidents can fuel drug or other substance abuse or simply stem from a disgruntled driver thinking he is owed some back pay.

In 2009 a driver was caught stealing bags of salad and vegetables from the back of his tractor–trailer in Brooklyn, New York. This is a classic example of an otherwise responsible driver who decided to make some extra money. In some cases, drivers have been known to drive their big rigs to their home to offload televisions and other electronics, later claiming they were victims of short shipments during the loading process.

Hijacking

In the United States, truck hijacking cases comprise less than 2% of all cargo theft activity. Defined as the in-transit theft of goods through the use of violence or threat of violence, hijacking of tractor–trailers is generally attributed to local gangs trying to make a quick buck when the opportunity arises. Professional cargo theft gangs such as those operating out of South Florida, New Jersey, or other cargo crime hotbeds understand that hijacking is a higher level of crime, ramping up more attention from law enforcement and dramatically stiffer penalties for convictions (not to mention increased risk of detection and capture due to the driver's presence at the time of the theft).

Hijackings take place most commonly in southern California, where gangs, including some small-time cargo theft gangs, tend to be more aggressive. From 2006 through 2010, over 40% of all hijackings in the United States were recorded in Los Angeles and San Bernardino counties.

While rare here, hijacking is a common MO in numerous other countries, including Mexico, Brazil, South Africa, Russia, Malaysia, and the Philippines. In these and other countries, its prevalence can be attributed to a complicated mixture of socio-economics, law enforcement presence and strategies, supply chain security practices, and the overall level of violent crime in each country. In Mexico, cargo theft occurs almost exclusively through the use of violence or threat of violence, with thefts of unattended cargo occurring only rarely.

Air

While product is virtually never stolen from aircraft, the airline and indirect air carrier (freight forwarder) cargo terminals that surround our major airports are rife with theft. As with rail theft, these incidents may not necessarily be listed as thefts from an air carrier because the product was in a facility when stolen, but there is no denying the desirability of product selected for shipping via air. Such product generally has a high value associated with it and some level of perishability equating to time–sensitivity. We would argue that many goods that are not susceptible to damage from temperature extremes are indeed still perishable. Think of brand name apparel that "enjoys" as many as six seasons in a single year. Due to the inherent higher freight costs, shippers tend to move goods in this mode only when there is a real value proposition. Therefore, shipments transported by air usually share the aforementioned characteristics, thus making them ideal targets for theft.

Rail and Pipeline

Theft from other modes of transportation such as rail, air, pipelines, and sea come in two general forms. First is pilferage from the transport mode itself. In the case of rail, that often involves people jumping onto trains when they are stopped or moving at very slow speeds, breaking security seals to "go shopping," and then throwing cartons from desirable ocean containers and intermodal trailers along the tracks so that their accomplices following behind in small trucks or vans can pick the stolen goods up. Second is the theft of product at a hub, such as a rail yard. While the first generally involves lesser volume of product loss per incident, the aggregate adds up very quickly and has a substantial impact on a nation's economy due to cargo theft. The latter method of theft may not be reported as rail theft due to the product being in a drop yard or other facility, even though it was moved via rail. This is explored more in Chapter 17: Rail and Pipeline Security.

There is no question that America is dependent on energy. Pipelines run across the country carrying oil and gas products. There are miles and miles of networked pipes that by the very fact that they cover vast distances and are in every corner of the United States make them vulnerable to tampering if not outright theft (people tapping into the lines) or attack and virtually impossible to protect.

Theft of equipment in the pipeline system is the biggest concern to those in the industry. From 2005 to 2007, over 500 cases of equipment theft involving pipelines were recorded in the state of Texas alone with losses estimated at $78 million.

Key Points

- For the purpose of this book, cargo theft refers to large-scale theft such as trailer or container theft and facility burglaries and robberies.
- Small-scale theft such as pilferage and "leakage" are typically not factored into cargo theft statistics cited.
- Warehouse burglaries are far more lucrative than full-truckload or container theft; however, the increased risks and complexities of warehouse burglaries keep this mode of theft between 4 and 5% of incidents each year.

- Truck hijackings and warehouse robberies are just full-truckload thefts, and warehouse robberies are akin to burglaries with the added component of violence or threat of violence during commission of the crime.
- Thefts in other modes of transportation can present a significant challenge to supply chain professionals, requiring comprehensive and flexible supply chain security programs.
- Theft in the rail industry, for example, has been occurring for over 100 years in the United States and today has simply taken on a different form than in years past, but is no less present and continues to have significant impacts on supply chain efficiencies, costs, and product delivery.

RISK vs. REWARD

INFORMATION IN THIS CHAPTER:

- Why theft gangs are dedicated to cargo theft
- Prosecution and sentencing
- Risk vs reward of cargo theft compared to other crimes
- Efforts underway to increase punishment for convicted cargo criminals

Go where the money is … and go there often.

Willie Sutton

Why Cargo?

Cargo theft, which rivals even the most grandiose white collar crimes, far surpasses the total losses from property crimes such as bank robberies, jewelry theft, and others. Given that cargo theft is such an underreported crime, industry experts are hard pressed to provide a precise annual price tag, although estimates range from $3 to $30 billion in the United States alone. What's more, only relatively small amounts of cargo are ever recovered and few cargo crooks are prosecuted and sentenced (Badolato, 1999).

The reason is that cargo theft is a very low priority for most policing agencies, including the Federal Bureau of Investigation (FBI), because by and large these crimes are nonviolent. Furthermore, professional cargo thieves in the United States are fully aware that the involvement of weapons would considerably raise the profile of their crimes to law enforcement and the judicial system. In the end, they choose to leave those sleeping giants alone by leaving the weapons at home.

As things now stand when thieves weigh the slight risk of capture against the extraordinarily high payoff for loads such as cell phones, pharmaceuticals, high-end clothing, and computers, action wins out every time. When the value of one of these loads can run as high as $40 million, and thieves can make 10 to 40 cents on the dollar (a fence makes about 50 cents on the dollar), it's easy to see why the scale tips in favor of theft. Even if they get caught, they may spend a few months in jail or get away with only probation (Eiserer, 2008).

In October 2009, several men were arrested in South Florida after being found in possession of $2.3 million in stolen cigarettes. A search of the residence of one of the suspects turned up product from almost all of the 22 reported thefts in Palm Beach County, Florida. In all, police found $13 million worth of stolen goods in his possession. In February 2011, after spending 16 months in the legal process, the cargo thief pleaded guilty to grand theft in Palm Beach County Court and was sentenced to 3 years' probation.

Three months prior, four coconspirators, two warehouse supervisors, and two truck drivers were convicted in connection with the theft of $200,000 worth of baby formula from a warehouse in Lehigh Valley, Pennsylvania. One of the warehouse supervisors, Daniel C. Vertilus, 24, of South Whitehall Township, Pennsylvania, was sentenced to 100 hours of community service, as he had no prior criminal history.

One of the drivers, Rene Chavez-Garcia, 45, of York, Pennsylvania, was convicted on nine theft charges and sentenced to 6 to 23 months in prison and 5 years' probation. The second driver, Angelo Rodriguez, 46, of Brentwood, New York, received 5 years' probation (Amerman, 2009). This is just one example of the punishments meted out to cargo criminals.

Bank Robbery vs. Cargo Theft (Electronics)

Of the 5531 bank robberies recorded by the FBI in 2009, 5246 were successful in that the perpetrators departed with money or other valuable property. The monetary loss to the banks ranged from less than a thousand dollars on the low end to an estimated high of $300,000. Of the total thefts recorded, the average bank robbery resulted in a $10,000 loss.

Also in 2009 there were 160 recorded cargo theft incidents involving electronics, with an average loss per incident of $870,000. Because cargo thieves earn 10 to 40% of the load's value, they made $87,000 to $348,000 per theft.

Of the $57 million stolen during bank robberies in 2009, law enforcement agencies recovered approximately 14%, while less than 3% of the $150 million in stolen electronics was ever found.

Cargo Theft vs. Bank Robbery

Even though bank robberies exceeded cargo thefts of electronics by well over 5000 incidents in 2009, bank robberies had a net result of $93 million less than cargo thefts, with an average value per incident of $10,000 compared to $870,000 (Figure 3.1).

Because of the immediate response to bank robberies by police and the FBI, the arrest rate is estimated at 60%. This percentage does not include bank robbers who got away but are later arrested for committing other crimes. Bank robbers get caught largely because their images are captured on closed circuit television systems during commission of the crime. These pictures are shared with law enforcement throughout the country and aired in the media, often resulting in a tip that leads to the culprit's arrest.

For cargo theft, the arrest rate is less than 4%. While arrests for bank robbery often occur because the perpetrators' pictures have been captured on camera and then disseminated to law enforcement, rarely do pictures factor into the cargo theft equation. With more than 70% of all cargo thefts occurring at truck

Cargo Theft vs. Bank Robbery

	Bank Robbery	Cargo Theft (Electronics)
Total # of successful thefts/robberies	5,531	172
Total losses	$57,000,000	$150,000,000
Average value per incident	$10,000	$870,000
Estimated value after being fenced	$10,000	$87,000 to $348,000
Amount recovered	$7,938,000	$1,500,000
% arrested	60%	< 4%
Average sentence	5 years	Probation

Figure 3.1 Data obtained from the FBI Bank Crime Statistics and FreightWatch.

stops or unattended/unsecured lots, criminal gangs face minimal risk of having their identity exposed.

One similarity between cargo theft and bank robbery is the low chance of being caught spending the money stolen or fencing the stolen product. Once stolen money leaves a bank, there is very little chance the thief will be caught spending it, even if the serial numbers are known to police and the bank's officers. The same is true with stolen cargo. With so many warehouses and ocean containers/trailers coming and going, the likelihood that stolen cargo will be recovered is minimal.

Sentencing is based on criminal history and the use of a firearm during the commission of a crime. Federal sentencing guidelines do not take the value of the loss into considerations, and thus loss amounts rarely play a significant role in sentencing. A bank robber who uses a note to commit a crime will receive a far lighter sentence than one who uses a firearm. Because cargo theft is almost exclusively a nonviolent crime in the United States, cargo thieves also receive less punishment, often suspended sentences with parole, despite the incredibly large loss suffered by the victim.

Identity Theft vs. Cargo Theft

According to the Federal Trade Commission, 9 to 10 million people fall victims to identify theft per year in the United States. On average, identity theft generates losses of approximately $50.8 billion in the United States alone (Javelin Strategy and Research).

Even though the number of identity thefts surpasses the number of cargo theft incidents, the average loss per cargo theft incident is considerably higher. For instance, single loads of electronics and pharmaceuticals are estimated at $870,000 and $3 million, respectively, whereas the amount of loss for identity theft ranges from $2000 to $5000 per incident. ("Fighting Back against Identity Theft").

Unlike cargo theft and bank robberies, it is difficult to estimate the number of identity crimes that are solved, as most incidents are reported by the victims only if financial harm is recognized or because of mysterious crimes appearing on an innocent person's criminal record.

In addition to monetary losses, identity theft also affects the victim's lifestyle. Because identity thieves tend to target people with good credit scores, years of creditworthiness can vanish in a matter of weeks, days, or even hours. As a consequence, even if the criminals pay a penalty or go to jail, the victims are not exempt from the difficult process of cleaning up their credit/

background records (Pearl, 180). Even though the consequences of cargo theft also go beyond monetary losses and result in order delays and customer dissatisfaction, most companies have cargo insurance and are able to recover at least a percentage of the value of the goods.

Similar to cargo crime, sentencing for identity theft is minimal. The average prison sentence for financial identity theft ranges from 3 to 5 years. In some states, criminals may serve no jail time, instead being required to pay a penalty ranging from $50,000 to $100,000 (IdentityTheft.com). Factors often considered in sentences for identity theft are the number of individuals/businesses affected and the financial loss.

Gene Franklin, a San Francisco-area man, was sentenced in August 2009 to 31 years in state prison following his conviction on more than 46 felony counts, including identity fraud. Franklin was accused of stealing the identities of more than a dozen people and using their financial information to buy property. Prosecutors estimated the value of his fraudulent purchases at $2.8 million, including a $685,000 house in Huntington Beach, California.

In September 2004, Philip Cumming was found guilty of identity theft and fraud and was sentenced to 14 years in prison. Cumming, a computer help desk assistant at a Long Island-based credit company, had access to clients' personal information, including usernames and passwords. Cumming not only stole client information to open bank accounts, he also downloaded credit reports and sold them to other identity thieves for as little as $30 each. The FBI investigation revealed that Cumming belonged to a large, international criminal organization that had been responsible for some 30,000 incidents involving identity theft and $100 million in losses (Swarts, 2004).

Similar to cargo theft, it is difficult to have a clear picture of identity thieves right after a theft is reported. Even with more traditional identity theft methods (such as the garbage method, where criminals acquire personal information by searching through trash cans and recycle bins), thieves are not able to be identified by their victims or witnesses.

Today, police face greater challenges trying to solve identity theft. Identity thieves are increasingly making use of the Internet with modern technology, allowing them to make their methods more sophisticated and harder to track. In the same way in which cargo thieves have resorted to the use of global positioning system jammers to thwart tracking devices, identity thieves prefer to use the Internet to access a company's bank account or to steal personal information at corporate and individual levels instead of going through garbage (Lacey and Cuganesan, 2004).

Cargo Theft Sentencing

In 2007, Carlos Alarosa, a native of Cuba, stole approximately 2800 Tom Tom global positioning units and an 18 wheeler in Dallas. The total value of theft was $842,000. Apprehended with the stolen load by police in Mesquite, Texas, Alarosa was convicted and sentenced to 5 years' deferred adjudication, meaning the offense won't count on his criminal history if he completes probation successfully (Eiserer, 2008).

Bank robbers and those who commit other high-visibility crimes do not draw tougher sentencing from the courts because their crime made the national news. Sentencing is largely based on their criminal history, as well as whether weapons were involved in the crime. Although law enforcement investigates all bank robberies intensely, perpetrators who made off with a few thousand dollars by passing a note to the teller will receive considerably lighter sentences upon conviction than those who brandished weapons inside the bank. In a similar vein, a convicted thief with no criminal history who stole a $12 million load without using a weapon will often receive no prison time, despite the value of the goods. For this reason, law enforcement agencies do not give high priority to even major cargo theft cases. It is simply not worth their time.

One strategy for correcting this problem is through appeals to legislators to stiffen the federal sentencing guidelines for cargo theft, asking them to factor in the potentially extreme impacts of such crimes on the national economy along with the recidivist nature of cargo thieves. The latter comes into play since left unchecked, with a veritable slap on the wrist, convicted criminals will otherwise be back on the streets the very next day.

Clearly the current process does not serve as a deterrent for cargo criminals, even those who are being processed by the judicial system. In 2010, several men stole four tractor–trailers loaded with cosmetics worth in excess of $4 million in Roanoke, Virginia. The criminals moved three of the trailers successfully, but were caught while attempting to paint over the distinguishing markings on the fourth. Of the gang members arrested, one had been arrested previously for the June 2009 theft of $10 million in pharmaceuticals that took place in Tennessee.

The four men arrested were Armando Canaura, 54; Jose Canaura, 44; Osvaldo Pedraza Roja, 48; and Denis Perez de Castro, 41.

On July 13, 2011, all four entered Alford pleas (an Alford plea is not an admission of guilt but acknowledges the prosecution has the evidence to persuade a judge or jury of conviction) of guilty to felony possession of stolen property with intent to sell or distribute (Adams, 2011). Each man received a suspended sentence and was placed on probation by the judge. The prosecutor for the case did not object when the defense requested that the convicted men serve their probation in Florida and be allowed to continue driving trucks for a living, which was granted by the judge.

To exacerbate the problem, the *Bloomberg BusinessWeek* article on cargo theft dated May 30 2011, "Cargo Theft: The New Highway Robbery" by Daniel Grushkin lists Jose and Armando Canaura and Perez de Castro by name as active cargo criminals from South Florida.

U.S. Sentencing Guidelines for Cargo Theft

Over the past decade the losses associated with cargo theft-related crimes have risen dramatically. One reason for the increase is that criminals involved in cargo theft see an opportunity for high reward with only minimal risks. Thefts of sought-after products such as televisions, cell phones, computers, and pharmaceuticals can allow them to reap significant paydays. Another factor causing an increase is the absence of sentencing guidelines or code under the Uniform Crime Reporting system that was specifically designated for cargo theft until the reauthorization of the Patriot Act in 2006. Furthermore, local and state police agencies often see cargo theft as a victimless crime because insurance companies reimburse victims for their losses.

There are, however, provisions to prosecute cargo theft gangs on the books. The following is a list of applicable federals laws that relate directly to cargo theft and racketeering:

- **Title 18 U.S. Code, Section 659:** Theft from interstate shipments.
- **Title 18 U.S. Code, Section 1951:** Interference with commerce by threat or violence.
- **Title 18 U.S. Code, Section 1952:** Interstate and foreign travel or transportation in aid of racketeering.
- **Title 18 U.S. Code, Section 1957:** Engaging in monetary transactions in property derived from specified unlawful activity (cash value greater than $10,000).
- **Title 18 U.S. Code, Section 1961 (1):** Definition of racketeering activity, to include any act or threat involving murder, kidnapping, gambling, arson, or robbery.

- **Title 18 U.S. Code, Section 2117:** The breaking and entering of a carrier facility, as well as breaking the seals of railcars and commercial trailers.
- **Title 18 U.S. Code, Section 2314:** Interstate transportation of stolen property of a value of $5000 or more.
- **Title 18 U.S. Code, Chapter 96:** Racketeer-influenced and corrupt organizations.

These regulations and guidelines, however, have proven to be ineffective, providing virtually zero deterrence to cargo theft gangs. Because of this, a group of pharmaceutical companies [Abbott Laboratories, Eli Lilly, GlaxoSmithKline (GSK), Johnson & Johnson, and Novo Nordisk] joined forces in 2010, forming the Coalition for Patient Safety and Medicine Integrity, to lobby Congress for stiffer penalties on cargo theft, specifically as it relates to the pharmaceutical sector. The result is a bill being sponsored by six U.S. senators that would grant police new investigative powers and tougher penalties on pharmaceutical theft (Eban, 2011).

Citing the 350% increase in monetary losses resulting from cargo theft since 2007 and the $76 million warehouse burglary in Connecticut, the senators introduced a bill in March 2011 calling for increased penalties on convictions for theft of medical products under the Racketeer Influenced and Corrupt Organizations law. The legislation would also give stiffer penalties for those who dilute and counterfeit stolen drugs, change the labels, or damage the drugs by storing or transporting them incorrectly.

In submitting the bill, the senators cited as a chief concern the repackaging of stolen, temperature-sensitive specialty drugs, and their reintroduction into the legitimate pharmaceutical supply chain—where consumers face significant risk of adverse medical effects from mishandled or relabeled drugs. A case in point occurred in 2009 following the theft in North Carolina of a full truckload of insulin valued at $10.9 million. The mishandling of the insulin and its later return to the legitimate supply chain resulted in the death of a Houston man, among other adverse effects on consumers.

Crime of Opportunity

While cargo theft is carried out most often by well-trained, highly skilled and focused gangs, it remains a crime of opportunity. The theft gangs, of course, go to great effort to ensure they are ready when the opportunity arises, often following the load for what could be hundreds of miles. In more than 98% of all cargo theft incidents in the United States, theft occurs when the load is left unattended.

Fortunately for the cargo criminal, there are countless numbers of trucks on the road every single day, and thus no shortage of opportunities to ply their trade. Cargo is moved throughout the United States 365 days a year, with loads stopping at truck stops, rest areas, drop lots, parking lots, terminals, roadsides, and any other place a trailer will fit.

Of course, for the theft to be a money-making enterprise, the criminals must steal something they can sell. As discussed further in Chapter 5: The Black Market, virtually anything of value to consumers can be sold and moved on the black market. Furniture, appliances, electronics, yard equipment, food, clothing, pharmaceuticals—the list goes on and on. All of these have a market and are regularly sought after by cargo gangs. With this seemingly endless supply of available targets, theft gangs do not have to work too hard to find loads they can steal and sell for a profit.

Another key component of cargo theft that makes this particular crime so attractive is the difficulty in catching criminals in the act. Cargo crime occurs almost exclusively when there is no one around, with no witnesses to the crime. In contrast, a bank robbery is guaranteed to have both surveillance camera footage and live witnesses, giving the police a head start in catching the offender. Once a bank robbery occurs, the surveillance footage is often on the local news within a few hours—not so in cargo crime. After a load is stolen, it may not be discovered missing for days, may not be reported to police at all, and the chances of having legible, actionable video footage of the criminals in the act are nearly nil.

Key Points

- Cargo theft is a low-risk, high-reward crime, with millions of dollars in product available to be stolen with very little risk of detection.
- Criminals can make 10 to 40 cents on the dollar for stolen loads, some of which are valued in excess of a million dollars.
- Cargo theft provides criminals with the opportunity to make substantially more money than bank robberies, with exponentially less risk of capture or incarceration.
- Arrest, prosecution, and sentencing levels for cargo theft are light, with little outcry from the public for increased law enforcement attention to this problem.
- Criminals caught with millions of dollars in stolen goods from cargo theft more often than not simply receive probation for their crime.

ORGANIZED CRIMINAL GROUPS

INFORMATION IN THIS CHAPTER:

- Major theft gangs in cargo crime
- Similarities and differences between gangs and their modus operandi
- Risk of theft based on geography and theft gang areas
- Role of the stolen cargo broker

Florida is the southeast point of what's been dubbed the Bermuda Triangle of cargo theft.

Barry Tarnef

Cargo theft gangs do not usually fit the traditional mold of organized crime. These loosely knit organizations rarely have a leader, as groups operate in small teams, traveling throughout their region (or country), each performing a specific task in order to acquire their targeted product. While power or control is often the underlying motivator for typical street gangs and organized crime groups, this is not the case with cargo theft gangs, who are motivated almost exclusively by money and the lifestyle that high-value thefts afford.

The leader of any job is traditionally the gang member who initially found the target or brought the opportunity to the gang. Because of this, cargo theft gangs are known for working extremely well together, with members performing their roles very efficiently.

In order for shippers, freight forwarders, carriers, and other supply chain and security professionals to combat these cells effectively, they must first learn how the gangs operate. They then must ensure that their employees receive cargo security awareness training on what to watch for and that these employees are constantly reminded to be vigilant. From suspicious activity around a distribution center or a truck stop, to paperwork with obvious mistakes being provided by a driver that is not known to shipping personnel, the vast array of methods used by theft gangs and methods by which they can be detected should be well known by anyone who operates within the supply chain arena.

Cargo thieves are not your usual run-of-the mill crooks. Certain skills and an understanding of the supply chain industry are required to successfully steal a loaded tractor–trailer or break into a distribution center. Gangs need personnel who know how to drive a truck, unhook a trailer, and are knowledgeable about the rules of the road when it comes to big rigs (Gonzalez, 2009).

Regardless of the mode by which cargo is stolen—whether from a warehouse, rail facility, air cargo facility, drop lot, truck stop, storage yard, or any other of the countless other places where cargo is stored or staged—if thieves steal the product in any kind of bulk, they are going to need to transport it via a tractor–trailer or container pulled by a tractor. This specificity to the crime of cargo theft creates a different dynamic than almost any other; the thieves must not only have the knowledge and skills to commit the crime, but also the ability to transport the product in a highly regulated environment.

Cargo theft gangs operate throughout the United States, focusing primarily on areas with high volumes of manufacturing and/or logistics operations. Rates of theft in relation to certain industries and the areas in which these thefts occur are quite predictable in fact. Consumer electronics and computer hardware and peripherals are commonly stolen in the Dallas area and in California (where numerous assembly and return centers are located). Pharmaceutical loads are commonly stolen in the Pennsylvania area (where a number of drug manufacturing sites are located) and in Tennessee (with its wealth of pharmaceutical distribution centers). For the major transportation hubs such as Atlanta, Chicago, Louisville, or Columbus, cargo theft tends to be more general, as theft gangs steal goods they can sell on the black market, but do not necessarily focus on one product type or industry.

Cargo Theft: 2006–2011

It is not by coincidence that the most prolific cargo theft centers in the United States are colocated with some of the country's largest seaports. With tremendous volumes of cargo moving in and out of the ports of Los Angeles/Long Beach, New York/New Jersey, and Miami, cargo thieves have a captive market not only for product selection, but also a ready-made thoroughfare for moving the product after it has been stolen (Figure 4.1).

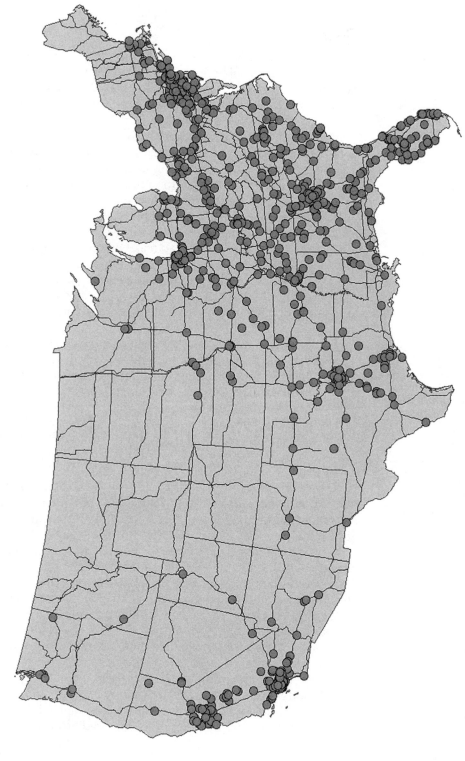

Figure 4.1 Cargo theft incidents in the United States from 2006 through 2011.

South Florida

In the modern era of cargo theft, no area has become more synonymous with this crime than South Florida. Referred to as this crime's epicenter, well-organized gangs, primarily from the Hialeah area near Miami, travel the country in search of high-value goods that they quickly transport back home and sell for significant profit and relatively little risk.

Cargo theft activity by these gangs became such a problem in the mid-1990s that the Miami-Dade Police Department joined forced with the Federal Bureau of Investigation, the U.S. Customs and Border Protection, the Florida Department of Law Enforcement, the Florida Highway Patrol, and the Florida Department of Transportation to form a South Florida cargo theft task force called the Tactical Operations Multi-Agency Cargo Anti-Theft Squad (TOMCATS). The task force is housed within the offices of the robbery bureau, cargo crimes section. This facility is used as the central clearinghouse for the collection and dissemination of all cargo theft information in the South Florida area.

South Florida-based cargo theft gangs typically operate in the eastern half of the country, although they will travel throughout the United States. "These groups are highly organized. For example, they will go to Kentucky, Texas, Georgia and other areas of the country to do surveillance on loads they want to take. They will rent vehicles in those areas, target locations to make thefts. They research it; they'll know whether to pursue a load if it's something they really want," said Lieutenant Twan Uptgrow, head of the Miami TOMCATS (Morasch, 2008).

Cargo criminals from Florida are well organized, but not in the traditional sense. While many are of Cuban descent, nationality or heritage is not necessarily the underlying factor in formation of a theft gang. TOMCATS officers say that in actuality, many smaller groups have formed their own partnerships based more on money-making capability than on traditional crime family hierarchy (Morasch, 2008). The theft rings often are described as "lateral" organizations that work together only through loosely based business relationships and less like traditional mafia families, Uptgrow said. Their less formal approach makes it tougher to take them down than a traditional crime organization.

Many rings are composed of people with international connections. These groups are rarely larger than 25 members and are run by leaders who live in multimillion-dollar homes and drive Land Rover SUVs among other high-dollar toys (Morasch,

2008). Thefts throughout the country are transported to South Florida and shipped out of the port of Miami.

The Cuban theft gangs of South Florida operated locally in the Miami area during the 1980s, targeting logistics providers, delivery services, and warehouses they could exploit. Later in the decade, the group began to expand their operations with thefts occurring along the I-95 corridor throughout the state being attributed to them as empty trailers from thefts were often found in the Miami area.

In the mid-1990s, the theft gangs of South Florida, perhaps due to the increased scrutiny of law enforcement or simply looking for a wider sphere of influence, spread their tentacles across the southeastern United States and became recognized as much more than a local problem. Thefts in other parts of the country conducted by these gangs may have occurred earlier but the police may have been confused as to whom the suspects were as they were not known nationally at the time, and the law may have believed they were dealing with indigenous (Puerto Rican, Honduran, Ecuadorian, Mexican) criminal groups.

As stated, they operate in most states east of the Mississippi and also in Texas. Additionally, several Miami groups have been arrested and convicted of cargo crimes in southern California and as far north as Beaverton, Oregon. These gangs were the first and remain the most prolific at traveling to the desired product source (manufacturing facility/DC) in order to facilitate the theft.

As with most successful ethnic criminal gangs, they have emigrated from a country with a dictatorial government and rarely accept anyone outside their nationality/heritage; gang members often have ties to the same village or province. Many of the skills that make them excel at criminal activity were learned in their home country while serving in the military.

As the efforts of law enforcement agencies and the Miami TOMCATS made operating in the South Florida area more difficult, the theft gangs took their show on the road, expanding throughout the southeastern United States and today are associated with theft incidents in almost every state.

Cargo theft gangs out of Miami are traveling significant distances in order to obtain goods and are transporting them back to their roots. Since 2008, over 75 thefts were associated with the South Florida gangs, with thefts occurring as far away as Chicago and Dallas.

Of the loads recovered in the Miami area, those with known values ranged from $300,000 to $6 million; three were shipments of liquid crystal display televisions, a known targeted commodity by cargo thieves (Figure 4.2).

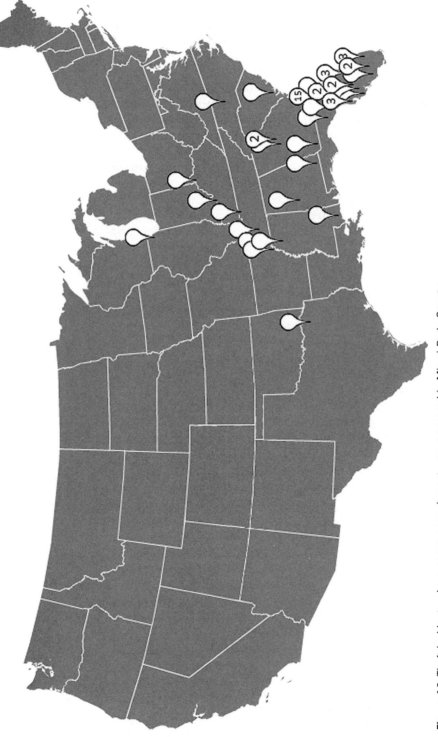

Figure 4.2 Theft incidents where cargo or equipment was recovered in Miami-Dade County.

While the South Florida theft gangs are generally associated with theft involving primarily consumer electronics and pharmaceuticals, assuming they target these verticals exclusively would be a mistake. When analyzing thefts in which the cargo and/or the equipment involved was recovered in South Florida, products ranged from food and beverages to clothing to tobacco and building materials. While the electronics and pharmaceutical sectors certainly give cargo theft gangs of South Florida a great way to earn a high return on their investment, these gangs are clearly willing to steal any item that can be sold quickly.

The majority of stolen product funnels back to South Florida where it is redistributed within the United States or exported. Outbound goods are shipped to this state's largest trading partners for legitimate goods, that is, Brazil, Costa Rica, Argentina, and other South and Central American countries. Other product is taken to New Jersey, where they also maintain warehouses and have buyers. A small percentage of product is staged at warehouses in the area where the theft occurred and then trucked directly to a buyer in a legitimate truck or, on occasion, via an unknowing legitimate carrier (i.e., the criminals literally contract with a valid transportation company to move the product).

These cargo criminals are certainly among the most creative in the United States. Through years of experience and a large number of successful cargo thefts, these gangs have been adaptive and ensure their success whether they are stealing an unattended trailer or breaking into a warehouse or distribution center. To demonstrate their creativity, these gangs have created some unique modi operandi (MO), such as videotaping alarm keypads to "capture" alarm codes, impersonating alarm company personnel, and tricking target company employees to divulge alarm codes.

In January 2011, a criminal gang broke into an empty warehouse space that was part of a larger facility occupied by several different companies. The criminals then broke through a wall that served as the barrier between the empty space and a company that stored cellular phones. The criminals made off with over $10 million dollars' worth of product.

Moreover, the gangs have begun efficiently separating pallets of stolen goods before they're fenced—in their version of less-than-truckload (LTL) operations. They divide full truckload shipments they have stolen into smaller quantities, moving them to different buyers in varying locations. By separating the stolen goods, this makes locating global positioning system-tracked loads more difficult, only adding to headaches police already face.

In 2008, according to Daniel Grushkin's article in *Bloomberg's BusinessWeek* magazine, an explosion of theft incidents were occurring in Palm Beach County, Florida, one of the counties immediately north of Miami-Dade along the eastern seaboard. With a growth from three incidents in 2007 to 22 in 2008, police began to really take notice. As mentioned in the previous chapter, one individual was arrested in possession of product from these incidents, all found in his house in Miami-Dade county, approximately 70 miles away.

During the investigation that led to the arrests and recovery discussed in the *BusinessWeek* article, an array of people were observed entering and exiting the same residence, many of whom had listed the home as their place of residence at various times, an intricate relationship with each other and the homeowner. Despite the numerous soft relationships that the homeowner had with known cargo theft gangs, at no point during the investigation was he observed committing any crime or even seen in or around industrial areas, truck stops, or other places in which cargo crime typically occurs. In fact, he was observed doing little more than fishing.

This showed the obvious levels of organization that exist within the South Florida groups, insulating members and leaders from criminal activity when possible and only getting involved as necessary to ensure successful completion of their thefts and fencing operations.

Groups such as these do not limit themselves to criminal activity in the southern region of Florida. In fact, the largest percentage of high-value goods targeted and stolen in the United States is attributed to South Florida (Cuban) cargo theft gangs. These aggressive gangs have managed to sustain high levels of activity since before 1993, leading to creation of the TOMCATS in 1996.

Their personnel, who generally are 20 years of age and older, include many former truck drivers from Cuba who are unemployed new citizens in the United States. Although most members are male, it is quite common for cargo theft gangs to use females as diversions or to gain entrance to those areas to which male members likely would be denied access.

The South Florida cargo theft gang members are assigned specific tasks. In this system, there is a leader, a truck driver, warehouse workers, thieves, a broker, and buyers. Within this system, all members generally are Cuban with the exception of the broker and possibly the buyer.

These cargo theft gangs are set in motion when they receive orders for certain products or commodities. In order to fulfill a particular order, their standard MO is to fly or drive to the location where their desired product is manufactured or stored and then rent an SUV locally. They will stay in a hotel near their target and conduct surveillance of the facility in order to determine the best way to steal the cargo. Options for theft include warehouse burglary, stealing a loaded trailer in the terminal yard, or following the load while in transit and then stealing the cargo when the driver stops. Although facility security measures often will cause cargo gangs to move on to an easier target, some groups will respond to these measures by using more aggressive tactics such as attempting to videotape door codes or cutting the phone lines.

Also, most of the full truckload and full container cargo theft incidents in New Jersey are committed by Cuban theft gangs. They have, on many occasions, been mistaken for Ecuadorians, Colombians, or Venezuelans—all common to the New Jersey area with regards to being active in the cargo theft arena. However, although these other ethnic groups are very prolific and well-known cargo thieves in the New York/New Jersey area, they specialize in thefts of high-value items (jewelry, watches, and small consumer electronics) from package delivery trucks (think FedEx and UPS) and LTL carriers, while making deliveries and pickups.

New York/New Jersey

In 2010, cargo theft in New Jersey increased by 143% over the previous year, growing from a midlevel state in terms of supply chain crime, emerging as the third highest state in the country for cargo theft rates.

Generally considered to be an area of old school organized crime as it relates to cargo theft, New Jersey has remained in the shadows of the big three states for cargo theft (California, Florida, and Texas) for the past decade, only in 2010 recording a level of theft that makes it one of the riskiest states in the country for in-transit cargo. Part of this sudden rise in crime statistics might simply be better data collection and reporting by the industry and law enforcement organizations, such as the New Jersey State Police cargo theft unit.

Regardless, there is no denying the incredible level of cargo theft activity occurring in the state and the efforts that industry professionals must go to in order to keep their cargo secure—both stored and in transit.

The most common form of cargo theft in New Jersey occurs from the local or regional distribution center on trucks destined for delivery at stores or retailers. Because of this, inside information remains a high concern (as it does elsewhere in the country) and enhances the need for transportation provider compliance with shipper security policies, such as not stopping while in transit, not leaving loads unattended, and not discussing the contents of their loads with other people.

Los Angeles Basin

Los Angeles is home to the highest rates of cargo theft in the country. Its seaports are a national hub for cargo, moving nearly 40% of the nation's imports (Gale Group, 2005) every year, which subsequently brings a tremendous volume of cargo theft activity with it. From 2006 through 2011, 21% of all reported cargo theft activity occurred in and around Los Angeles. In fact, Los Angeles and San Bernardino counties combined to account for one-quarter of all cargo theft activity in the United States.

With these alarming statics comes some confusion and debate regarding how cargo theft is classified based on mode of transportation. With an incredibly high volume of sea freight in the area, many are perplexed at the high rates of containers being stolen, as seaports, particularly after September 11, 2001, are considered substantially more secure than other nodes in the supply chain. This line of thought is quite accurate. While inside the ports, cargo is safe, particularly after the security upgrades that came post-September 11; once the cargo leaves via truck (or rail), however, cargo thieves lie in wait, knowing the load will stop eventually, giving them the perfect opportunity to steal the cargo.

Extremely common locations for theft in Los Angeles are the yards that service the maritime and intermodal rail industries. Hundreds of thousands of loaded containers, waiting to be picked up and shipped, are virtual fish in a barrel for theft gangs.

In California, gangs from Central and South America, including MS-13 (also known as Mara Salvatrucha), are active in the cargo theft arena (Palmer, 2009, p. 1169). Known for their violence in other criminal matters, these gangs are known as the few involved in cargo theft willing to hijack trucks and risk the increased police response and potential stiffer sentencing.

The aggressiveness of cargo theft gangs in Los Angeles, also including the Mexican and African-American contingents, is becoming well known to the supply chain community, with the majority of violent cargo theft incidents occurring here. While violence comprises less than 2% of all cargo theft activity, Los Angeles accounts for approximately 40% of all hijackings and warehouse robberies.

Four days before Christmas in 2010, a group of armed thieves hijacked over $2.5 million in computer products transiting through Inglewood, California. This incident came on the heels of a transportation company being robbed by six armed men just outside of the Los Angeles International Airport. The gunmen held the employees while trailers were opened and searched, eventually departing with almost a million dollars in consumer electronics.

Others

While theft data analyzed by state provide excellent trends at the macrolevel, the ability of supply chain and transportation professionals to see cargo theft incidents down to the county or city level is crucial if they are to adjust in-transit security policies and keep their cargo secure. Los Angeles, Dallas/Fort Worth, San Bernardino, Miami-Dade, and Memphis were the top five metropolitan areas for cargo theft in the United States over the past 5 years. Jacksonville, Florida; Cook County, Illinois (Greater Chicago area); Hudson County, New Jersey; Fulton County, Georgia; and Middlesex County, New Jersey, rounded out the top 10.

Each of these areas, along with an array of other major and mid-major U.S. cities, is plagued by cargo theft from external gangs operating in these areas, as well as local theft criminal gangs. While professional cargo theft gangs will travel significant distances from their homes to seek out high-value cargo, steal it, and then return to their local area where their brokers or buyers are generally located, supply chains must also deal with local theft gangs (those that specialize in cargo and those that will target low-hanging fruit in the supply chain). These local gangs are ever present in a majority of cities throughout the country and account for a significant of theft volumes in the cities discussed, often hitting loads happened upon and easy targets derived through inside information.

When analyzing cargo theft state by state, cities such as these listed earlier serve as the focal points with rates of theft decreasing quickly as one moves away from the metropolitan areas (Figures 4.3 and 4.4).

The Dallas/Fort Worth Metroplex is a veritable mecca for cargo thieves seeking consumer electronics. With dozens of manufacturers in the area, along with countless suppliers, logistics providers, the Alliance corridor, Dallas/Fort Worth International Airport, and three interstates, thieves have no lack of available cargo to target and steal. Local theft gangs in the

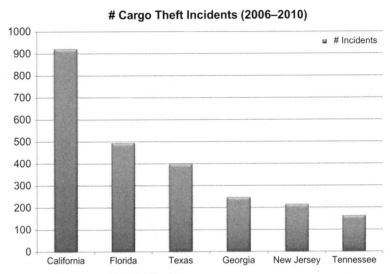

Figure 4.3 Courtesy of FreightWatch.

Major Risk Zones (Number of Thefts 2006–2010)
Los Angeles (518)
Dallas/Fort Worth (243)
San Bernardino County (168)
Miami-Dade (158)
Memphis/W. Memphis (110)
Jacksonville, Fla. (74)
Cook County, Ill. (61)
Hudson County, N.J. (55)
Fulton County, Ga. (54)
Middlesex County, N.J. (50)

Figure 4.4 Courtesy of FreightWatch.

Dallas area are known to target the Alliance corridor, known for shipping and receiving high-end electronics through its private airport. Product stolen from this area has been found for sale on the black market in Central and South America, showing the connection between the theft activity in north Texas and Latin American theft gangs, which also includes the Cuban gangs out of South Florida.

When analyzing cargo theft rates compared to the general population of a city, there is no riskier place for in-transit cargo than in Memphis and the surrounding communities.

Chicago, the county seat for Cook County (one of the riskiest counties in the country for cargo theft), accounts for double-digit rates of theft in the supply chain every year. With a long history of theft and the railroad system in Chicago due to the significant volume of rail activity in the city, over the road trucking crime has been on the rise. Industrial products (including metals), auto parts, and tires, as well as electronics and tobacco, are all commonly targeted in the greater Chicago area.

In 2010 and 2011, Louisville emerged in the supply chain consciousness as a hotbed for cargo theft activity. Even though its rate of theft remained far below those of places such as Los Angeles, Dallas, and Miami, cargo theft gangs were spotted frequently in the Louisville area with numerous incidents of facilities being probed.

In Louisville, one of the main attractors for cargo criminals is the presence of the UPS hub that naturally brings with it extraordinary volumes of cargo. As with the FedEx hub in Memphis and the substantial supply chain hubs present in cities such as Los Angeles, Miami, Chicago, and Jacksonville, so with the increase in supply chain operations came the cargo criminals. With this increase has come additional gangs beyond the traditional South Florida groups, to include eastern Europeans and other local gangs, all attempting to make money on the backs of the supply chain operations in and around the Louisville area.

In April 2011, several men were spotted conducting surveillance in an industrial complex in Louisville. A description of the suspects' vehicle was circulated throughout law enforcement and industry personnel. The same suspects were subsequently spotted in two other vehicles, and then on July 7, 2011, a full truckload of cell phones was stolen, valued at approximately $1 million.

While it is unclear if the gang spotted repeatedly by authorities in the area is responsible for this theft, there is no denying the substantial increase in cargo theft gang activity in and around Louisville to include the theft of loads originating in the city that were subsequently stolen when left unattended while in transit.

The Broker

Cargo theft is not a random crime. While earlier criminals in this particular industry may have been prone to conducting "pot luck"-style thefts, that mode has given way to active targeting of high-value, easily moveable loads for sale on the black and gray markets. The process of fencing, however, is rarely handled directly by the theft gang. Instead, this process, and subsequently the direction and targeting by the theft gangs, is often handled by an individual commonly referred to as a broker. Brokers make their living in the business of finding, acquiring, and fencing stolen products for profit.

The majority of the time, cargo thieves know what they are stealing. They acquire inside information, understand the trucking and shipping industry, and take advantage of it. They also have a buyer already lined up (Gonzalez, 2009).

Under this process, brokers find buyers for product through a variety of methods and locations. This can occur after the theft has occurred or beforehand. In the case of the latter, the broker develops a buyer for a load or product that has yet to be stolen, in which case the broker then tasks or hires a cargo theft gang to seek out, find, and steal the in-demand goods.

For loads that have been stolen prior to a buyer being acquired, the cargo is stored by the theft gang and made available to brokers and buyers. The process to sell can be in bulk to individual buyers or in smaller portions, all the way down to individual piece sales through a variety of means discussed further in Chapter 5: The Black Market.

Cargo theft in the United States is becoming far less random and increasingly specific. Many loads stolen are targeted actively by gangs in what is referred to as theft-to-order scenarios. Simply put, brokers or buyers place an order with a cargo theft gang for a particular product. The gang then conducts its research, locates the desired product, and steals the cargo at the first opportunity.

Key Points

- The most prolific cargo theft gangs in the United States originate in South Florida, New York/New Jersey, and the Los Angeles area.
- Historically, gangs would operate in their local areas; however, increased pressure from law enforcement agencies and increased security-hardening measures by the supply chain industry have caused gangs to operate across larger geographical regions.
- Gangs can specialize in certain industries; however, thefts of product generally occur in the areas that they are manufactured or distributed.

- Many metropolitan areas and large logistics hubs are under attack by both local gangs seeking high-value cargo and regional/national criminal groups.
- Cargo theft gangs are not the ones selling the goods once they have been stolen; in fact, individuals known as brokers are largely responsible for arranging the sale of goods once merchandise is made available to them.

THE BLACK MARKET

5

> *The black market was a way of getting around government controls. It was a way of enabling the free market to work. It was a way of opening up, enabling people.*
> **Milton Friedman, economist**

When a theft occurs, the reason for the crime can be seen from one of two perspectives. The stolen product is either for the use and enjoyment of the thief or the stolen product is to be sold for a profit. If the motivation is the latter, then the product has to be sold, a process known as fencing. Fencing, loosely defined, is the act of stealing or buying stolen goods at a significantly reduced price in order to resell the goods for a profit. In the case of cargo theft, the goods are virtually never for the theft gangs themselves (although it is common for them to keep some of the product for personal use at times), therefore requiring the load to be moved and sold.

Once a load of cargo is stolen and moved to a secure area for storage, the next step is moving it to the broker, or to the location directed by the broker, to sell on the black market, move back into the legitimate market, or export to another country. Typical venues for fencing of goods have traditionally been pawn shops and flea markets. For cargo theft gangs and their brokers, places such as flea markets certainly are an option for moving their newly acquired goods, but are difficult to scale and run consistently. Therefore, other means of moving high volumes of product are used.

Being able to determine where exactly stolen cargo ends up is next to impossible, but stolen goods have been found on Internet auction sites, small retail stores, and discount outlets (Eiserer, 2008). Companies that profit from the purchase and sale of large volume products are prime conduits (either knowingly or unknowingly) for stolen cargo, where bill of sales, identification, or other requisite documentation showing product authenticity are not required. Once in possession of the stolen goods, thieves are able to distribute their product through brokers or so-called "ghost" companies, which have developed extensive networks of clients. These fly-by-night operations are often locally registered firms that close up shop after less than 2 years in business and promptly reopen under new names (Chavez and Tello, 2009).

Bulk purchase and sale on the black market, e-fencing, exportation to another country, and secondary wholesale markets are all commonly used methods for off-loading stolen cargo without detection or being traced back to the broker.

E-fencing

With the proliferation of the Internet came the ability to move massive amounts of stolen product with limited interaction and virtually complete anonymity. While the traditional fence is the person who knowingly purchases stolen goods in order to resell it at a later date, the movement of stolen goods through the Internet is often referred to as e-fencing. E-fencing is particularly common in online auction sites such as ebay.com and Craigslist, with others popping up on the Internet seemingly on a weekly basis. These sites have become so commonplace in today's society that it has become second nature for people to go straight to the Internet in search of their desired product, often landing them in online bids.

While the concept of fencing product has existed for centuries, the explosion of electronic options has made the task of selling stolen goods significantly easier for the criminal and far more difficult to monitor and prevent for the loss prevention professional and law enforcement community.

According to CNBC in January 2007, e-fencing is a $37 billion business, resulting in conflicts between retailers and online market sites as to who is responsible for keeping stolen goods from these legitimate market places. While online market sites take the position that moving stolen product through their sites is a quick way of getting caught, prosecutors and law enforcement alike see these avenues as a quick means to move product without the requirement for face-to-face contact when making a sale.

Some obvious benefits of moving stolen goods over online as opposed to traditional locations include anonymity, decreased interaction with potential buyers, and, most importantly, physical separation from the event to avoid detection and apprehension. The identity of the e-fence can be vague or completely secret pending on the chosen website's requirements. Criminals can use this to their advantage by spreading product across multiple sites with multiple people using a variety of payment methods available, all with the goal of ensuring that the true identity of the seller remains unknown.

In addition to increased security for the criminals as they sell product, doing so through online sources is more lucrative for them as well. In a study by Wholesale Central, online shoppers were found to pay approximately 70 cents on the dollar compared to purchases made at physical locations (flea markets) where the rate was substantially lower.

For the cargo criminal, the opportunities for e-fencing exist beyond the individual or small bulk sale, with sites and companies in the business of purchasing large quantities of items for resale in smaller quantities at higher profits. These goods are moved most frequently under the guise of excess or overstocked product from established distributors and then moved into the legitimate market for sale to the public.

Export

It should be no surprise that South Florida, New York/New Jersey, and Los Angeles are three of the major cargo crime zones. With the presence of major ports comes an endless stream of goods for thieves to seek out and steal within hours of being off-loaded from ships.

Thieves can also use these ports as part of their own supply chain, moving stolen cargo out of the United States to their overseas buyers. Cuban gangs have an affinity for cargo from the Alliance corridor in Tarrant County, Texas. Stolen goods from this area have shown up as far away as Central America (Eiserer, 2008). Cases have been recorded of stolen cargo from the United States appearing in countries such as Venezuela, Brazil, Argentina, Paraguay, and Guatemala.

While supply chain crimes, such as smuggling, terrorism, and theft, are of marginal concern in Costa Rica, the country is still known for being a popular destination for stolen cargo. These goods are often exported to Costa Rica for sale on the local market and for repackaging under phony company names and sold back into the legitimate markets of the United States and European countries.

When discussing the exportation of stolen goods to Latin America for sale, the most significant topic that commonly arises is the presence of the terrorist group Hezbollah and their recorded activities in South American countries. The connection between stolen goods and terrorism is a commonly held belief, although there have been no recorded connections between gangs that steal cargo and products that end up funding terrorist groups. While such a connection is certainly possible after multiple degrees of separation, it is important to note that by all accounts, cargo theft in the United States is a monetary crime and not a proven avenue for terrorist activity.

Secondary Wholesale Market

The U.S. supply chain is a vast network of manufacturing, distribution, transportation, freight forwarding, third-party logistics providers, and countless other touch points that products transit before finally reaching the shelf. When product is stolen and fenced, it enters an undefined area where stolen goods are moved from person to person, finally reaching the consumer through illicit, untraceable channels.

There is, however, an alternate method of fencing product that takes stolen goods from the black market and moves them back into the legitimate supply chain, eventually reaching the retail outlet, pharmacy, or any other of the countless places of business where goods are purchased every day. A common way for this to happen is for a secondary wholesale company, usually operating within close proximity, to purchase stolen goods, often knowingly, and then reselling them to another wholesaler or to a retailer as legitimately acquired goods.

It only requires one company, such as a distributor, willing to purchase cargo without questioning its origin. In the United States there are an almost endless number of companies that operate slightly off the mainstream of cargo movement, making their living buying and selling goods, taking advantage of every opportunity to acquire goods at a substantially discounted rate to then turn around and sell them for profit.

This is particularly true in the pharmaceutical sector, where thousands of secondary wholesalers make their living trading among each other, fulfilling client orders, and moving hundreds of millions of dollars in pharmaceuticals annually. This particular area went largely unregulated for years and is a prime area for illicit (stolen or counterfeit) goods to reenter the supply chain, eventually making it to the pharmacy or hospital where it is then provided to the consumer.

This process is far more common than people realize, with illicit goods finding their way onto retailers' shelves after passing hands numerous times until finally reaching a legitimate channel partner in the supply chain. As such, the victim who lost the cargo fails to benefit from the sale, experiencing a number of downstream costs, and the consumer unknowingly purchases stolen product, which can result in a number of possible negative consequences to include mishandling, health issues for food and pharmaceutical product, and more.

Anchoring

On March 14, 2010, a pharmaceutical manufacturer suffered a $76 million warehouse burglary, the largest recorded in the United States. The criminals executed a well-orchestrated, well-timed plan, catching the company off guard. By analyzing behaviors in criminality, as well as black market supply and demand, the question is asked; could this theft have been predicted?

There are various contemporary theories that aim to explain the nature of crime by studying the factors that influence a person's behavior (Van Zandt, 2009). One of these is the concept of anchoring—a term that describes the marrying of a criminal or criminal group to a certain crime, or victim type, due to the logistics, established infrastructure, or experience of the criminals with completing the crime successfully.

A criminal or criminal element who steals a certain type of product for the first time must then put time and effort (and potentially money) into creating a system for turning that product into cash (fencing). Once that system has been established, the criminal will continue to use the established method for obtaining money from a particular stolen product until it is no longer viable. In essence, they become "anchored" to that system. Once a criminal has found a method for making money, what is the likelihood of him changing? What does it take to make him change to another method or product?

There are psychological and sociological principles that explain what causes criminals to commit crimes and to make modifications in their behavior (Schmallyer, 2009). Criminals will make changes in the methodology used to commit crime when punishment, rewards, or other alternatives stimulate or force them to change their conduct; even greed and poverty play a major role in the decision-making process of a criminal. When greed is the primary motivation rather than necessity, criminals target commodities in high demand or those in which the price is expected to increase (Schmallyer, 2009).

The principle of *behavioral conditioning*, under psychological theories, states that the frequency with which a crime is committed can increase or decrease through punishment and reward (Schmallyer, 2009). However, in the case of cargo theft, evidence shows that when government attempts to stop crime by imposing stricter punishments, it also motivates some criminals to evolve and change their methods. In this case, the threat of punishment would not meet its objective, which is to stop crime, due to the fact that these punishments are being applied to well-established criminals who adopted this type of lifestyle and do not plan to change it. Additionally, existing laws and punishment for cargo crime pale in comparison to other comparable property crimes, providing no disincentive for thieves to stop. To use business terminology, the barriers to exit are high and incumbents are more likely to adapt rather than cease activities.

CASE STUDY: U.S. PHARMACEUTICAL CARGO THEFT

In the first half of the 2000s, high-value cargo theft in the United States was centered predominately on the high-tech sector. With significant increases in electronic thefts occurring, organizations such as the Transported Asset Protection Association (established in 1997) emerged, encouraging information sharing and increased supply chain security both in situ and in transit (over the road).

During this time, thefts in the pharmaceutical sector were occurring more sporadically, with companies suffering losses at an extremely low rate, falling well within acceptable loss ratios. It is argued, however, that during this time, cargo thieves were in the process of establishing methods for fencing stolen pharmaceutical products. Using experience in selling high-tech goods, thieves were able to find buyers (brokers) and systems for exporting stolen pharmaceutical products to Latin America for sale or resale back into the U.S. supply chain.

Once established, the level of pharmaceutical theft activity exploded in 2005, with rates doubling each year until 2009 when they appear to have leveled off, although the total value of losses experienced in 2009 nearly doubled.

During this time frame, pharmaceutical cargo theft in Europe was relatively limited, with minimal reports throughout the industry. In late 2009 and early 2010, however, reports began to emerge of extremely high-value thefts occurring in western Europe, often with product being moved into eastern Europe for sale. Overall, however, pharmaceuticals are rarely targeted in Europe, largely due to socialized medicine throughout the continent, while what thefts do occur are mostly of lifestyle drugs and others that can have a high value in eastern Europe.

There are several notable points to be made about pharmaceutical theft rates in the United States. First, companies with established in-transit security policies that go above and beyond industry standards have had their losses reduced to virtually zero for all loads that fall within these protocols. For loads that are shipped without these measures, theft rates remain consistent with the industry averages. For targeted loads inside a hardened supply chain (i.e., criminals experience an increase in the likelihood of failure or capture), data suggest that criminals prefer to find an alternate target to obtain similar products at less risk. Second, through collaborative efforts with law enforcement agencies, a significant amount of stolen product has been recovered by pharmaceutical companies. It has been argued that the recovery of product increases the level of desire for product by cargo thieves as their "sale" was unable to be completed.

Example

On May 2, 2009, a known cargo theft gang was discovered to be staying at a motel in Plainfield, Indiana. At the request of the Miami-Dade Cargo Theft Task Force, the Plainfield police department set up surveillance on the gang and followed them for approximately 48 hours. During that time, the theft gang drove in and around several manufacturing and distribution centers in the area.

On Sunday, May 4, the gang left Plainfield, heading east toward Pennsylvania, and local police relinquished surveillance. On the same date, a tractor–trailer loaded with $37 million worth of pharmaceuticals also left Plainfield, Indiana, heading east toward Pennsylvania.

Within 24 hours later, the load was stolen at a truck stop on the Pennsylvania turnpike while the driver was paying for fuel. Upon discovery of the theft, the driver notified the state police whose barracks was adjacent to the truck stop, and a patrol was dispatched.

The thieves, who were known to be well versed in cargo theft deterrence measures, had parked the tractor–trailer a few miles away in order to test for covert tracking devices that may be aboard. The dispatched state police trooper discovered the load and the criminal element escaped.

This creates several points that should be addressed.

a. The product aboard the trailer (mostly antidepressants), based on the concept of active targeting, has a known value on the black market.

b. The cargo theft gang knows what company manufactures these products and has an understanding of their supply chain and current security protocols.

c. Due to recovery of the load, the gang was unsuccessful in completing the transaction into the black market, thus the demand remains and is potentially greater.

On March 14, 2010, the same company suffered a $76 million dollar warehouse burglary of the same products that were stolen during the May 5, 2009, in-transit theft.

Based on this concept, cargo thieves have limited reason to stop stealing cargo, and as supply chains become more secure (or if laws and potential punishment became more severe), it is more likely for criminals to merely adapt their strategies to account for these new conditions than it is for them to cease stealing cargo altogether.

Recessionary Impact

During the recent recession, a significant concern among those in the logistics industry was the possibility of cargo theft rising due to a "down" economy. While cargo theft rates continued to rise during this time (+13% in 2009, +4.1% in 2010), on a year-by-year basis, the rate of growth was actually lower than in the previous years of the decade. While researching this particular topic, what the author discovered was an apparent willingness of consumers to purchase goods with the knowledge (or strong possibility—goods for sale at prices way below market value) that the product may have been stolen.

According to a June 2009 article in *Brandweek* magazine entitled "Copying Machines," intellectual property firm Marks and Clerk questioned companies on the topic of illicit goods and found that 80% of respondents believed that any sense of progress in consumers purchasing goods through legitimate channels would be easily undone by a recession. "In other words, a bargain speaks louder than morality." Simply put, when recession hits, people seek better deals, including the purchase of stolen goods.

"There's concern that in the current climate, low-price fake goods will be of increased interest to consumers looking to make their money go further" (*Economist*, 2010, p. 18). In the same environment where counterfeit goods are knowingly being purchased by consumers for fractions of retail costs, so too are stolen goods being sold at comparable low rates, but with increased demand over counterfeits as the product is from the original manufacturer and brings with it the quality lacking in knockoffs.

In addition to the loss of sale by manufacturers due to the purchasing of stolen goods, most companies are also faced with the dilemma of providing lower cost products to remain competitive during times when consumers are seeking better deals. Less expensive alternatives are becoming a necessity for manufactures in fear of losing their consumer base. Adding to the impact of a recession is the proliferation of e-commerce, making the moving of stolen goods easy and extremely profitable for theft gangs and their brokers.

Between the burgeoning of electronic fencing and other methods for moving stolen goods through the black market and into the legitimate market, combined with consumers' desire to stretch their buying power, cargo criminals have a significantly easier time selling stolen goods while reducing their risk of exposure or arrest.

Key Points

- A number of methods exist for moving cargo once it has been stolen—from e-fencing to exporting to reintroducing it into the legitimate supply chain; the end goal is for the product to reach a consumer.
- Exportation of stolen cargo is very common, especially to South and Central America for sale on the local market or for repackaging and sale back into the U.S. and European economies.
- Once criminals have found an industry or product type to steal and have developed an effective means for fencing the product, there is a high probability they will continue to target these or comparable goods and move them using the same methods until those means are no longer viable.
- While minimal evidence suggests that recession impacts will cause an increase in cargo theft, studies have shown that consumers are more willing to turn a blind eye when purchasing product that may have been stolen.

6

INTERNATIONAL CARGO THEFT
A Warning for the United States

INFORMATION IN THIS CHAPTER:

- Variations in cargo theft outside the United States
- Common modi operandi around the world
- Predictive modeling for supply chain risk
- Understanding risk based on regional or international boundaries

It is no surprise that the cargo theft hot spots in the world coincide with countries that play a significant role in the global and our domestic supply chains, such as Mexico, Brazil, South Africa, Malaysia, and the majority of Europe. Where these countries differ from the United States is the common use of violence involved in cargo theft. Hijackings, weapons, and assault are commonplace in these countries but violence is almost never associated with cargo theft in the United States. There are multiple reasons for this disparity—mainly the general crime culture, laws regarding the use of violence, and hardening of the supply chain.

As supply chains are hardened in the United States, however, there is an argument that violence may increase as cargo criminals become more aggressive out of necessity to steal high-value goods successfully. On February 27, 2011, a group of 15 armed gunmen raided the Unigen Corp. electronics facility in Fremont, California. The gunmen forcibly locked all the employees in a high-value cargo security cage while they loaded a tractor–trailer full of components before making their getaway.

While such instances are still considered a rarity in the United States, they certainly occur in several countries overseas where they are considered more the rule than the exception.

Malaysia, for example, has the highest rate of cargo crime in the Asia-Pacific region, which is centered primarily along the north–south highway corridor, where large amounts of precious metals and electronics are moved every day. Cargo thieves in

71

Malaysia are very aggressive, and because laws make the use of a firearm during the commission of a crime punishable by death, they resort to using knives and machetes while they hijack loads. This technique, however, makes the criminals more aggressive; as their bladed weapons do not share the intimidation factor of a loaded gun, it is not unusual for the thieves to become more physically engaged with the driver or facility employees during the commission of the robbery.

Cargo to and from China has traditionally not been targeted for theft; however, shippers frequently suffer from losses through pilferage (particularly at seaports), along with intellectual property right theft and counterfeiting. Over the past few years, however, full-truckload thefts have been on the rise, but still nowhere near the rates of other Asian countries such as Malaysia, the Philippines, or India.

The high-reward, low-risk nature of cargo theft is not limited to the United States. In many countries, criminals caught stealing cargo face minimal punishment. In 2007, a man in Melbourne, Australia, received two and a half years in prison for stealing $10 million in cigarettes from a customs-bonded facility, the equivalent of 1 day in prison for every $11,000 worth of product stolen. If he had not been caught, the theft would have cost the Australian government approximately $2.3 million in lost tax revenue alone.

Europe

Cargo theft modi operandi (MO) in Europe are conservatively 5 to 10 years ahead of those in the United States in terms of tactics and aggressive behavior (Burges, 2006), where cargo theft remains largely a nonviolent crime. During the late 1990s, cargo theft in Europe began to increase significantly, resulting in awareness for shippers, forwarders, and carriers throughout the continent, which led to hardening of the supply chain. As product became more difficult to steal, cargo thieves became more aggressive with nonviolent theft giving way to hijackings, weapons use, forced police stops, and kidnappings.

The United Kingdom, France, Italy, Germany, and The Netherlands all report high rates of cargo theft annually, comprising an estimated 80% of all cargo theft in western Europe. Intrusion, pilferage, hijackings, and a variety of other MOs were seen throughout the continent as cargo thieves actively seek high-value goods and move them quickly across international lines and onto the black market.

While the overall number of full-truckload or container thefts has increased year after year for the past decade, the number of thefts from vehicles (chiefly intrusions) has declined. Accordingly, the loss value per incident continues to rise as cargo thieves seek a higher return for their efforts. Thieves are stealing more expensive goods, committing larger scale thefts, and continuing with aggressive tactics as needed to succeed in the commission of their crimes. In the United Kingdom, the average value per theft incident increased an estimated 70% from 2009 to 2010.

In July 2009, a truck loaded with tobacco products was forced to stop in Hamburg, Germany, by two men in a black Volkswagen. Armed with a handgun, the driver of the VW forced the truck driver to get out and then handcuffed and put him in the trailer. They took the truck to another location where they transferred the cargo into another trailer and made their getaway.

Thieves in England are arguably the most aggressive of any European country. It leads the European Union (EU) in terms of violence across all crime categories with cargo theft being no exception where violence during the commission of freight theft is often considered to be the norm, not the exception, as is the case in the United States.

In contrast to most of the Western Hemisphere, where cargo theft incidents are primarily thefts of entire trailers or ocean containers, the most common MO in Europe is referred to as intrusion. Intrusion is the act of breaking the lock or security seal of a trailer or slashing the panels of the ubiquitous soft-sided "curtain" trailers and stealing as much of the cargo as possible before discovery. Intrusion also refers to breaking into a cargo storage facility to steal product. Incidents of fake police checkpoints, diverted drivers, violence, and forged paperwork have all been recorded by pharmaceutical and electronic companies in Europe.

Intuitively, reported cargo theft is highest in countries that actively compile statistics and participate in cargo theft incident-sharing programs. The vast majority of cargo theft data is derived from law enforcement sources, and countries with dedicated agencies to deal with cargo theft (such as TruckPol in the United Kingdom) no doubt have better cargo theft data than countries that don't. Thefts throughout eastern Europe and Russia are far more difficult to track as data are sparse, with mostly anecdotal information being provided. The lack of verifiable and quantifiable statistics exists throughout the global supply chain, continuing to make the development of a clear picture of the scope and magnitude of this international problem nearly impossible.

The United Kingdom is one of the most active countries addressing and combating cargo crime in Europe. According to *Freight Industry Times*, an estimated 40,000 truck crimes are reported annually in the United Kingdom, mostly in England's nine regions. These crimes, according to the industry quarterly publication, account for £500 million worth of stolen trucks and cargo.

TruckPol, the U.K.'s national freight crime intelligence unit, however, estimates higher losses. It says that each instance of freight crime averages more than £25,000 per loss. Just as discussed earlier, product loss is just part of the total extent of the economic damage, as it can also adversely affect client trust and loss of business. Of course the converse holds true—meaningful benefits can accrue to companies with better supply chain security, leading to fewer thefts and, principally, more profitable sales.

One aspect of over the road security that differs in Europe, particularly the United Kingdom, from that of the United States, is vocal support for the development of secure truck stops. In a European survey taken in 2009, 66% of respondents rated the availability of secure truck stops as poor or very poor, while none rated them as very good (Falkner, 2009). There were 793 truck thefts recorded in the fourth quarter of 2008, which is approximately the total number of thefts recorded for the entire year in the United States.

According to the World Bank's Logistics Performance Index (LPI), the United Kingdom is one of the top 10 logistics performers in the world. Results of a 2009 survey (released in 2010) ranked the United Kingdom No. 8 worldwide, moving up one position from the previous year, with Germany garnering the top spot, scoring a composite 4.11 out of a maximum score of 5.

Strategically located in the center of Europe, linked to Scandinavia via the Jutland Peninsula and claiming some of Europe's most advanced road and rail networks, Germany sees more cargo pass through it than any other country on the continent. This factor also makes it one of Europe's hot spots for cargo theft. That said, theft reports from Germany decreased in 2010 as compared with 2009, although this could be more the result of a drop in crime reporting than to an actual decrease in cargo thefts.

Regardless, according to the World Bank's most recent LPI, Germany ranked No. 1 worldwide in the survey, scoring 4.11 out of a total possible of 5.

Germany took serious steps in 2010 to address its chronic shortage of secure parking places for trucks. Projects have been undertaken to expand rest areas and to create more than 8000 secure parking spaces for trucks along several major highways.

Another effort aimed at improving logistics operations saw progress in 2010. The North Sea Freight Intelligent Transport Solutions project hosted a workshop in June at the Port of Bremerhaven to demonstrate how the system would work and to showcase the range of information expected to be made available to drivers and transport operators via this system. Among its objectives is to allow drivers to plan and adapt their activities by supporting them with route-related information, including live traffic updates, crime hot spots, secure parking areas, weather alerts, and truck-specific road conditions.

Cargo theft in France continues to be on the rise, according to the government's Central Office for the Fight Against Itinerant Delinquency. Their latest report estimates that cargo crime in 2010 increased to 1600 thefts with a total loss of €31 million.

Although France is known for underreporting of cargo crime, it is nonetheless clear that the country remains a high threat area for cargo crime in Europe due to factors such as its size, geographical location, and high level of economic development. Continued incidences of cargo theft in 2010 and 2011 made France a hot spot within the EU again.

The majority of cargo thefts occur in northern France, especially in Ile-de-France (Paris metropolitan area), Champagne-Ardenne, and Picardy, although the Languedoc-Roussillon region and the Rhone Valley in the south are also affected by this type of crime.

Thieves also are known to run trucks off the road or force the driver to stop by posing as police or customs agents. At other times thieves simply block the road using two or more vehicles.

Some sophisticated criminals have been known to fraudulently create transportation companies, get hired to move a shipment, and then simply drive off with the cargo, never to be seen again. As in other areas of western Europe, violence occurs occasionally during the commission of cargo thefts.

For example, on October 8, 2010, a truck driver hauling 24 pallets of cigarettes was hijacked in Croissy-Beaubourg. According to reports, two armed assailants forced the driver to stop by waving guns at him. The driver was then kidnapped by one of the assailants while the other drove the trailer to another location, where accomplices were waiting. Although police arrived on the scene quickly, the thieves managed to escape with half the load.

Goods most targeted by cargo thieves in 2010 were electronics, building/industrial materials (including metals), clothes/shoes, and consumer care products. As in other European countries, thefts of metals have increased. Most of the incidents were thefts from vehicles parked in rest areas along major international and national roads, with thefts from warehouses also prominent. In 7 of every 10 in-transit incidents, thieves slashed the trailer's side curtain or cut off the security seal while the driver was either away from his vehicle or sleeping in it.

Thieves have somewhat altered the profile of cargo crime in Spain recently as they switched their focus to products that tend to net them higher profits and also expanded their repertoire of MOs. Thieves there are known for using aggressive and unusual tactics, including stealing from trailers while the vehicle is in motion.

Regions reporting the highest number of cargo thefts in 2010 were Catalonia in the northeast, Madrid in the center, and Andalusia in the south. Together these regions accounted for more than 50% of all cargo theft incidents in the country.

Early in 2010, in Catalonia, opportunistic thieves forced open the trailer doors and stole a load of liquid crystal display televisions from a truck parked at a Figueres service station during a heavy snowfall. Also in this region, an entire trailer loaded with consumer electronics was stolen in the town of Terrassa. The theft occurred after the driver parked the truck less than a mile from his pickup location and went home for lunch. The driver discovered the theft only after police notified him that the truck was parked irregularly. The loss was estimated at €275,000 ($346,514 USD).

Methods used by cargo theft gangs in Spain are among the most varied in Europe. The most daring by far is when they hit a targeted truck while it is in motion, often at night. As depicted in the Spanish newspaper *El País*, one of the thieves' vehicles moves in front of the truck in order to slow it down. Then, thieves traveling closely behind in a pickup or similar vehicle jump from the hood to the back door of the truck, where they saw or force open the lock. (In some reported cases last year, thieves actually harnessed themselves to the target truck.) The thieves then pass the cargo from the truck to their accomplices in the cargo bed of the pickup, repeating this action until several have been loaded. These thefts often are discovered only after the trucker arrives at his destination. Loads of computers, televisions, and food products were reported stolen by thieves using this MO (Figure 6.1).

Russia is one of the hot spots for cargo theft in Europe. Well-organized, heavily armed and at times well-connected gangs operate throughout the country, often hijacking trucks and kidnapping drivers at gunpoint. In addition to cargo crime, endemic corruption and infrastructure deficiencies remain as serious impediments to the supply chain. The lack of serious investment in Russia's aging road and rail networks is hindering

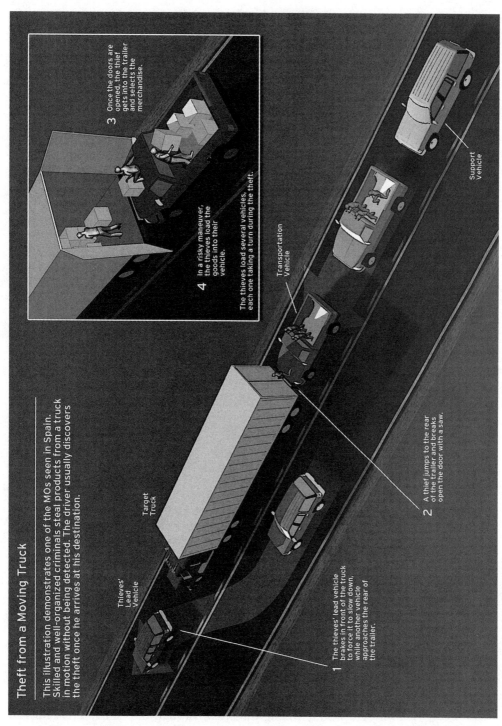

Theft from a Moving Truck

This illustration demonstrates one of the MOs seen in Spain. Skilled and well-organized criminals steal products from a truck in motion without being detected. The driver usually discovers the theft once he arrives at his destination.

Thieves' Lead Vehicle

Target Truck

Transportation Vehicle

Support Vehicle

1 The thieves' lead vehicle brakes in front of the truck to force it to slow down, while another vehicle approaches the rear of the trailer.

2 A thief jumps to the rear of the trailer and breaks open the door with a saw.

3 Once the doors are opened, the thief gets into the trailer and selects the merchandise.

4 In a risky maneuver, the thieves load the goods into their vehicle.

The thieves load several vehicles, each one taking a turn during the theft.

Figure 6.1 Courtesy of FreightWatch.

logistics operations. Moreover, their crowded and poorly maintained highway system presents problems for the road transport industry. In its 2010 Corruption Perceptions Index, Transparency International, an independent organization that monitors business corruption worldwide, ranked Russia as the most corrupt nation among the developed economies.

For the logistics industry, corruption can affect the efficient and safe flow of goods along every link/node of the supply chain when organized crime and corruption have penetrated both public and private sectors. Strong relationships with officials from customs and other regulatory bodies are essential to those companies wanting to avoid losses.

Media reports from the country last year indicate that government efforts to fight crime and corruption are growing. Earlier this year, more than 50 international companies operating in Russia signed a pact pledging intolerance to bribery. Russia and Europol have also started negotiations on a cooperative plan to combat transnational criminal activities.

Cargo theft in Russia regularly involves guns and/or violence, as armed hijackings and robberies are common while most thefts occur while cargo is in transit. Russian thieves force drivers to stop by pretending to be police or customs officers.

That is not to imply that stationary vehicles are ignored. Five masked and armed men stole 13 tons of caviar from a truck parked in an unsecured area near St. Petersburg. The driver and a security guard hired to escort the truck were kidnapped and later released in a suburb. The loss was estimated at nearly $650,000.

Mexico

Since 2007, cargo theft in Mexico has taken on new and more sophisticated patterns. Small-time gangs have evolved into specialized rings that are employed by organized criminal groups to target specific high-value shipments that can be resold easily through the informal market across the country (Chavez and Tello, 2009). Cargo crime in Mexico is extremely violent. There is a history of assaults throughout the country, for example, in the state of Veracruz, due to the large volume of goods imported and exported through the port.

Mexico City serves as the country's supply chain hub, with inbound lanes traveling east–west from the nation's seaports, while a tremendous amount of goods transit north–south to and from the United States; the so-called "Golden Cross." With so much product being transited through this single area, Mexico

City has arguably the highest rate of cargo theft per geographic size than anywhere in the world, with an estimated 1000 cargo theft gangs operating in the Federal District alone. This criminal activity is having an impact. According to the Mexican Association of Insurance Companies, insurance premiums for policies covering cargo damage and theft increased $1 million in a single year (Chavez and Tello, 2009).

Products targeted in Mexico are similar to most other countries, where electronics, building materials, high-end clothing, and food are all commonly sought after by cargo thieves. Gangs operate by developing relationships with distributors and/or transport company employees. The thieves also infiltrate the companies to gain access to information on shipments and transit routes.

Driver give-ups are common in Mexico due to the propensity for violence used by criminal gangs. Information flight is also common. Armed escorts, armored cabs, and duress systems (such as real-time communications, remote engine kill switches, or panic buttons) are the only protection against armed criminals and a successful hijacking. A driver in Mexico without some or all of these countermeasures is virtually helpless to keep his cargo secure. In contrast, just remaining with a load in the United States generally is all it takes to keep criminals at bay.

The intense conflict between drug cartels and the Mexican government since the turn of the century has affected all facets of society. In addition to cargo theft, natural disasters, and infrastructure deficiencies, drug-related crimes present a serious financial threat to the supply chain and transportation industry. In 2010, transportation companies in Mexico experienced a 12% increase in security costs (e.g., security cameras and surveillance systems) and cargo insurance rates also rose by 20% in some states with high cargo theft activity.

Drug-related violence has particularly affected northern border cities, such as Nuevo Laredo, Reynosa, Tijuana, and Ciudad Juarez, all major conduits for cross-border trade. The cartel's effort to control trafficking access routes into the United States is the main reason for the constant and deadly fighting.

Cargo theft activity is rampant in central Mexico. This is also the region where products stolen across the country most often end up being sold on the black market, particularly in the boroughs of the Federal District. In 2010, half of all cargo theft occurred in the Federal District and the states of Mexico, Jalisco, Puebla, Veracruz, Hidalgo, and Nuevo Leon.

Despite the elevated cargo theft risk in some states, only certain cities contribute to this status. For instance, in the state of

Coahuila there is a high risk of cargo theft; however, the majority of incidents take place in the cities of Monclova, Torreon, and along the Saltillo–Monterrey and Monclova–Monterrey highways. The rest of Coahuila state experiences low levels of cargo crime.

According to FreightWatch International, Cities with the highest cargo theft activity include Mexico City, Guadalajara, Puebla, Monterrey, Pachuca, and Queretaro. Additionally, theft activity on highways between and within certain states (Queretaro–Mexico, Puebla–Veracruz, Guadalajara– Colima, Mexico–Puebla, Saltillo–Monterrey, San Luis Potosi– Queretaro, Mexico–Veracruz, Guadalajara–Michoacan, Pachuca–Sahagun City, and Nuevo Leon–Tamaulipas) is worth noting by shippers, transportation intermediaries, trucking companies, and anyone with logistics responsibilities.

Food and beverage items were the most stolen commodity in Mexico in 2010, with one apparent anomaly—loads of sugar, followed by building and industrial materials and automotive parts, especially in the states of Jalisco, Michoacan, State of Mexico, and the Federal District. Also, agricultural products such as cereals, grains, seeds, and beans were among the most targeted.

Mexican organized cargo theft gangs have developed sophisticated methods to steal loads. As in many Latin American countries, Mexican cargo thieves develop working relationships with, or threaten, warehouse and distribution center employees in order to obtain cargo routing and schedule information. This, of course, allows them to plan and execute thefts with minimal risk of capture by police.

Many gang members also find employment in warehouses and trucking companies (usually as drivers or security guards) to obtain the necessary information. When they steal the truck, they make police and cargo owners believe that the driver was the victim of a hijacking.

One method—gang members wearing police or military uniforms to conduct fake truck safety inspections—continues to be among the most popular in Mexico. This MO allows them to find out the type of products inside the trailer before deciding whether to proceed with a theft.

Central and South America

Central and South America have booming cargo theft markets. They buy stolen goods from the United States and sell them on the black markets locally or elsewhere. Most cargo stolen in the United States is exported to countries such as Paraguay,

Venezuela, Colombia, Brazil, Argentina, the Dominican Republic, and Costa Rica (Palmer, 2009, p. 1169) where it will be either sold domestically or repackaged and returned to the United States, appearing as legitimate product, and thereby reintroduced into the U.S. supply chain.

Supply chain risk as a whole in Central and South America continues to vary, sometimes widely from country to country, with Brazil, Guatemala, and Venezuela ranking among the most dangerous. Shippers and freight forwarders continue to be keenly aware of these variances, as transportation providers can at times be very selective as to which countries they will cross into and which ones they will not.

Cargo theft gangs in South America are generally organized, with in-depth planning, well-honed methods for eluding police, and intricate networks for fencing stolen goods. While violence or the threat of violence is common, some countries such as Guatemala report a larger percentage of drivers being injured during theft incidents than countries such as Brazil, where cargo crime is so common that interaction between the driver and the thieves has almost become routine.

Electronics, including computers, cell phones, and high-definition televisions; pharmaceuticals; food products; metals; and tobacco are commonly targeted goods in Brazil. Brazilian cargo thieves will use fake police, corrupt police, and violence (to include deadly violence)(Burges, 2009b, p. 46) to get what they want. In March 2008, a security manager of an electronics manufacturer in Jundiai and his family were kidnapped while at a shopping mall. The kidnappers held his wife and children while their associates forced the manager to enter the warehouse, allowing the criminals to overtake the facility and hold all of the employees as hostages. As a result, more than 100,000 components and 2000 laptops were stolen.

Criminal gangs in Venezuela and Guatemala continue to rank among the highest countries for cargo theft using the topography and road infrastructure to easily block convoys of trucks, move stolen products into secluded areas for storage, and then sale on the black market.

The majority of cargo theft incidents in countries such as Brazil, Venezuela, Argentina, and Guatemala are classified as hijackings. Thieves use violence or the threat of violence to stop trucks en route and steal the goods—often along with the truck and trailer.

There is at least one bright spot in Latin America, however; to combat cargo theft in Colombia, the federal government has developed a national strategy through its law enforcement organizations to target cargo theft gangs and influence the various factors that contribute to criminal activity, investigating incidents vigorously, conducting 800 in 2010.

In Brazil, the southeast region accounts for 81% of all cargo theft in the country. The level of industrialization and high freight volume in Sao Paulo, Minas Gerais, and Rio de Janeiro states provide an opportunity for thieves targeting loads traveling along highways connecting major industrial cities.

Official cargo theft statistics indicate a total of 5198 cargo thefts in Sao Paulo state over a 9-month period representing a total loss of R$207.8 million ($125.9 million USD). The highest number of incidents, just over one-half, occurred in the capital, Sao Paulo, with another 38% taking place on highways around the city. Cargo theft has been consistent since 2008, with only minor fluctuations.

Despite a decrease in the total number of thefts occurring during the first three-quarters of 2010 compared with the same period in 2009, there was a corresponding uptick in the value of the stolen goods.

Brazilian cargo thieves know that most trucks are equipped with global positioning system (GPS)-tracking devices and attempt to circumvent the devices by installing towing equipment or trailer hitches on their vehicles. They make off with only the trailer, gambling that the GPS remains in the tractor they have left behind. More tech-savvy cargo thieves are starting to use GPS signal jammers in order to thwart logistics security.

Cargo thieves in Brazil are violent. In every attack, they kidnap the driver until the stolen load is transferred to a secure location. If provoked, they will beat the driver severely.

Advanced cargo criminals try to develop relationships with warehouse employees, police, lawyers, and custom agents in order to obtain false documentation and information about types of loads and routes. They also forge strong alliances with buyers of stolen goods and deliver products to them through intricate distribution networks that rival those of legitimate businesses.

In Argentina, the attention given by law enforcement to cargo theft is higher than in other South American countries. Federal, provincial, and local law enforcement agencies, together with victimized companies, often work together from the moment a theft is reported. However, the number of theft incidents exceeds their collective ability to solve all cases or even to prevent fast-acting thieves from delivering a load to a buyer or getting it onto the black market.

In order to minimize losses from cargo theft and thus avoid rate increases, insurance companies operating in some provinces of Argentina now require trucks to have GPS devices or escorts as a precondition for getting coverage.

According to Argentina's Chamber of Commerce of Logistics Operators (CEDOL), in 2010, an average of five to six truckloads of cargo were stolen per day on highways connecting large cities. The CEDOL estimate an annual average of 1800 to 2200 cargo incidents with an average loss per incident of $250,000.

Currently, 72% of all cargo thefts occur in Buenos Aires Province, which is composed of the city of Buenos Aires and its outlying districts, as well as the surrounding Federal Capital district. However, industry reports state that cargo thieves are expanding to other provinces, with increases noted in Santa Fe, Mendoza, San Juan, Formosa, and Entre Rios. According to police reports, six districts in Greater Buenos Aires account for 56% of all cargo theft in the area. These are La Matanza, Mercedes, Moron, San Isidro, Almirante Brown, and Quilmes. Two other districts within this region, San Martin and Lomas de Zamora, also consistently report high rates of cargo theft.

Wednesdays and Fridays show the highest incidences of cargo theft, at 24 and 22%, respectively. The frequency of incidents on Mondays and Tuesdays are both at 17%, with Saturdays and Sundays only a combined 20%. Moreover, 70% of all incidents take place between 6 a.m. and noon, while 14% occur from noon to 6 p.m. and 8% from 6 p.m. to midnight.

Consumer electronics, primarily televisions, cell phones, and laptop computers, continue to be the most desirable goods to thieves, accounting for one-third of all thefts.

The consumer care and tobacco category comprised 22% of the total stolen, with perfume and cigarettes favorite targets. Building/industrial (13%), food/drinks (11%), and pharmaceuticals (6%) round out the rest of the list of notables.

According to the newspaper *La Nacion*, 90% of loads stolen in Argentina in 2010 consisted of products that had been ordered in advance. Thieves seek loads based on their client demands. In 2010 and 2011 the most targeted products within the food and beverages category were agricultural products, mainly cereals, soybeans, and sugar cane. Also, truckloads of soft drinks, snacks, and alcohol were among the most targeted.

According to CEDOL, 41% of all cargo theft in Argentina occurs within the Greater Buenos Aires area, while 26% occurs in the Federal Capital and 11% in the interior of the country, with Santa Fe and Cordoba topping the list in the interior.

Although recent industry reports show an increase in the number of thefts in the central Argentine province of Cordoba, some companies operating in the province have witnessed a dramatic *decrease* in thefts since 2008. Thanks to law enforcement efforts, these companies no longer see cargo theft as one of the main problems for their supply chain and transportation industry; instead, other crimes, such as drug trafficking and bank robberies, are the major threats in the province.

Argentine cargo thieves are among the most sophisticated in Latin America, and technology, including the use of GPS jammers, plays a key role in their MOs. Some gangs also are known to seek technical assistance from professionals in the use of GPS jammers to discover other useful methods to thwart technology advances coming from the security industry.

Argentine cargo thieves are organized gangs with hierarchical and complex structures. As such they are known to assign roles to specific gang members for all phases of the operation, such as intelligence gathering, planning, attack, sales, and distribution. Furthermore, the theft gangs often have ties with terrorist organizations and powerful drug cartels.

Although thieves are well-armed in Argentina, the use of violence is rare during attacks. Given the already strong law enforcement focus on cargo crime, thieves tend to avoid the violent hijackings that may result from the increase in highway surveillance, stricter punishments, and longer prison sentences. However, if drivers do not respond to intimidation or other nonviolent tactics, the criminals will not hesitate to act swiftly and cruelly.

Thieves have the necessary tools, such as trailer hitches and towing equipment, to carry out the theft quickly. They move the load to the next truck stop or another safe haven where they can unload the cargo.

Guatemala's Public Ministry estimates that Guatemala City alone experienced an average of 18 cargo thefts per week in 2010. It is no surprise, then, that companies operating in the capital regularly protest what they consider inadequate police protection against cargo thieves.

Next to Guatemala City, the cities with the highest cargo theft rates were Palin in Escuintla and the Santa Ana municipality in Peten. Guatemalan police reported that an average of 200 truck hijackings occurred each month, at a loss of $2 million, in the four regions comprising the southern coastal region of Escuintla, Santa Rosa, Retalhuleu, and Suchitepequez.

In Guatemala, most thefts occur on the main national highways, with some of the worst spots for cargo crime along the Inter-American (CA-1), the Atlantic (CA-9), and the Pacific (CA-2) highways. Although police patrol these roads, their efforts are sporadic and generally limited to populated areas. Due to the continued threat from cargo thieves on these highways, companies are requiring that their vehicles travel in convoys, both organized and informal.

Like other countries that experience high rates of cargo theft, trucks in transit and warehouses are the most common targets of thieves. Guatemala's well-armed gangs all tend to use the same MO when attacking trucks. They intercept their target and force the driver to stop by using or threatening violence. Some gangs are known to steal the truck along with the cargo and then sell the truck's parts on the black market.

Compounding the cargo theft problem in Guatemala are cases that involve collusion by corrupt police and/or employees of warehouses and transport companies. For example, Guatemalan authorities identified a powerful cargo theft gang they believe has been operating for years along the Atlantic Highway. Specializing in stealing loads of food and drink products, clothing and footwear, and auto parts, the criminals are adept at obtaining insider information as to the types of products being transported and the trucks' routes.

On November 17, 2010, the National Civil Police arrested five members of the Guatemalan military during the theft of a truckload of food, beverages, and consumer care products along the northern section of the Atlantic Highway.

Police also recovered a stolen truckload of food products worth $48,000 USD at a cargo thieves' garage. Three additional stolen loads of automotive parts and fabric were also recovered.

Africa

The continent of Africa is wrought with cargo theft. While South Africa often gets the most attention for high rates of violence and cargo theft (Burges, Global risk, 2009, p. 47), that is mainly due to its being the most industrialized country on the continent and therefore offering increased abilities to measure and track crime. Based on numerous crime statistics and estimations, western Africa (including Nigeria, Niger, Liberia, Cote d'Ivoire, Ghana, Togo, Benin, and Cameroon) has the highest risk of cargo theft in the continent.

South Africa is plagued with theft and violent crime. Statistics specifically regarding cargo theft are not maintained in South Africa, but hijackings of trucks and freight are far more common than the nonviolent versions of cargo theft seen in the United States and Canada. That being said, cargo theft has been rising in South Africa, particularly in the areas around the airport in Johannesburg. This increase in cargo theft rates and hijackings has reached the point of being "unacceptable." According to an eyefortransport September 11, 2008, article, "South Africa [is] becoming a no-go transit route for foreign shippers." In the article, eyefortransport went on to report that the convenience of transporting through South Africa is outweighed by the "financial risk due to cargo theft."

According to FreightWatch International, it is important to note that the frequency of hijackings that occur in South Africa far exceed the rates of traditional "nonviolent" cargo theft in virtually every other country where such data exist.

Asia

Asia presents extremely diverse levels of cargo theft and risk to supply chain operations. Malaysia and the Philippines both report frequent incidents of in-transit cargo hijackings, with violence or the threat of violence being used in commission of the crime. In contrast, China experiences a far different form of cargo crime, with small-scale pilferage considered rampant and intellectual property rights at the core of multinational business concerns.

There's little question that cargo theft and supply chain risk have increased throughout Asia over the past decade. As manufacturing and logistics functions continue to operate at high levels, the overall appetite for obtaining products at less expensive prices grows. India is becoming increasingly noted for large-scale theft incidents, including truck hijackings and warehouse robberies. While these trends continue to be of concern, it is important to note that the rate of theft experienced throughout Asia is at a significantly lower rate than seen in countries such as Mexico, Brazil, and South Africa.

China presents a wide array of security problems for manufacturing plants and distribution centers. Political, labor, and social unrest are tightly controlled in a more reactive than preventive mode, while inconsistencies and unpredictability in regulatory enforcement are the norm. The central government's limited control over the regulatory whims of regional and local governments, where corruption is rampant, exacerbates this problem.

The government is now reasserting its authority over directing energy and economic policy in certain strategic industries, such as energy, aviation, and possibly financial services. There is also a move to direct investment and trade relations from southeast to inland China. China has long stood out as a country at very low risk for cargo theft. However, corporations have seen a definite increase in theft numbers since 2009.

Pilferage has always been an issue in China, with items stolen in free trade zones or at seaports and airports prior to a load's shipment overseas. Throughout 2010, however, reports of full-truckload thefts increased steadily, presenting logistics managers with a security problem that was largely unheard of in years past.

The major high-tech manufacturing centers around Shanghai, Beijing, and Tianjin began to see shipments targeted, mainly involving finished consumer electronics and microprocessors. Law enforcement and media in these areas reported cases in which criminals followed loaded trailers in order to steal full or partial loads.

An MO seen before in China, and in certain countries in Europe, continued to be an issue in 2010, particularly in southern China. In this MO, criminals steal cargo from loaded trucks that are in motion on highways. As Figure 6.1 illustrates, criminals board the moving truck, break into the trailer, and then offload the cargo into a trail vehicle—all without the driver's knowledge that theft is transpiring. One report indicated that this MO was used four times in quick succession on the highway system near Heyuan city.

Also in 2010, Hong Kong saw increases in thefts of wine and other alcoholic beverages after this region eliminated all duties on wine. Criminal activity subsequently increased as thieves attempted to smuggle the stolen alcoholic beverages into mainland China.

As in the past, pilferage and larger thefts from ports and free trade zones in 2010 saw the products reintroduced into the Chinese market through means that avoid taxation. It is at this point that many counterfeit products are introduced into the supply chain to be sold as legitimate products.

It is well known, of course, that China's massive counterfeiting operations reach well beyond the country's borders. In 2010, U.S. customs conducted more than 14,000 seizures of counterfeited products originating in China, far more than from any other country. Additionally, one report showed that 64% of all seized counterfeit goods in the EU originated in China.

Malaysia, which manufactures a significant amount of goods, especially those of the high-tech variety, is one of the countries in Asia with the highest rate of cargo theft—violence or the threat of violence is often involved. The major manufacturing centers around Penang and Kuala Lumpur especially have attracted organized criminals, including the long-active Mamak gang, which turned to cargo theft after high-tech manufacturing increased.

Facing increasing rates of cargo theft in the country, the Malaysian government stepped up law enforcement efforts, specifically monitoring heavily transited routes and cargo theft gang activity, and focused on improving interagency coordination. In several cases, police presence in a certain area, and thus officers' quick response to a theft in progress, prevented loads from being stolen. For the same reason, some criminals were arrested, and the cargo fully recovered, within minutes of a theft.

Initial reports in 2010 indicated significant success by authorities in curbing cargo theft activity, as theft rates fell dramatically in the first half of the year. However, despite law enforcement efforts—and more stringent in-transit and facility security measures—cargo crime continues to be a significant problem, with hijackings occurring on a weekly basis.

Complicating the issue are reports of collusion between local police and criminal gangs, which thwarts efforts to curb cargo theft activity and creates a level of distrust between industry and some local agencies. According to the Asia Economic Institute, Malaysia remains one of the riskiest areas in Asia in terms of cargo theft. Although perceptions are beginning to change, further action to combat cargo crime will be necessary.

Thieves in Malaysia commonly target high-value products. Hence, building/industrial, electronics, food/drinks, and consumer care product types were most favored by thieves in 2010. In the building/industrial category, precious metals topped the list, while cosmetics were most targeted in the consumer care category.

Thefts of precious metals occurred in transit and at the site of delivery, suggesting that either loads were being followed for long distances or the thieves had previous knowledge of delivery times and the cargo being transported.

As in previous years, thefts across the country occurred both in transit and at warehouses. Most in-transit thefts involved armed hijackings, with criminals either threatening violence or using violence in order to stop trucks and steal their cargo. Thieves also staged truck break-ins to get at cargo in 2010.

Among the many issues facing the supply chain industry in India are infrastructure deficiencies, including the lack of paved roads connecting major industrial cities with the rest of the country, cargo theft at the hands of well-armed thieves, and corrupt law enforcement officials and industry employees who collude with cargo criminals.

Although the Indian government approved several projects for future improvements on roads and railways and set up dragnets on some of the worst highways for cargo crime, little headway was made on any of these fronts in 2010. As in previous years, efforts to nab the worst of the cargo theft gangs and opportunistic criminals failed, and the number of incidents increased in some states.

Meanwhile, 2010 perhaps will be remembered for its outbreak of iron thefts, principally in the central Indian state of Uttar Pradesh. Nationwide, thefts of iron in just the second half of 2010 were valued at $13 million. Although no figures were provided, this reportedly far exceeded such thefts in previous semesters.

Given that 65% of all cargo is transported by road in India, the nation's roads—paved and unpaved—are hot spots for cargo criminals. However, warehouses and freight forwarding yards are also frequent targets. Furthermore, although stolen loads are often recovered in other countries, such recoveries are rare in India, even when authorities are alerted immediately to a theft.

The central and north-central regions of India, especially Uttar Pradesh and Madhya Pradesh states, reported increases in cargo thefts in 2010. Additionally, the risk remained high in regions throughout India's upper half.

For instance, the number of theft incidents increased along National Highway 22 (NH22) near the city of Jabalpur, Madhya Pradesh. In this area, thieves tend to target trucks traveling on unpaved roads connecting to the NH22. Most incidents occur late at night when police surveillance is limited. Although Jabalpur police were aware of specialized cargo theft gang operating in this area, efforts to capture any of the gang members or discover where they keep the stolen merchandise failed.

Cargo theft in this country is mainly the domain of opportunistic criminals who take advantage of isolated trucks or loads left unattended. However, there are also many sophisticated gangs that operate in an organized manner. In all cases, thieves are well-armed and can be violent.

Organized gangs are known to collude with corrupt police and/or employees of warehouses or freight forwarding yards. Employee payoffs in return for information regarding cargo arrivals and security measures in place allow thieves to plan their attacks.

Additionally, organized thieves tend to store stolen cargo in illegal warehouses before selling it on the black market or distributing it to existing clients. Police in the Dhule District, Maharashtra state, discovered several illegal warehouses reportedly operated by an extremely violent, powerfully armed gang. The outgunned district police apparently did not confront this gang.

Within the building/industrial product type, steel and scrap iron were among the most targeted products in 2010. In fact,

Indian government authorities have expressed their concern over the $13 million in losses resulting from stolen truckloads of iron in the second half of 2010.

Placed on alert to this rising problem, police established security checkpoints to inspect commercial trucks on highways where the greatest number of iron thefts had occurred, including near the hot spot city of Varanasi, Uttar Pradesh state. Although several drivers were held for lack of proper documentation, none of the gangs targeting truckloads of iron was captured.

According to industry reports, some thieves have begun to target iron with the intention of selling it to state-owned Indian railways (IR). In January 2011, an IR employee was apprehended in the midst of negotiating with a cargo thief. Both the thief and the IR employee were arrested. Police have been unable to determine whether the thieves responsible for the increase in iron theft belong to a single large gang or multiple independent gangs.

Regardless, iron thefts have continued into 2011. For example, a truck loaded with 13 tons of scrap iron was stolen in the city of Mandi Gobongarh, Punjab state, in January. The truck disappeared from a restaurant parking lot while the driver was having a meal.

Conclusion

One of the most common trends that differ when analyzing cargo theft around the world compared to the United States is the presence of the driver when the crime occurs. When assessing cargo theft in Europe, Mexico, South America, and Asia, in almost every case, the driver is present when the crime occurs, requiring the criminals to force the driver to separate from the load. Whether through violence or simple threat, these criminals take a more overt and aggressive action that is rarely seen in the United States, where cargo theft is almost exclusively nonviolent, occurring while loads are left unattended.

Key Points

- While cargo theft in the United States is almost exclusively nonviolent, that is not the case in other parts of the world, including Mexico, Brazil, South America, Russia, South Africa, and throughout Europe.
- The reason for the high levels of violence in cargo theft in other countries is complicated and goes deeper than supply chain security and operations; however, these do have a direct impact on the methods used by criminals to steal cargo.

- Even for countries that border each other, the methods and rates of cargo theft from one country to the next can change dramatically.
- As the supply chain become increasingly hardened to prevent supply chain theft, industry professionals can expect thieves to alter their tactics, targeting, or level of aggressiveness in order to obtain the product they need to sell on the black market.
- It is critical to understand the various changes in supply chain risk from country to country (or region to region) and ensure that in-transit security policies are adjusted accordingly.

7

PRODUCT TARGETING

INFORMATION IN THIS CHAPTER:

- What products are popular for cargo criminals to target
- Cargo theft data analysis
- Supply and demand—a criminal's perspective
- Active targeting—how thieves steal the right cargo

> *By the time I grew up, there was thirty billion a year in cargo moving through Idlewild Airport and believe me, we tried to steal every bit of it.*
>
> **Henry Hill, *Goodfellas***

Cargo thieves steal every variety of products imaginable. Computers, cell phones, aspirin, cigarettes, wine, energy drinks, steak and lobster, lawn chairs, appliances, furniture, auto parts, you name it. If the American consumer has a use for it, a cargo criminal will steal it.

The author has been tracking cargo theft for FreightWatch since 2006 with the goal of determining the kinds of products cargo thieves go after, where the thefts occur, and the monetary losses that result from these crimes. When possible, based on the information available; date and time of the theft; city, country, or state of the incident; location type; thieves' modus operandi; product stolen; and its loss value are all recorded. The ultimate objective is to better understand cargo theft to be better able to provide meaningful intelligence and forward-thinking analysis to mitigate risk and prevent cargo theft.

The analytics allow tracking a variety of trends or patterns, including geography, method of theft, locations (truck stops, parking lots, terminals), and, the most critical information, the type of product stolen. As trucks travel down the road, the cargo they contain is the number one factor determining whether it will be targeted by thieves. Other factors could influence the likelihood that a theft occurs, but the product itself is the key driver for criminals.

While cargo thieves will steal literally anything, there are certain requirements that the product must meet. First, there has to be a demand for the product on the black or gray market. If the criminals (or brokers) cannot sell the stolen merchandise, then it is of no value. Also, the higher the demand, the easier the product is to sell, and therefore more desirable to the theft gang. Second, the more valuable the product is, the more likely it is to be targeted. High-definition televisions are more desirable than traditional sets; prescription drugs are favored over generics and designer clothes over low-cost brands.

Before going forward the reader needs to know that there is no universal product classification system in use by those who track theft data. For example, some list cell phones, televisions, and computers individually, while the system developed at Freight-Watch groups cargo into product categories such as electronics, consumer care, and building/industrial products in order to keep the listing manageable. A "miscellaneous" category was also added for products that do not fit neatly into any other category or when a shipment contains several types of goods like one would see in a less than truckload move.

The FreightWatch classification system, which the author used for this book, divides cargo into 11 product types:
- Alcohol
- Auto/parts
- Building/industrial
- Clothing/shoes
- Consumer care
- Electronics
- Food/drinks
- Home/garden
- Miscellaneous
- Pharmaceuticals
- Tobacco

It should also be noted that cargo theft data are fragmented because there is no centralized reporting mechanism in the United States (or elsewhere for that matter). Even if police and sheriff's departments around the country shared cargo theft reports with one another, or a single data repository, which they do not, many theft incidents are never reported to authorities at all. Whether it's for fear of negative publicity, a desire to avoid the hassle of police involvement, or another reason, many victims simply are averse to reporting cargo theft incidents. And yet logistics and security professionals would benefit from up-to-date and accurate cargo theft data. This dichotomy has led to the creation of a number of disparate cargo theft collection and distribution systems across the country. Even when combined, the information may not offer the most complete picture of cargo theft in the United States. However, it does provide a pretty decent snapshot, giving us theft trends and ratios of thefts by product type and locations, and pinpointing cargo theft hot spots.

Because of this lack of a single cargo theft data source, the author has spent six years collecting information from cargo theft task forces, insurance companies, online newspapers, and victims themselves, all in the attempt to capture the clearest picture possible of cargo theft within our national supply chain.

In 2010, FreightWatch recorded 899 incidents of cargo theft in the United States. In each case, the incident was categorized by product stolen, city and state of the theft, location of the theft if known (truck stop, parking lot, terminal, and drop lots, to name a few), and reported value of the loss. Figure 7.1 shows the level of thefts from 2006 through 2010.

While the number of incidents grew steadily each year, the average value per incident over that time increased by 108%. However, that only tells part of the story. Cargo theft trends are a push and pull between criminals seeking high-value cargo and those law enforcement and industry security specialists developing ways and means to reduce losses.

While the total volume of cargo theft in 2006 was significantly lower than the years following (310 incidents in 2006 vs. 899 incidents in 2010), cargo criminals were very successful in seeking high-value cargo that year. Possibly the tipping point in the logistics industry, the year cargo theft prevention registered in the

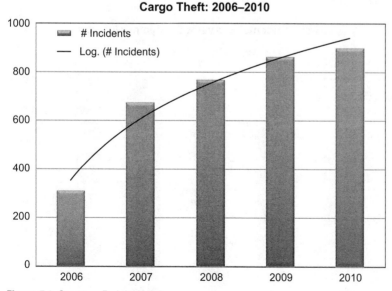

Figure 7.1 Courtesy FreightWatch.

minds of shippers of high-value cargo, as well as the companies handling, storing, or transporting them, was in 2006 when there was an inordinately large number of catastrophic (over $1 million) losses.

That year, 20 such incidents were recorded, representing 6.5% of the annual total. In comparison, in 2010 the 28 incidents of the same magnitude made up just 3% of the thefts.

The average loss per incident peaked in 2009 for a variety of product types, including electronics and pharmaceuticals. As shown in Figure 7.2, it reached $591,000, surpassing every other year studied.

From 2006 through 2010, electronics were the most targeted product type, variously accounting for between 19 and 38% of the total. Only in 2010 did thieves not target electronics more than any other product type. That year, the food and beverage product type accounted for 21% of all cargo theft incidents, whereas electronics loads dropped to second, with 19% of all incidents (Figure 7.3).

Pharmaceutical thefts grew exponentially from 2006 to 2008, increasing a whopping 283% (from 12 recorded thefts in 2006 to 46 incidents in 2008). Since 2008, the rate of growth has been almost flat, with one additional incident in 2009 and three additional incidents in 2010.

The average loss per incident has been volatile, with a low of $1.13 million in 2007 to a peak just under $4 million 2 years later (Figure 7.4). For additional data and analysis of cargo theft in this particularly high-value industry, see Chapter 9: Pharmaceuticals.

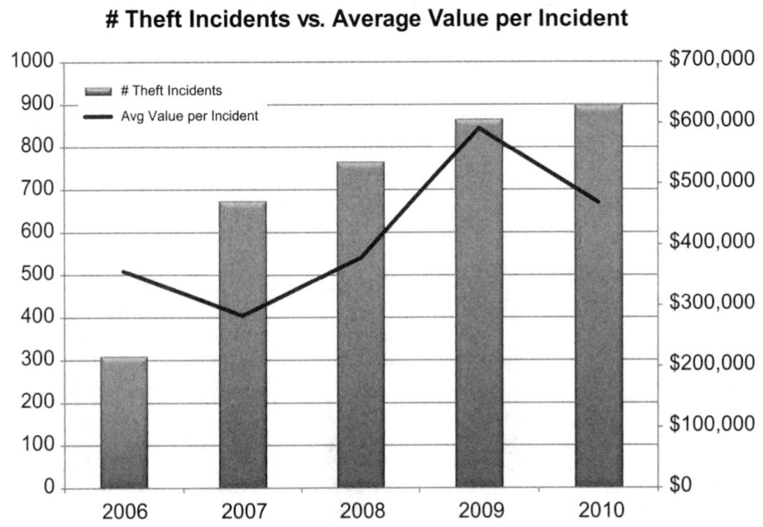

 # Theft Incidents vs. Average Value per Incident

Figure 7.2 Courtesy FreightWatch.

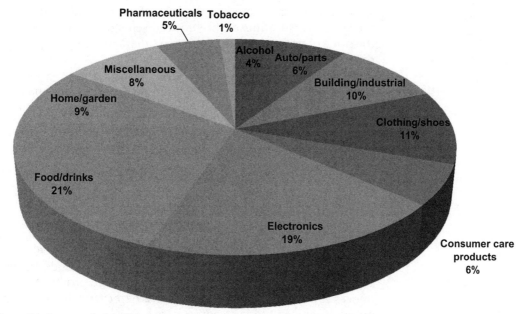

By Product Type: 2010

Figure 7.3 Courtesy FreightWatch.

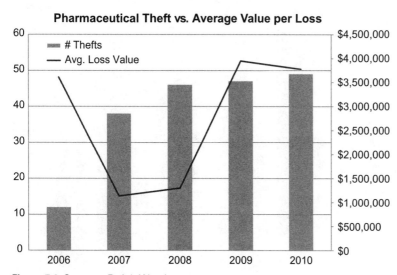

Pharmaceutical Theft vs. Average Value per Loss

Figure 7.4 Courtesy FreightWatch.

Product Demand

As in any capital market, the laws of supply and demand are the key drivers for those who buy and sell stolen goods. As such, the price of products on the legitimate market clearly plays a vital role in the desirability of cargo.

Over the 2010 Labor Day weekend, a group of thieves entered the S.H. Bell Company yard in Baltimore, Maryland, and made off with six trailers loaded with high-value metals, including nickel and copper, valued at $1.82 million. The theft was hardly an anomaly that year, as 43 cargo theft incidents involved metals, for an estimated $17.4 million in direct losses.

Not coincidentally, the value of copper and other precious metals had skyrocketed in 2010. Figure 7.5 demonstrates the correlation between the value of copper and the rate of its theft.

This trend toward targeting high-value merchandise is not isolated to a single industry or product type. Cargo theft gangs are becoming increasingly selective in the products they steal, often traveling unheard of distances to attain the desired goods. Instead of more readily available generic or lesser value products, cargo thieves are going after more expensive name brands, which are more attractive to today's consumers.

Price, of course, is not the only factor thieves consider before selecting targets. A demand has to exist as well. One factor is the

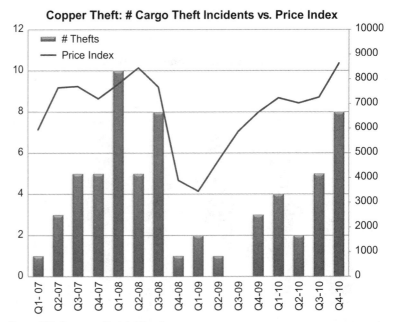

Figure 7.5 Courtesy FreightWatch.

increased marketing efforts of manufacturers and retailers, as consumers are driven to higher end goods and are less willing to settle for a similar (generic) product. The products people are enticed to purchase appear on television and newspaper ads, the Internet, and even on NASCARs race cars are the exact same products that cargo thieves are going to steal. In this market-driven economy, criminals will opt for in-demand merchandise that will fetch them the best return.

This is especially clear in markets in which new products emerge regularly, such as the electronics industry. As new cell phones and computers are rolled out, thieves, like the rest of us, quickly lose interest in outdated models. The pharmaceutical sector is another good example of the power of advertising on consumer buying habits, and ultimately on the products that thieves target. As the miracle drugs to alleviate aches and pains and improve the overall quality of people's lives exploded over the past few years, so too did consumer demand. This desire is reflected directly in the rate of cargo theft. Cargo thieves are no different than legitimate for-profit enterprise in that they must understand their markets and the products they will be able to sell at a premium. Because of this, high-demand products are targeted and then sold at discounted rates on the black and gray markets, netting thieves huge amounts of money for a few days of work.

Additionally, cargo thieves are becoming more sophisticated, conducting preoperational surveillance, knowing where products are made and stored, and acquiring inside information through various means. This has increased the range that thieves are willing to follow a load due to the increased confidence that their efforts will result in a large payday. After putting in the effort to find and travel to the load's origin, following loads longer distances is now less of a drawback for cargo thieves.

Product launches are prime opportunities for cargo thieves to achieve a significantly higher margin. When a new cell phone, computer, or gaming console is set to hit the market, cargo thieves often increase their operations in and around areas where these products are made, stored, and shipped with the goal of stealing a full truckload of them and then getting the items to their outlets at/before the official launch date.

Active Targeting vs. Pot Luck

In the late 1990s and early 2000s, cargo thieves were far more opportunistic. In those days most of them were content with the "pot luck" approach at truck stops, where they would steal any accessible rig and then determine whether the product inside could be fenced. While not terribly efficient, this modus operandi (MO) posed a minimal risk to cargo thieves and required little or no preoperational efforts on their part. The drawback, however, was that loads were often sold for minimal profit or were simply left abandoned because they had no "market" value. The desire for increased profit drove cargo thieves to actively target higher end products that could be fenced easily.

Of course, this method of cargo crime involves more investment; gangs now have to gather more intelligence, travel, be more persistent in tracking in-transit cargo, and take greater risks in stealing the goods.

CASE STUDY: THEFT IN CLUSTERS

Cargo theft often occurs in clusters. These clusters can be geographically based (a rash of thefts happening in a short period of time in a small area), product based (multiple thefts of the same product type occurring in a short time period), or MO based [numerous thefts occurring with a similar (often rare) MO being used].

Sometimes, on rare occasions, a cluster of thefts will occur that meet several of these categories. In November/December 2011, a rash of thefts occurred that were targeting gaming consoles. A common target for cargo criminal, especially during the holiday season, gaming consoles are moved quickly by criminals and sold on the black market effortlessly for extremely high profits. This was a classic example of product-based clustering.

Additionally, details surrounding these thefts placed each theft either within close proximity to Memphis or the cargo had departed the Memphis area as the point of origin before the theft had occurred. In fact, each of these thefts involved trailers and cargo that had all departed the same distribution center in Memphis, Tennessee (Olive Branch, Mississippi). This example of geographical-based clustering was not only very apparent to the victim in this string of thefts, but also provided significant evidence of the potential for insider information compromising the security of these shipments (i.e., criminals being provided shipment information in order to accurately find, follow, and steal these high-value loads).

Often, cases of clustering involve a particular theft gang, such as the South Florida cargo theft gangs. In this case, evidence was traced to theft gangs from New Jersey (where the cargo from the first theft was recovered by the state police), and additional cargo from these thefts was discovered in the Miami/Hialeah area. While a connection between gangs in New Jersey and Florida has always been relatively known, cases such as this only help confirm this apparent link.

A case such as this creates not only a substantial headache for shippers as cargo lost in mass during the holiday season can put a significant strain on the supply chain and generate the potential for lost sales and damaged relationships with retailers, but could also have significant impact on the bottom line for the freight forwarder that could possibly lose a significant customer as a result of the potential security breach.

This case also demonstrates the willingness of cargo criminals to continue targeting and stealing loads even though law enforcement agencies are aware of their activity. The first load of gaming consoles was recovered within days of the theft by the New Jersey State Police, before any of the subsequent thefts had occurred, but the criminals continued to target and successfully steal loads from the Memphis logistics center, stealing in excess of $5 million in product.

Finally, this case reaffirms the notion that if a supply chain is targeted or hit successfully by a theft gang, every effort should be made to discover why and how the theft occurred and what can be done to prevent it from occurring again in the future. Too many times shippers feel that after a theft or attempted theft has occurred that they are no longer "on the hook" for gang targeting, but nothing could be further from the truth as criminals will continue to exploit weaknesses in a supply chain until they have filled their orders or that weakness is eliminated.

Components of Active Targeting

Active targeting refers to the method used by professional cargo criminals to steal a particular product. The process works as follows.

The broker or buyer places an order with the cargo criminals for a product type or a specific item. The theft gang conducts research to determine where the product is manufactured or distributed. The gang then chooses which facility to target, assembles the necessary team, and travels to the location, usually in a rental car or two acquired by an acquaintance of the team (often female). Finally, the gang will rent a room at an inexpensive motel near the targeted facility.

The gang will then conduct surveillance of the facility to determine the flow of goods in and out, shipping schedules, and other intelligence that will help them select the trailer that contains their target.

During the information-gathering phase, gang members will seek insider details through a number of methods from the more simplistic fishing or purchasing information from employees (sometimes purchasing information), seemingly wandering into facilities pretending to be lost and seeking directions, or attempting to be hired as a temporary employee. On rare occasions, more elaborate means have been devised with some thieves going so far as to place hidden cameras near doors to record entry codes.

Once the gang has the intelligence it needs, members move into an operational mode by trailing the truck. Historically, thieves would go as far as 200 miles before giving up and selecting another load. In recent years, however, they have been known to follow a desired load more than 500 miles just waiting for the driver to stop and create the vulnerability ("cargo at rest …") they seek. Then they pounce.

Because cargo theft continues to be a nonviolent crime, thieves generally wait for the driver to leave the load unattended before they move in to steal the entire tractor–trailer. Gangs are proficient at an almost endless array of creative means for gaining access to locked tractors and getting them started for a quick exit.

Once stolen, the truck is driven a short distance to an out-of-sight place and the tractor is unhooked and another tractor, usually stolen a day or two before the job and swept clean of any form of tracking device, is then attached to the trailer and the load is moved to its destination.

After his 2009 arrest in California, one suspected cargo thief told authorities he primarily targeted facilities that would preload trailers and leave them in their lots overnight, preferably over the weekend. By going after these loads, the criminal was able to move the cargo a significant distance before it was ever discovered missing and reported to police. He even acknowledged having been stopped by police on several stops for traffic violations. In each case he was allowed to continue on his way because the police had no way of knowing he was transporting a stolen load.

Cases such as the previously mentioned Plainfield, Indiana, incident illustrate the lengths to which theft gangs will go in order to find, "case," track, and eventually steal high-value cargo. No longer do criminals operate only within the general areas where they live or limit themselves to following loads over short distances. Today's cargo criminal has a far different mentality—one consistent with what the general public would deem appropriate for a modern business enterprise.

Key Points

- Cargo theft is a market-driven crime. Organized theft gangs will seek out, target, and steal products that are most desired by the consumer, and therefore easiest to sell for a high profit on the black market.

- By understanding market demand, price fluctuations, and new product releases, manufacturers and shippers can predict the risk of being targeted by thieves and adjust their supply chain security program accordingly (for more information, see Chapter 11: Determining Risk).
- Although truck stops and other unsecured parking areas continue to be the most common location for thefts to occur, organized theft gangs rarely use "pot luck" methods to steal cargo any more.
- Shippers and transportation providers should not underestimate the lengths to which criminals will go following loads across the country in order to steal them at their first opportunity.

8

HIGH TECH

INFORMATION IN THIS CHAPTER:

- Historical perspective of cargo theft
- Introduction of industry collaboration to combat cargo theft
- Analysis of theft trends in high-tech sector
- Discussion about the most targeted items by cargo criminals

Background

Cargo theft as we know it today began during the high-tech boom of the 1990s, with the proliferation of the computer industry by companies such as Compaq, Dell, HP, and others. With this boom came a new-found problem, cargo theft, which was largely unrecognized as it slowly crept into our supply chain until the problem became rampant, causing significant and adverse financial and operational impact on these companies.

During the latter half of the 1990s, security in the high-tech industry centered primarily on manufacturing sites preventing internal theft. There was minimal effort to reduce in-transit theft or burglaries from third-party warehouse facilities.

In April 1997, Gary Alton, then divisional security manager at Compaq Computers, received a call from one of the company's logistics managers. Thieves were running roughshod over Compaq's supply chain, stealing computers and laptops seemingly at will and something had to change.

Compaq, it turned out, was not the only company suffering such losses. Discussions between Alton and Don Greenwood at Sun Microsystems, Steve Lund at Intel, and others indicated an industry-wide problem. With this recognition came a decision to have an informal meeting in Phoenix in July 1997. Compaq, Sun Microsystems, Dell, Intel, HP, and Texas Instruments all attended with 35 representatives from 25 different companies showing up.

The initial meeting ended with a clear agreement that their industry was under attack and in desperate need of a proactive approach to securing their supply chains, including facilities and in-transit lanes, and that the manufacturers had to lead this effort.

A second meeting was hosted later that year in Boston where the Technology Asset Protection Association (TAPA) was formed, chaired by Mr. Alton, with the goal of sharing information, developing supply chain security standards, and reducing losses from theft and pilferage.

Direct losses were not the only problem this sector was facing. Theft of components and accessories added an entirely different dimension to the problem, as manufacturing centers failed to receive needed components on time, slowing the production process, resulting in lost revenues, profits, and customers.

TAPA's emergence, however, was only part of the required response. The size and breadth of the U.S. supply chain still left cargo thieves with countless opportunities to steal goods as physical and procedural weaknesses became known, human errors occurred, and lapses in security arose. Cargo theft rates still grew. In 2004, the Los Angeles County Sheriff's department investigated 284 thefts, an increase of 20% from 2003 (Gale Group, 2005).

2006 through 2010

From 2006 through 2010, FreightWatch recorded 896 cargo theft incidents in the electronics sector, accounting for more than $512 million in direct losses. While the annual number of cargo thefts moved considerably in the electronics sector from year to year over the 5-year period (peaking at 221 incidents in 2007), the net result was an overall increase. At the same time, however, the percentage of electronics thefts in relation to all cargo theft in the United States declined significantly.

In 2006, electronics comprised 38% of all cargo theft incidents, while years later this product type accounted for only 19% of the total—for the first time dropping to second place on the list of most stolen products (Figure 8.1).

Not surprising, given their "Big Three" status, California, Florida, and Texas recorded the highest levels of cargo theft activity in the electronics sector from 2006 to 2010. Tennessee, Illinois, and Georgia followed with New Jersey just behind on the 5-year argument (Figure 8.2).

The theft of electronics is far more likely to occur in and around Los Angeles, Miami, and Dallas/Fort Worth. In fact, 34% of the thefts in these three metropolitan areas involved electronics loads, as compared to roughly 20% nationwide.

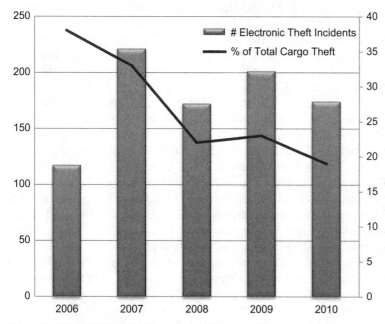

Figure 8.1 Courtesy FreightWatch.

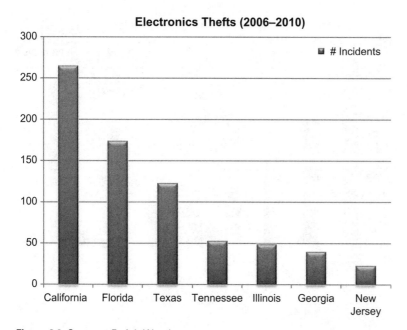

Figure 8.2 Courtesy FreightWatch.

When looking at the county level for electronics losses, Los Angeles County, Miami-Dade County, Dallas/Tarrant counties, and San Bernardino County collectively accounted for 41% of all electronics thefts in the country over this time (Figure 8.3).

Memphis/West Memphis (Shelby/Crittenden counties) was the fifth most active area in the country for thefts in this industry. Cook County (Greater Chicago area), which was the site of nearly every electronics theft incident recorded in Illinois, was next in line.

One of the most surprising discoveries, given its status as one of the nation's hot spots for cargo theft, was the relatively low number of electronic thefts in Fulton County (Atlanta). In this sector, Fulton County placed ninth, even trailing Texas's El Paso County and Florida's Duval (Jacksonville) County. Indeed, Fulton County earns its overall high rate of cargo theft as a result of thefts in other industries, such as food/drinks and building/industrial, and a large number of thefts of all product types in the Atlanta general area, but outside the county lines.

Although the number of cargo thefts was higher every year after 2006, the increase was not steady. An examination of theft totals on a yearly basis reveals an almost cyclical pattern (see Figure 8.4), as rates increased and then decreased every other year consistently.

The average loss per incident was less consistent, with varying percentages of growth each year from 2007 to 2009, followed by

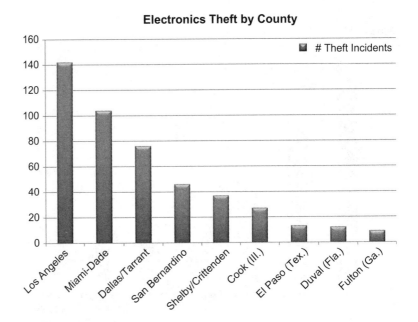

Figure 8.3 Courtesy FreightWatch.

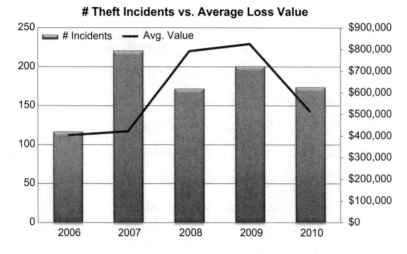

Figure 8.4 Courtesy FreightWatch.

a substantial decline in 2010. The most dramatic change occurred from 2007 to 2008, when the average value of an electronics theft jumped from $421,900 to $791,900, a 71.1% increase.

It has long been understood and now proven through analysis of cargo theft data since 2007 that cargo is more at risk over weekend periods than during the middle of the week. This absolute, however, does not hold true when looking specifically at the electronics industry.

While thefts occur with somewhat increased frequency over weekend periods, Tuesday and Thursday both experienced higher rates of theft than Saturday. Still, the highest levels of theft of this product type were recorded on Friday and Monday (Figure 8.5).

One possible explanation for this deviation from traditional cargo theft patterns is the level of targeting of electronics products by cargo criminals—a result of the degree of desirability of these products on the black market. The opportunity to fence coveted products quickly provides added incentive for aggressive cargo thieves to work midweek. Additionally, the electronics sector as a whole, now well versed in the dangers of cargo theft, is less likely to leave high-value loads stationary during the weekend.

Most Targeted Items

The popularity of electronics is easy to understand, as people now view them as necessities, buying them at an astonishing pace over the past decade. Televisions, smart phones, laptops, tablet

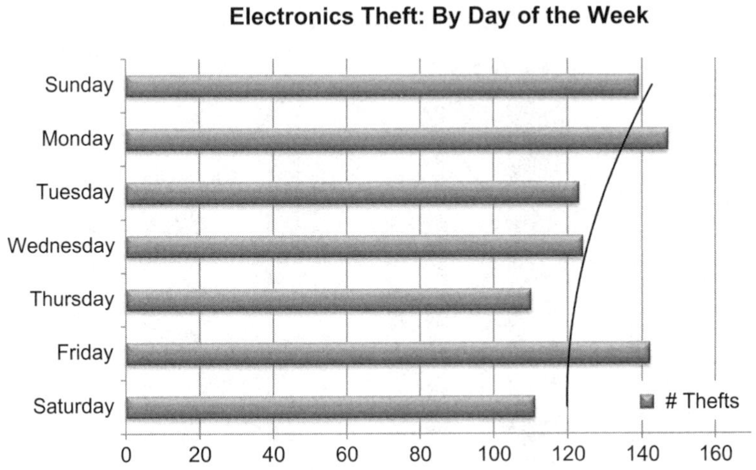

Electronics Theft: By Day of the Week

Figure 8.5 Courtesy FreightWatch.

PCs, gaming consoles, and software are all commonplace in the U.S. economy, with an ever-increasing demand.

According to a survey conducted in March 2010, 91% of all Americans (approximately 275 million people) use mobile phones, up 15 million users from the same survey conducted the year prior, and up from just 82% in November 2007.

An additional 15 million consumers of mobile phones in just a single year is a clear indication of the incredible demand for high-end electronics—iPhones, Androids, and Blackberries—expensive items people will gladly purchase for a lower price, thus creating a significant black market demand. In fact, the demand is so high that many insurance companies are unwilling to insure full truckloads of mobile phones due to their extreme value and the rate at which cargo thieves target them. The average load of mobile phones can range from $1 million to in excess of $3 million, rivaling pharmaceuticals and tobacco products in value, but far surpassing each for demand and ease of sale on the black market.

Similarly, with 99% of all Americans owning a television, and with more than 80% of the population having multiple sets in their households (not to mention those in businesses, restaurants, bars, hotels, and other public places), there is little surprise that TVs are the most sought-after product by cargo criminals in the United States. With over 300 loads of televisions stolen since 2007, criminals are frequently successful at seeking, tracking, and acquiring large quantities, with flat screen and high-definition models being the most popular.

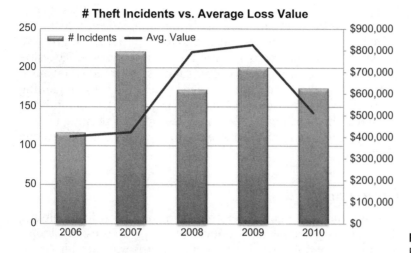

Figure 8.6 Courtesy FreightWatch.

Cell Phones

The volume of cargo theft within the cell phone industry has been inconsistent since 2007. The highest number of thefts of this product (a subset of the electronics product type) occurred in 2007, with 26 recorded incidents, followed by 21 incidents in 2009. However, although 2007 ranked first, it was last in average loss at $802,700 per incident. By comparison, 18 theft incidents were recorded in 2010, with an average loss value of $3.65 million (Figure 8.6).

By state, Florida (27), California (12), and Texas (12) all recorded double-digit theft incidents, with Tennessee (6), Kentucky (5), Illinois (4), and Georgia (4) rounding out the top seven. By city, Miami recorded 16 theft incidents of cell phones from 2006 to 2010, the most on record. This was followed by Fort Worth with six loads, Memphis with four loads, and Los Angeles with three.

Televisions

When compared to any other specific item, televisions are the most commonly stolen item by cargo thieves in the United States. With over 250 recorded theft incidents since 2006, televisions are the easiest items to sell on the black market with no service and activation requirements that accompany computers, laptops, or cell phones; televisions are extraordinarily easy for consumers to acquire and begin using within minutes of their purchase.

On July 7, 2008, a shipment of high-definition televisions arrived in Miami, Florida, as part of a new product launch.

Stopping briefly for fuel and to use the restroom, the truck driver returned to find his rig, along with the load, stolen, a loss estimated at $4 million, one of the largest television heists on record.

While television loads generally have a lower average value ($375,000) than other electronics, such as cell phones (average value: $1.9 million), laptops (average value: $590,000), or gaming consoles (average value: $730,000), their marketability is so immense that stealing television loads is akin to printing money as they almost guarantee a speedy and successful sale on the black market.

Computers

Computers and computer equipment are historically among the most targeted of all products by cargo thieves. Desktops, laptops, notebooks, hard drives, and accessories are all stolen throughout the United States with little geographic concentration and done so routinely month after month. Companies such as HP, Dell, Toshiba, Sony, IBM, and Lenovo continually update and alter their supply chain security programs attempting to stay ahead of criminal elements targeting their cargo.

With the boom of personal electronics in the late 1990s and early 2000s, computers were among the most sought after of all items by cargo criminals. Companies manufacturing, assembling, and transporting items within the computer sector quickly realized they were under fire from these gangs, leading to the eventual creation of the Technology Asset Protection Association and other similar groups that continue to thrive today.

With emerging technologies, new products, and a consistent demand by consumers, the ability of criminals to move computer-related products on the black and gray markets is high, with good profit margins for the gangs and their brokers while enjoying the minimal risk of arrest and prosecution associated with cargo crime.

Chips, Chip Sets, and Memory Devices

Historically, computer chips have been highly sought after by cargo criminals. The value to product size ratio is higher than any other electronics equipment and rivals most pharmaceutical products. High-end computer chips packed into a shoebox-size carton can easily be worth seven figures, making their desirability for cargo criminals and their brokers unmistakable.

At approximately 8:45 a.m. on Sunday, February 27, 2011, fifteen armed gunmen entered the gated property of Unigen

Corp. in Fremont, California, by cutting a hole in the fence. Armed with automatic rifles and handguns, the suspects, all dressed in black, accosted employees, binding, gagging, and securing them in the company's cargo security cage. The suspects then proceeded to steal flash memory chips, a theft valued at $34 million.

According to multiple experts in the electronics field, a take this large would be too much for sale in the U.S. market, making export to foreign buyers a likely scenario, possibly China. Before the product could be exported, however, law enforcement was able to track down the product through a variety of sources and methods, eventually recovering all the stolen cargo and arresting 9 of the 15 suspects. Additionally, two men arrested were identified as Pierre Ramos and Leonardo Abrium—employees at Unigen Corp.

The investigation was spearheaded by REACT—a multicounty technology crime task force led by the Santa Clara County District Attorney's Office (Benedetti, 2011). The quick action by the team and key leads culminated in the product recovery and the arrests made.

Consumer Electronics

Consumer electronics are extremely popular for cargo criminals to steal, as with the other products listed earlier, due primarily to the demand by the consumer and their ease of sale on the black market. Televisions (discussed previously in this chapter), gaming consoles, and book readers are constantly on the thieves' radar. From 2006 to 2010, over 200 consumer electronics loads were stolen in the United States with another 18 loads of gaming console and software (games).

A recent subset of consumer electronics is book readers such as the Amazon Kindle and the Barnes and Noble's Nook, as well as tablets such as the iPad and various other similar products. A sea container of book readers can be worth up to $2.5 million—a significant take by criminals for a product that is extremely easy to move on the black market or reintroduce into the gray market.

Key Points

- The modern era of cargo theft began with significant losses to the high-tech industry.
- This spike in cargo theft led to creation of the Technology Asset Protection Association, the first industry group formed specifically to combat over the road and facility cargo crime.

- Criminals highly motivated to acquire cutting-edge and newly created products will deviate from normal trends to acquire them, including thefts from highly secured facilities and yards.
- Televisions are the most commonly stolen type of electronics.
- New products being introduced into the market are at extreme risk of being targeted by cargo thieves and should be given special security consideration during both storage and distribution.

9

PHARMACEUTICALS

INFORMATION IN THIS CHAPTER:

- Attractiveness of the pharmaceutical sector for cargo thieves
- Cargo theft trends in the pharmaceutical sector
- Methods of theft, storage, and sale of stolen pharmaceuticals
- Impact of supply chain complexity and cargo security

> *It was quickly no longer a matter of "if" we were going to get it, but a matter of "when."*
>
> **Kenneth Obriot, Wyeth Pharmaceuticals**

On June 17, 2009, a driver pulled his tractor–trailer into a TravelCenters of America truck stop approximately 5 miles off of Interstate 40 in Denmark, Tennessee. Having just completed a 5-hour leg of his trip from a distribution center in Louisville, Kentucky, to a medical supply wholesaler in Memphis, he was anxious to stretch his legs and fuel up. He filled up and then went inside the truck stop to pay the cashier and grab a quick shower. When he returned a short time later his entire rig, along with $10 million in prescription drugs, was gone—a loss of approximately 100 times that of the average bank robbery, and one that would ultimately cost the shipper, a foreign-based pharmaceutical manufacturer, an estimated $47 million in product recalls.

Cargo theft of the pharmaceutical industry has exploded since the turn of the century. Although thieves in Canada, Mexico, Brazil, and a few other countries occasionally target this sector, no other country has experienced anything like the boom seen in the United States, particularly since 2007. In 2010, this sector recorded 49 cargo theft incidents, a 287% increase over 2006 levels.

One argument for the spike in thefts is the emergence of heavy marketing of prescription drugs designed to do everything from improve a patient's quality of life to treat life-threatening conditions. With television commercials and other advertisements promoting the benefits of a vast array of new and improved drugs, consumers are now driving demand for many of these

115

products rather than the medical professionals who prescribe them.

Another argument for this demand could be the high value of the drugs themselves. With consumers struggling to afford name brand medications and the ability to move stolen goods easily into the legitimate market through secondary wholesalers, cargo thieves have a variety of methods for moving these high-value goods at substantial profit.

The result has been an explosion in cargo theft incidents throughout the pharmaceutical sector.

History

Although cargo theft has existed to some degree in the pharmaceutical industry since the late 1990s and earlier, organized cargo criminal groups started targeting loads in earnest in 2006.

Kenneth Obriot of Wyeth Pharmaceuticals in Madison, New Jersey, began tracking cargo thefts involving the industry in 2005, logging every pharmaceutical theft that occurred in the United States. Obriot began recording these incidents after his company, which had not experienced any thefts previously, lost two loads to thieves in 2004, both the result of what was then called "driver error." These "errors" involved breaks in established protocol, such as leaving a load unattended and dropping the load (i.e., detaching the trailer from the tuck and leaving it). Both thefts occurred off of the major transportation arteries in areas where it would be difficult for opportunistic criminals to find high-value cargo. Cargo thieves were now apparently targeting and trailing pharmaceutical loads. Previously, cargo theft in the pharmaceutical industry was considered more of an acceptable risk due to low quantities being stolen at very infrequent intervals. When thefts did occur, it was indeed more a case of "our time" or bad luck rather than overt targeting by cargo theft gangs.

While dealing with his company's two losses, Obriot became aware of thefts suffered by Abbot Laboratories and Bayer Pharmaceuticals around the same time. Comparing notes on the incidents, Obriot and his peers at Abbot and Bayer quickly realized similarities among the incidents, including the thieves bringing their own tractor to transport the loads, targeting products that were sold readily on the black market, and stealing the load the first time it was left unattended, revealing a more systematic approach by the thieves.

Obriot recorded a pharmaceutical theft at a truck stop in late 2005, followed by a two-trailer theft only a few weeks later from the same truck stop as the first theft incident where his company was victimized. He shared this information with Bob Monteiro of Pfizer and Chuck Forsaith of Purdue Pharmaceuticals, and they realized that the industry needed a means of sharing information to prevent incidents like the dual thefts from the same truck stop.

With Pfizer as its host, the pharmaceutical security group—later named the Pharmaceutical Cargo Security Coalition (PCSC)—held its first meeting in fall 2006 in New Jersey, with 40 professionals representing mainly pharmaceutical manufacturers in attendance. After opening the meeting with a few words, Pfizer's Bob Monteiro asked the attendees to share their experiences of losses they had suffered. The room went quiet for a few minutes before the chatter of small side conversations began to spread. Monteiro, realizing the open discussion he had anticipated was not forthcoming, took the podium again. This time he pointed out that everyone in the room was experiencing the same problem, cargo theft, and everyone in the room wanted the same thing, to make it stop. The best way to get there, Monteiro insisted, was for the professionals to share their experiences. With those words, a few hands reluctantly went up. Rick Demberger of GlaxoSmithKlein was the first to open up about a loss his company had recently experienced. After Demberger, others began to speak up one by one, until it dawned on everyone that each of the stories was resoundingly familiar. With that realization, the PCSC was born.

The next meeting, hosted by Purdue Pharmaceuticals' Chuck Forsaith 6 months later, drew more than 100 attendees, including a handful of security vendors. Meetings have been occurring consistently ever since then, the most recent in late 2011, with more than 300 people participating.

Pharmaceutical companies, like any others, dislike having their dirty laundry aired in the public. Add to that their inherent public trust issues along with the heavy government regulations involved. Within 48 hours of a pharmaceutical theft, a company can be sure that two agents, one from the Drug Enforcement Administration and one from the Food and Drug Administration (FDA), will come calling. This level of oversight provides additional motivation for the industry to harden its supply chain and seek out innovative ways to secure cargo and keep potentially dangerous substances away from unsuspecting consumers.

2006 through 2010

According to data collected by the author and reported by FreightWatch, Pharmaceutical thefts grew substantially from 2006 to 2008, increasing by 283% (from 12 recorded thefts in 2006 to 46 incidents in 2008). Since 2008, the rate of growth has been almost flat, with only one additional incident recorded in 2009 and two more the next year. Despite the rate of growth in pharmaceutical thefts since 2006, the average value per incident has fluctuated significantly, from a low average of $1.13 million in 2007 to the highest at $3.95 million in 2009.

While Tennessee ranked sixth in total cargo theft incidents since 2006, the state recorded the highest number of thefts in the pharmaceutical product type over the same time period, with 25 thefts. Florida was second with 20, and California was third with 17. Also noteworthy, Pennsylvania, fourth in pharmaceutical thefts with 16 theft incidents, ranks just 16th in total cargo theft (Figure 9.1).

At the county level, the Memphis area (Shelby and Crittenden counties) recorded the most pharmaceutical theft incidents with 20. Los Angeles County was second with 11, while Dallas/

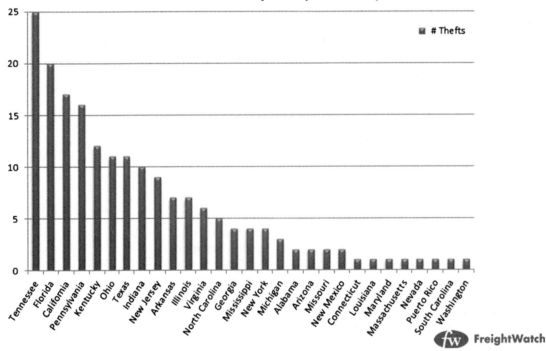

Figure 9.1 Courtesy of FreightWatch.

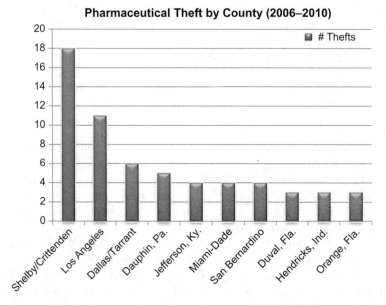

Figure 9.2 Courtesy of FreightWatch.

Fort Worth (Dallas and Tarrant counties) was third with 6. Of particular note, Dauphin County (Harrisburg), Pennsylvania, ranked fourth in pharmaceutical thefts over the 5-year period, even though the Harrisburg area ranks very low for cargo theft overall (Figure 9.2).

October stands out as the highest month for pharmaceutical theft incidents, recording 23 total incidents in that month from

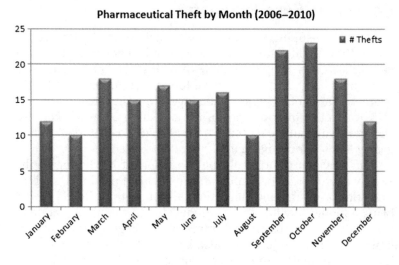

Figure 9.3 Courtesy of FreightWatch.

2006 to 2010. September, the second highest month for thefts in this sector, only ranked 10th for all cargo theft during the same 30-day period (Figure 9.3).

Full truckload thefts accounted for 87.8% of all pharmaceutical incidents since 2006. During the same period there were 12 hijackings, nine warehouse burglaries, and a single robbery.

Extreme Value

Given the prices of prescription narcotics on the streets, it is no surprise that there is such a high demand for pharmaceuticals on the black market. In a June 1, 2011, article featured in CNN *Money Magazine*, Parkia Kavilnaz compared the street price of prescription drugs with their price when sold legally. The disparity between the two was shocking.

According to the report, one pill of Oxycontin will cost $50 to $80 on the black market, while the cost is $6 per pill at a pharmacy. Oxycodone is another example that costs $12 to $40 on the street compared to the same $6 retail price. While both pills cost the same in a legitimate market, prices can vary significantly on the black market, largely based on demand and what people are willing to pay to acquire these narcotics through illicit channels. A tablet of Vicodin costs a mere $1.50 from the pharmacy, but can run $5 to $25 per pill on the black market. When the price for a prescription drug jumps from 2 to 12 times its normal value, and when criminals can obtain it at virtually no cost to them, the draw is clear. Why wouldn't criminals be attracted to this high-reward, low-risk venture?

Consumer Care Products

When developing the cargo theft database for FreightWatch, the author decided to separate consumer care from pharmaceuticals, as this category includes any products that are used on a person's body, such as creams, lotions, perfumes, and toothpaste, but are not designed to be ingested or injected.

The level of theft activity in the consumer care market also showed a substantive increase from 2006 (8) to 2010 (54), a staggering 575% jump (Figure 9.4).

This obvious trend could be the result of hardening of the supply chain for higher value pharmaceutical products, such as prescription drugs and narcotics. Although these loads would bring a higher pay day for criminals, due to the higher value of these drugs on both legitimate and illegitimate markets, consumer care products are also sought after due to their high level of desirability, and ease of sale, on the black market.

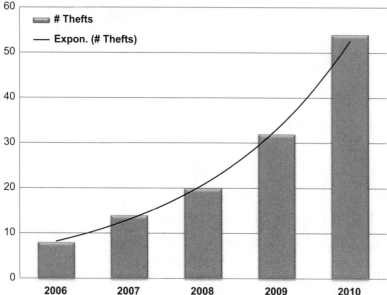

Figure 9.4 Courtesy FreightWatch.

During the 2006–2010 period, criminals stole consumer care products most predominantly in the counties and states in which cargo theft rates typically are high. Thus, Los Angeles, Miami-Dade, San Bernardino (California), and Duval (Florida) counties all made the top seven (Figure 9.5).

Middlesex County, New Jersey, recorded the second highest number of consumer care thefts, with 11. While New Jersey has emerged as a hot spot for cargo theft in the United States, incidents in the state are generally spread across all product types. This second-place ranking, however, clearly indicates the existence of a market for these products in North Jersey (Figure 9.6).

Other counties with high rates of consumer care thefts include Los Angeles, Miami-Dade, San Bernardino, Duval (Jacksonville, Florida), and Dallas. The presence of Los Angeles and San Bernardino are worth noting, as neither is present on the high theft rate list for pharmaceutical products.

Complex Supply Chain

Reprint from Cargo Security International—October 2009—with permission

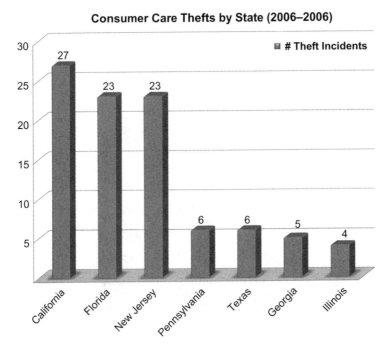

Figure 9.5 Courtesy FreightWatch.

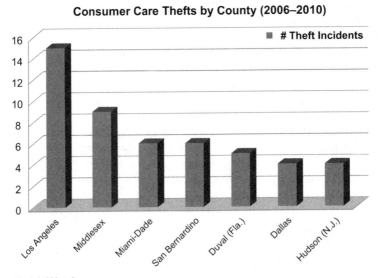

Figure 9.6 Courtesy FreightWatch.

Risks in the Pharmaceutical Supply Chain

While in-transit cargo theft within the pharmaceutical industry has persistently existed, the attention drawn to it, as well as overall values of those types of thefts, until recent times remained relatively low. Beginning, however, in 2005, the industry experienced a sharp rise in theft rates, which has seemingly continued to rise to the present day. Many factors are involved, to include the inherent risks involved in shipping consumable products, the complexity of the unique pharmaceutical supply chain, as well as the unusually high values that can be attributed to certain pharmaceutical products. This issue has caused both logistical and security personnel within the pharmaceutical discipline to become more intensely focused in attempting to protect the world's pharmaceutical supply chain.

The pharmaceutical industry has an inherent risk that is comparable to—and some would argue greater than—other industries such as electronics and tobacco. The most significant source of this risk lies primarily with products that are consumable: i.e., something a consumer would ingest, apply to, or use in conjunction with the body. As with anything that is considered "consumable" there are potential risks if the product is not maintained properly, stored at acceptable temperatures, or otherwise mishandled. If distributed by personnel that are not properly licensed, have contractual authority, and/or trained, these risks only increase.

Pharmaceutical product distribution is unique when compared to other commodities. Rarely does a manufacturer sell their products directly to an end-user or patient. Manufacturers typically sell products in bulk to drug wholesalers—examples being companies like McKesson, Cardinal Health, and AmerisourceBergen. The wholesalers, whose profit margins are somewhat less than a manufacturer, then sell the products to pharmacy retailers—examples being CVS, Walgreens, and Wal-Mart—as well as hospitals and other medical institutions. The retailers, in turn, sell to the end-users or ultimate consumers. This multiple-touch model presents an increased risk of theft within the supply chain and is noticeably different from other typical commodities.

Certain pharmaceutical products, for example, "biotech" type drugs used to treat those with medical issues such as cancer, literally take years to research, develop, and receive government approval for distribution. The processes used to manufacture these products are extensive, as well as very costly. Environments in which these products are manufactured are required to meet extremely high standards for processing, quality assurance, quality control, cleanliness, and overall accountability. Many in the discipline of pharmaceutical manufacturing follow established and required GMP (Good Manufacturing Processes) to remain compliant with government regulatory programs. All of these processes, whether the product is the high-end example of a prescription-required biotech drug, or a product purchased simply over the counter (OTC), those required processes add to the costs associated with manufacturing and distribution of that particular consumable product. Hence, those additional costs drive up the overall value of a pharmaceutical shipment—large or small.

In certain instances, the overall cost of an in-transit theft can easily exceed the original value of a particular shipment. To better comprehend that point one must understand that pharmaceutical products are manufactured in "lot" sequences, with each lot individually numbered for track and trace purposes. In certain instances an entire "lot" might be shipped in one conveyance, all at the same time. More commonly, however, that is not the case. Goods under a particular lot designation are more typically shipped multiple times, over an extended period of time, by numerous conveyances.

The largest, most valuable shipments of pharmaceutical products are those associated with the original manufacturer. Typically these are full truckload shipments that, because of their overall value and insurance requirements should receive a high degree of attention when it comes to in-transit security. Even today, unfortunately, this is not always the case.

As with every commodity, the concept of there being no "silver bullet" solution for supply chain security rings ever truer in the pharmaceutical sector. The multi-touch model of the pharmaceutical supply chain, coupled with the extremely high value of the product, brand reputation issues, and the multiple methods of shipping and distributing product create an environment that requires flexibility and creativity for both the logistics and security staff to ensure each shipment is as secure as possible.

By Chuck Forsaith and Dan Burges

Beyond Full Truckload

While the industry continues to make great strides in securing large-scale pharmaceutical shipments and storage facilities, criminals continue to adapt their targeting techniques that plague the industry and create a multimillion-dollar drain on manufacturers and their transportation and logistics partners.

Adding to the problem are reports of drug shortages in the United States. According to the University of Utah Drug Information Service, in 2010 there were 211 vital drugs reported as being in short supply (Aleccia, 2011). This not only drives demand (and price) in legitimate markets, but also skyrockets demand through illegitimate markets, making these drugs more appealing to cargo criminals and their middlemen due to the exponential profits that can be made by selling them into gray markets. As practitioners and consumers increase their demand for pharmaceuticals, so drives the market for criminals, middlemen, and others willing to skirt regulations to move product at low or no cost to them in order to sell it for high profits—even when placing consumer safety in jeopardy.

Deception and Counterfeit

Not a single pharmaceutical manufacturer anywhere in the world sells its products directly to a pharmacy, hospital, or other consumer retail outlet. Rather, they all go through wholesale channel partners. These distributors/wholesalers purchase product in bulk for sale to the retail outlets or to other, smaller distributors, and so on down the line the product goes, moving through a potentially complex supply chain with numerous touch points before finally reaching the consumer.

This complex process opens the door for dishonest entities to steal product and introduce the goods into the marketplace all under the disguise of legitimacy.

Deception occurs when stolen products are sold as legitimate product to a distributor, normally small ones eager to turn a profit; once purchased by them, the product resumes its "legitimacy" even though it is stolen, bound for legitimate outlets such as pharmacies and hospitals.

In 2009, an 85-year-old resident of Maryland was taking a litany of drugs for various ailments. Each day her husband would line them up on the kitchen table, ensuring that each dosage was correct and administered at the right time. One of these was an injectable medication that is prescribed for Alzheimer's, the ailment that prevented her from being able to administer her own medicine, so her husband did it and since he did so every day, he could readily see the results of the medication.

One day on the phone with his son, the father mentioned that the Alzheimer's medication hadn't been working like it used to. The son, a security executive for a pharmaceutical company, offered some words of encouragement, but over the weeks as they continued to chat, the father brings it up again—the medication isn't working like it used to. Finally, on the third time, the son flies to Baltimore and collects the medication from his parents and brings it back to his company's headquarters where there is a testing laboratory.

Their discovery was that his mother's Alzheimer's medication was, in fact, water, introduced into the pharmaceutical supply chain by someone, somewhere, that made its way to a reputable pharmacy and then purchased by a patient in need.

The introduction of stolen goods into the supply chain, without evidence of alteration or tampering, remains a struggle for the pharmaceutical sector as they not only strive to protect their intellectual property and sales, but, more importantly, to protect their customers and the consumer.

Secondary Wholesale Market

The complexities of a pharmaceutical supply chain create opportunities for criminal enterprises to profit by exploiting the intricacies. Nowhere is the system more vulnerable than the secondary wholesale market. As discussed in Chapter 5: The Black Market, this legitimate marketplace is filled with unscrupulous people, unlicensed distributors, and businesses willing to cut corners (and overlook product efficacy issues) to turn a profit.

In the pharmaceutical supply chain there are the manufacturers, the primary distributors (including McKesson and Amerisource Bergen), and a host of secondary wholesalers. This secondary market can range from multimillion-dollar legitimate companies to unlicensed dealers buying and selling prescription drugs from their bedrooms.

With corrupt wholesalers and middlemen ready to acquire stolen goods, forge pedigree documents, and eventually sell the product at full market value to unknowing and unwitting pharmacies (and by extension consumers), cargo security in the pharmaceutical industry is quickly moving from a "nice to have" into a "must have."

In fact, according to the MSNBC report where over half of hospitals and pharmacies willingly and knowingly purchase drugs from gray market vendors (Aleccia, 2011), there is no lack of demand for companies willing to obtain drugs through less than legitimate means and move them into the consumer market. Gray-market suppliers take advantage of the ongoing shortages, monitoring drug availability and then exploit the vulnerable supply chain, according to Mike Cohen, president of the Institute for Safe Medication Practices. This, of course, leads to worries that the drugs sold to hospitals and pharmacies may be of questionable quality, may not have been handled properly, or may be counterfeit or stolen (Aleccia, 2011).

Reputation

Consider the husband of the Alzheimer's victim discussed earlier in this chapter. Even though the manufacturer of the medication had no direct complicity in the substitution do you think the man ever felt quite as comfortable injecting his wife with that drug again?

Reputation is vital to the well-being of every company, but perhaps no more so than to those in the pharmaceutical industry. As the makers of powerful medications, some of which are injected directly into the bloodstream, drug makers work feverishly to earn and keep our trust. One cargo theft, if the result is tainted or mishandled product, can undermine years of work and millions of dollars in marketing, especially if the product causes severe adverse reactions or, worse yet, fatalities.

In 1982, seven people in the Chicago area died after taking Tylenol that had been laced with potassium cyanide, a lethal poison. The case was investigated by local police as well as the Federal Bureau of Investigation (FBI)—who named the case

TYLMURS. The poisonings involved Extra-Strength Tylenol capsules, manufactured by McNeil Consumer Healthcare, a subdivision of Johnson and Johnson. The pills were laced with potassium cyanide. A reward of $100,000 was offered by Johnson & Johnson, but has never been claimed.

Because the affected product had come from different plants and all the deaths occurred in the Chicago area, tampering during the manufacturing process was ruled out. Instead, the culprit was believed to have entered various grocery and drug stores over a period of time, removed Tylenol product from the shelves, added the poison, and then replaced the product back onto shelves. Eight bottles in total were discovered as being tampered with the poison during this case.

As with the Tylenol case, a product that creates adverse medical reactions, even at no fault of the manufacturer, can have significant consequences that are not resolved easily. Johnson and Johnson went to great strides to keep the public informed, find the guilty parties, and ensure that consumer safety and confidence were restored, and restored quickly. In fact, Johnson and Johnson's actions were praised throughout the industry and media as the ideal way in which such situations should be handled and is used frequently in business schools as a case study in how companies should respond to public relations disasters.

In such incidents where pharmaceutical product results in adverse medical reactions, if overt criminal activity is not known or cannot be proven, the manufacturer, not the unknown criminals, is often considered to be responsible. This is also true in the case of cargo theft when product is mishandled but ends up back in the normal stream of commerce. Even when companies go to every length possible to recall product and keep them off the shelves, it is still the manufacturers names associated with the harmful products and the conditions that resulted from consumers taking the mishandled or tampered drugs.

Consumers will remain at risk as long as stolen drugs are brought back into the supply chain regularly, with no guarantees, of course, that they are being handled properly during the detour. They exit the manufacturer and the consumers are at risk. "No one is selling Lipitor on the street," the FBI's Tom Hauck was quoted as saying in a March 2011, *Fortune* article (Eban, 2011), illustrating the point that these products need to be moved back into legitimate retail outlets to be sold. Whereas a consumer buying drugs on the street should understand they are taking a risk by doing so, those purchasing from a pharmacy do so with the impression the drugs they are buying are safe, but that might not always be the case. While the product moves through the vast array of secondary wholesalers, most of them legitimate, but some who readily welcome stolen drugs onto their docks, the drugs can lose their potency quickly and even turn toxic.

According to the *Fortune* article, Americans are rarely informed about cases in which consumers are harmed or become sick after taking stolen medications they have purchased from legitimate outlets.

In 2009, some consumers suffered adverse medical reactions after taking insulin purchased at two different pharmacies, one in Texas and one in Ohio. The insulin sold at both pharmacies came from a single stolen load. Despite the warnings and recall notices by the insulin manufacturer and the FDA, one company purchased the vials from a secondary wholesaler and then sold them to consumers through pharmacies.

Such instances are not uncommon. Because the warning system and recall process is manual (meaning there is no automatic system for detecting recalled products), stolen drugs can slip through the system, putting both consumers and manufacturers at risk.

To help combat this problem, Abbott Laboratories, Eli Lilly, GlaxoSmithKline (GSK), Johnson & Johnson, and Novo Nordisk announced formation of the Coalition for Patient Safety and Medicine Integrity in early 2011. The group seeks to amend laws governing cargo theft in general (and specifically in the pharmaceutical sector) as discussed in Chapter 3: Risk vs Reward. The change in criminal penalties to better reflect the risk to consumers is a key component of their mandate, as cargo criminals—even those stealing millions of dollars in pharmaceuticals—rarely see jail time and have no incentive to help investigators in stopping this seemingly endless criminal enterprise.

Proactive cargo security programs that ensure traceability throughout the supply chain, to include monitoring of temperature and other required controls, vendor compliance, and rapid response in the event of a theft, can save a company tens if not hundreds of times over the cost of such a program by preventing stolen and tampered drugs from reaching the consumer.

Key Points

- Pharmaceutical shipments are among the most sought after by cargo criminals.
- There are fewer shipments of pharmaceuticals than of product types such as electronics and building materials. This is one

reason why pharmaceutical thefts comprise a smaller percentage of the overall total.

- The average pharmaceutical shipment is worth in excess of $2 million.
- Many drugs stolen through cargo theft end up back in the legitimate supply chain. In most of these cases the drugs were not stored/handled per protocol.
- Cargo theft affects the pharmaceutical industry well beyond the cost of stolen loads. Brand reputation, product recalls, and overall consumer safety are all issues affecting this sector's bottom line.

THE TRUE IMPACT OF CARGO THEFT

INFORMATION IN THIS CHAPTER:

- Analysis of downstream costs of cargo theft
- Impacts of cargo theft beyond monetary loss
- Special implications for the pharmaceutical sector
- Role of insurance companies in curbing costs

The cost of cargo theft is ultimately paid for by the consumer. For decades, corporations have factored into their pricing the expense of cargo theft and other shortages. The consumer has no ability to know how much is added to the retail price to account for these losses, but there is no denying that these costs are passed on and paid for at the cash register.

With every cargo theft, a value is assigned to the loss by the manufacturer or product owner. Typically this value represents either the retail price of the load or the replacement cost, the cost of manufacturing. Most companies see this amount as the total loss experienced in the theft—the total impact. But the declared value of the loss is only one small part of the total impact of cargo theft. Costs associated with replacing the load, loss of market share, increased insurance premiums, and, in some industries, product recalls and loss of brand trust all must be factored when analyzing how cargo theft impacts a company's bottom line.

While it is very tempting for supply chain professionals and researchers in this space to affix a number to these tangible and intangible costs, the broad range of variables involved make this task virtually impossible but certainly no less real. With lean manufacturing, just-in-time delivery expectations, outsourced warehousing and distribution, and companies becoming more risk averse, the true financial loss due to cargo theft must be multiplied several times over the product value. Other downstream costs include product replacement, administrative time and expense, loss of market share, recall and/or destruction of goods in certain industries, and increased insurance premiums.

Product Replacement

Replacing stolen product gets priority. Whether shipping to a retailer or directly to the consumer, once an order has been made, the shipper has the expectation that the right product will be delivered to the right place and on time. When goods are stolen en route, it is their responsibility to replace that product as quickly as possible, while bearing the extra expense. Even in business-to-business sales, where customers are aware of the risk of cargo theft and its effects, losses in the supply chain are not seen as a legitimate excuse to delay order fulfillment.

The replacement process delays the manufacturing schedule, as time is dedicated to making the products for a second time instead of creating new ones. In addition to the temporary drop in efficiency resulting from product replacement, the manufacturer endures overhead costs and perhaps equipment changeover and maintenance during the replacement process.

This repetition decreases the revenue-to-expense ratio, yet this is rarely, if ever, factored into the loss associated with a stolen load, but clearly has a direct impact on a company's bottom line.

Even more downstream costs, such as the time spent by employees handling the associated administrative processes, are rarely, if ever, considered. While employees are remaking the product that was stolen, the company is incurring employee costs for product that is being made a second time, essentially working at a zero efficiency rate. While not an overwhelmingly high monetary figure by itself, these expenses, when combined with all others involved, clearly add up.

Employee Time and Expense

When replacement goods are being made, the manufacturer is paying for the personnel's wages and benefits. There is also a significant administrative burden. For each stolen load, an array of customer service and administrative staff must deal with getting the product replaced, but often their hours are not included in the cost of the loss. Further, the product receives expedited shipping at no additional cost to the retail customer or intended consignee (the manufacturer bears the cost) in order to minimize the delay and limit customer dissatisfaction. This, too, adds to the monetary burden.

The time expense of replicating a stolen load is not the only one involved. Simply identifying what product has been stolen can be a difficult task, especially for large shippers with multiple loads on the road at any given time. Once the theft is reported by the transportation provider, the manufacturer must assign a manager to the task of determining which load was stolen and the product involved. This process literally has the manufacturer starting from scratch as they receive information from the carrier and begin the lengthy process to have the stolen product identified for replacement as soon as possible—a process that can take up to a week in some cases. Once it is determined what product was stolen, each business unit affected by the loss is contacted and informed of the lost product so they can place their exchange orders, contact the affected customers, and arrange for expedited shipping.

Customer service hours spent with the consignee (the company that would have received the shipment) is another factor to consider. Ensuring that the replacement order is processed as well as expedited manufacturing and shipping is applied.

Market Share

With lean manufacturing and direct build models, such as computers built to the specifications of the customer, in vogue, the time from production to shelf (or direct customer) is reduced significantly. This also results in companies keeping minimal components or product in reserve. While these models are designed for efficient and cost-conscious supply chains, cargo theft can clearly wreak havoc as there is almost no wiggle room between order and delivery times. Loss of market share, customer dissatisfaction, reduction in brand loyalty, and other "hidden" costs drive up the real monetary extent of cargo theft several times, many multiples for industries such as pharmaceuticals and consumer care products.

First is the loss of market share—the percentage of total sales volume in a market captured by a brand, product, or firm. With the interruption in time to market caused by cargo theft, product is kept off the shelf. Unless there is an unbreakable allegiance, customers will purchase a similar product manufactured by another company because it is available. The cargo theft not only prevented a company from selling its product but it may have created a sale for one of its competitors.

There are numerous ways to describe the consumer decision-making process. A common one is illustrated by the traditional "funnel" diagram shown in Figure 10.1.

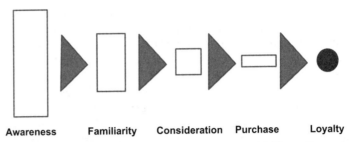

Awareness   Familiarity   Consideration   Purchase   Loyalty

Figure 10.1 Recreated based on the traditional funnel by *McKinsey Quarterly*.

Consumers are made aware of a product through marketing, advertising, and, in many cases, word of mouth. As consumers become more familiar with a product and consider a purchase they will do so if it is available. If it meets their expectation, the consumer becomes loyal to the product. Focusing on price, product, placement, and promotion, marketing drives the consumer to the purchase. Cargo theft, however, is a significant interruption to this process. If the product does not arrive on time, then "placement" is lost. Additionally, prices will increase to account for the loss costs. This effect not only lowers the likelihood of purchase but also increases the probability of the consumer switching to a competing product.

"Consumers are loyal when there is convenience and/or a real need," according to Lenora Greene, managing director of Kick-Start Marketing, an Austin-based marketing firm with a national client list. When convenience is lost because a product is not on the shelf, then loyalty can diminish quickly and even end as competitor products are purchased instead and the opportunity for a new loyalty begins to grow. This does not apply to all products, according to Greene, as those with a "culture" around them have consumers who are willing to endure delays and other inconveniences (e.g., Apple). Brands are increasingly playing a role in self-identity and self-expression in contemporary consumer culture. By associating with a particular brand, an individual can portray a desired image. Apple is an ideal example of this concept, revolutionizing the way in which consumers interact with products by marketing user-friendly, personalized, and stylish consumer electronics. Through product development, listening to customers, and aggressive marketing campaigns, Apple embodies creativity, individuality, and convenience, while allowing consumers to establish their own identity. So, in some instances, loyalty will outweigh convenience; however, those products without a culture will lose this strong consumer attachment.

Customer Retention and Retrieval

Another cost endured by the victims of cargo theft is replacing lost customers. It is significantly less expensive to keep a customer than to acquire a new one. According to studies, the cost of acquiring a new customer can be six times the costs of keeping an existing one. When a consumer switches from one brand to another, getting that customer back is a long, difficult, and expensive process.

Loss of market share due to cargo theft is exacerbated if the theft occurs during a product launch due to loss of a competitive advantage and a concomitant drop in initial sales. Months of marketing efforts preparing new product launches, driving potential sales, and customer expectations can lead to nothing if the company is unable to deliver. Companies that rely on retail space for their product depend on a manufacturer delivering on time. When the product does not arrive, the space will be filled by a competitor who will not give it back readily.

For "direct build" companies, the customer has already purchased the product and has an expectation of on-time delivery. If the company is unable to meet this expectation, consumer dissatisfaction can result in the order being canceled, a refund being issued, and loss of a future sale. Past purchasing experience plays a significant role in consumer behavior; this was listed as the most significant influencer in a 2009 article entitled "Defining Brand Loyalty and Its Relation to Customer Satisfaction" by Christina Pomoni, a financial adviser and marketing expert. It is important to note that bad experiences typically resound louder than previous positive ones. Poor experiences can dissuade consumers from returning to a company with which they did business previously. In summary, these downstream effects are extremely difficult to quantify, but clearly have an impact on a company's profitability and are losses experienced in addition to the value lost from cargo theft (Serafine et al., 2005).

Loss of Sales

Another issue is erosion of the customer base due to the introduction of stolen products into the marketplace. Brokers who sell stolen cargo often do so through shell companies, allowing them to introduce these goods into the legitimate marketplace. To accomplish this, the broker uses legitimate companies, often shell companies under the broker's control, to sell stolen product to wholesalers and others in the distribution system as legitimate goods. Customers, prepared to purchase a computer or cell phone from an established retailer, find the product available to them at a substantially reduced price, albeit through illegitimate means almost always unknown to the consumer. This flow of stolen goods into the market displaces legitimate sales, resulting in losses that must be accounted for in the cost of doing business. So while consumers receive the product from a retail outlet, the manufacturer does not benefit from the sale.

Additional Costs for Other Sectors

These costs apply to virtually any product affected by cargo theft. Of those feeling the highest levels of impact, the electronics and pharmaceuticals industries are the most impacted.

Worldwide, electronics are one of the most sought-after commodities by cargo thieves, and the industry commonly uses just-in-time manufacturing and direct build models in which customers have multiple purchasing options and brand loyalty is an important component of future sales. In 1999, the Rand Corporation conducted a study examining costs of high-technology hardware thefts. While cargo theft was not the direct focus of the study, the authors stated "… over 70 percent of the reported losses occurred while product was in transit" (Dertouzos et al., 1999, p. xiii). The study examined the added financial burden of cargo theft on society, stating:

> If such a firm experiences hardware losses valued at $1 million, its indirect losses, including increased security investments and lost sales, would total an additional $1.8 million. Also, sales would be displaced from other firms, amount to another $1.0 million in loss to the industry at large. Finally, customers would suffer losses totaling $2.4 million as firms raise prices in reaction to the higher cost of doing business. For this example, total costs to society are over six times the original hardware costs. For the products that are most likely to be preferred targets of thieves, these other costs can be even higher (Figure 10.2; Dertouzos et al., 1999, p. xiv).

While the figure of 6.2× the load value is a good reference point for determining the overall monetary impact of a theft, actual figures can vary based on the load value, type of product stolen, and other variables on which consistent monetary values are difficult to determine. Additionally, although the high-tech sector was the focus of the Rand study, other industries face an entirely different array of problems and impacts resulting from cargo theft. Food and beverage manufacturers have to contend with Food and Drug Administration regulations and the real

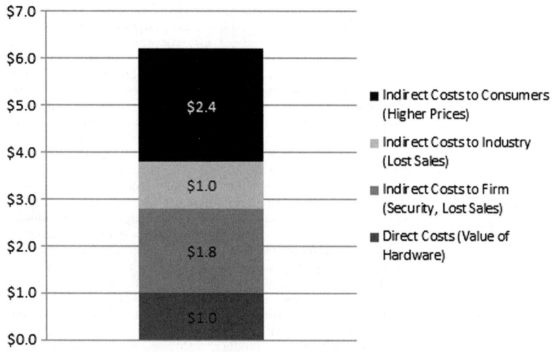

Figure 10.2 Recreated from Dertouzos et al. (1999, p. xiv).

potential for recalls and product destruction in the event of theft. While not subject to theft incidents, spinach and peanut butter recalls in 2009 and 2010 led to widespread removal of these products from shelves nationwide, draining dollars due to added costs and a steep decline in sales. Tobacco companies are often the victims of counterfeiting operations, along with tax evasion schemes (selling tobacco products without required tax stamps) through the use of stolen cargo. In October 2010, two men were arrested for transporting $3 million in stolen cigarettes in Carlisle, Pennsylvania, charged with possession of stolen property and tax evasion. The pharmaceutical industry is similarly vulnerable. In fact, of all industries, the pharmaceutical manufacturing sector may feel the most profound impacts of all when it comes to cargo theft.

Pharmaceutical Sector

Product Safety

For consumer safety reasons, most pharmaceuticals, especially ingestible drugs, cannot be reintroduced into the supply chain once the "chain of custody" has been interrupted or broken. For example, if a shipment of pain medication is stolen, it can never be reintroduced into the supply chain (never be delivered to a pharmacy or placed on store shelves)—even if it is recovered shortly after the theft. There have been cases where a trailer of pharmaceutical products was recovered almost immediately with the tamper-evident security seal still intact, no temperature excursions, or handling irregularities noted and was allowed to proceed on to the consignee and eventually to market; however, such instances are rare and require near instantaneous recovery in order to not be sent to destruction.

This is true even when the product is recovered with the cargo door seal intact and/or no temperature control issues are associated with the product. The break in the supply chain creates an ethical situation for the pharmaceutical company that mandates that the product be destroyed. In the event that product is recovered quickly, such as in the example that a covert tracking device was aboard, the company still has an ethical obligation, in additional to legal requirements, to only put products on the market that are guaranteed to be safe for consumption and handled within established specifications.

When a unique product, such as cancer medications of extreme high value, is stolen, especially one that has very specific handling requirements, such as refrigeration or light limitations, pharmaceutical companies will initiate a recall of all product with the same manufactured "lot number," as they cannot assure that the drug the consumer is purchasing is the one that arrived through the legitimate supply chain, as opposed to the stolen product having been reintroduced into the supply chain through illegitimate means. Some drug companies are helping to reduce this loss by creating lot numbers in smaller batches, often only the size of a shipped trailer load, to minimize the cost and potential damage if such a load were to be stolen.

Consumers inherently entrust drug companies with their health and have an expectation that the pharmaceutical companies will not allow product that is tampered with or handled unsafely to be sold. A firm that is slow to react when a recall is necessary not only faces potential litigation, it exposes itself to long-term reputation damage (Cheah et al., 2007, p. 428). In the case of some biotech products, unsafe storage, such as loss of temperature control, could make it potentially toxic, even if it were never physically tampered with. These issues make chain of custody and proper standards of care a necessity for the pharmaceutical industry while such measures are not as necessary in other industries.

Public Relations

The person who coined the term "there's no such thing as bad press" probably made his or her living getting company names in the media. In reality this is patently not true, as bad public relations have had devastating effects on corporations. According to a 2004 *Journal of Business Communications* article by Dwane Dean, it can often lead to a corporate crisis—a nonroutine event that threatens an organization's goals (Dean, 2004, p. 192), which must be handled quickly to minimize the longer term damage. "The corporation will lose social legitimacy if it is seen as being irresponsible, dishonest, breaking the law or acting in a manner that exhibits little concern for the community" (Dean, 2004, p. 193).

Cargo theft in the pharmaceutical industry can create an environment for significant bad press if the theft of certain products is not handled properly. Ingestible and injectable pharmaceuticals present the greatest liability exposure to pharmaceutical companies, especially those drugs with strict handling requirements, because of their potential lethality if mishandled and then passed to the consumer through illegitimate means. If a stolen drug is taken by a consumer and he or she has an adverse reaction, the company will have to answer for the safety and security of their manufacturing and distribution, along with their postloss handling of the situation.

Beyond the monetary loss associated with a product recall, there are potential diminutions of overall company value and shareholder wealth. While a pharmaceutical company can keep such recalls relatively low in volume if lots are produced at smaller quantities, research has shown that the stock market reacts negatively to product recalls (Davidson and Worrell, 1992, p. 472).

Brand Name Trust

Pharmaceutical companies know that consumer trust in their brand name is critical to their survival. Negative reports in the media can threaten that trust and require proactive measures be taken any time product is stolen that could potentially be harmful to the consumer. Actions that go beyond what is required by law, embracing a more socially responsible attitude, and striving to do what is best for their client base can have significantly positive long-term effects, even if such actions are expensive and time-consuming.

The classic example of a company going beyond the minimum requirements when faced with recalls on a massive scale is McNeil Consumer Products (a subsidiary of Johnson & Johnson) and their handling of the tainted Tylenol bottles that killed seven people in the Chicago area. Many market experts thought that Tylenol would never be sold again; however, due to the efforts of Johnson & Johnson, the company recovered quickly and Tylenol continues to be one of the top over-the-counter drugs in the company. The company's handling of the crisis is considered by experts to be one of the best in the history of public relations.

When the tampering was discovered, Johnson & Johnson immediately put customer safety over company's profit and other financial considerations. Johnson & Johnson quickly alerted consumers across the country not to consume any type of Tylenol product and not to resume using Tylenol until the extent of the poisoning could be determined. In addition to stopping all manufacturing and distribution of Tylenol, as well as ceasing all advertising, Johnson & Johnson recalled all Tylenol from the market, a total of approximately 31 million bottles, valued in excess of $100 million.

These timely actions by Johnson & Johnson, and the company's willingness to put the customer first in their decision making, are credited with the survival of the Tylenol product line and its continued success in the market today.

Product Recall and Destruction

Product recalls and the destruction process place additional costs to a company that has suffered a loss if required. Retrieving thousands of bottles of product from drugstores across the country takes time and is an administrative burden. Companies such as GENCO Pharmaceutical Solutions specialize in product recall and destruction, taking the administrative burden from the manufacturer. They conduct the process from beginning to end so that the manufacturer does not have to, including actions such as consignee contact, product collection, lot number verification, and destruction.

Destruction of pharmaceuticals is most commonly outsourced to companies that specialize in drug returns and destruction. Despite the savings to the manufacturer that outsourcing provides, this process prevents destruction activities from being conducted by organic assets, resulting in the entire process being a 100% cost add-on to the total cost of the theft incident.

Insurance

Many in the manufacturing and logistics industries think cargo theft is an "insurance issue" handled through the claims process. Unfortunately, it is not that simple. Cargo may be insured at every point along the supply chain, and in the event of a theft, a claim will be made by the entity with the insurable interest (usually the owner of the product at the time of theft) against their insurer on some cost basis, depending on the policy terms and conditions. However, the effects of the theft do not stop there.

Normally, every stakeholder within the supply chain—manufacturer, third-party logistics provider, transportation provider, and every other channel partner that handles, stores, or transports the cargo—will have some insurable interest and thus should have some form of coverage for protection in the event of loss or damage. Cargo insurance is generally provided either by the shipper (seller) or by the buyer and includes (but is not limited to) in-transit portions of the supply chain. For example, stock throughput policies can cover products almost cradle to grave from raw materials used in their manufacture to the finished goods while in storage, distribution, and retail stores until sold.

Coverage

Cargo can be insured a number of ways, including the product's retail cost, replacement cost, or other variant. Insuring for replacement costs does not include the loss in sales and the transportation/freight costs incurred, but insurance premiums for this type of coverage are lower and thus can be attractive to a shipper or buyer who sustains minimal losses. The shipper can also insure the product for the wholesale cost, accounting for what the product would have sold for had it reached its destination and the sale had been completed. An alternative to replacement cost insurance, these policies provide a larger monetary reparation for the shipper, but such policies come with higher insurance premiums.

According to Barry Tarnef, a senior loss control specialist and assistant vice president for the New Jersey-based Chubb Group of Insurance Companies in business since 1882 and with a global reach (Chubb is one of the nation's leading property and casualty insurance companies), most manufacturers and product owners insure cargo using a "cost plus" method to be compensated for all expenses involved in a catastrophic loss (such as a full-truckload theft). Under this method, insurance policies will cover cost, insurance, and freight (CIF) plus 10 or 20%. CIF covers the cost of manufacturing the product, the cost of the insurance, and the cost of transportation (or freight). Tarnef states that the plus 10 or 20% covers the unknown and unplanned costs inevitably encountered when dealing with a loss, including employee time required to submit claims, lost time, and other often unquantifiable losses incurred. This additional coverage also allows the company to recoup at least a small portion of the missed sales.

Ownership

The terms of sale determine whether the seller or the buyer owns the goods and thus can make a claim against their insurance company when a theft occurs. For example, if the terms of sale are Ex Works (EXW), stating that the buyer (consignee) owns the goods once they have left the seller's (shipper) premises and the cargo is stolen in transit, then the buyer will file a claim. The buyer's insurer after paying the claim then has the right to go after (subrogate) the negligent party, usually the transportation provider, trying to recoup a portion of the claim or its entirety. In most cases, however, transportation companies contractually limit their liability for damage or loss, even if gross negligence (such as leaving a tractor running, unlocked, and loaded with high-value cargo) is involved.

Determining who is financially responsible for cargo at each point in the supply chain can be tricky. In order to codify transfer of ownership and risk of loss/damage, a set of trade terms, referred to as International Commerce Terms, or most commonly INCOTERMS, was developed by the International Chamber of Commerce and adopted by most countries. INCOTERMS reduce or remove the uncertainties that arise from different interpretations of responsibility. The scope of INCOTERMS is limited to matters relating to rights and obligations of the parties involved in the sale with respect to the delivery of goods. There are 13 different terms, each of which helps users deal with different situations involving the movement of goods. Figure 10.3 provides a relatively simple version of the INCOTERMS.

Also, INCOTERMS only apply to international transactions; in the United States, the Uniform Commercial Code governs sales terms so the reader should reference those when talking about shipments within the United States only.

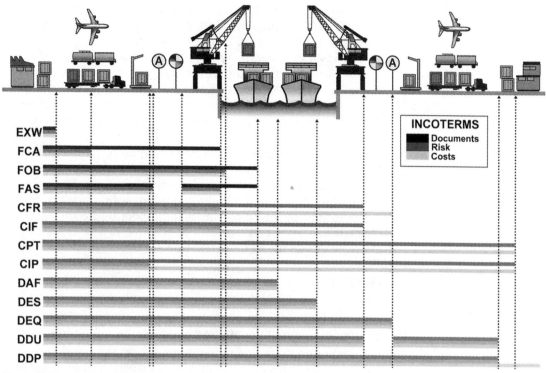

Figure 10.3

Investigations

After a loss has occurred and a claim submitted, the insurance company will begin an investigation once the claim is submitted. Significant delays in filing the claim, however, can severely hamper recovery efforts and these are not unusual. According to Brandon Stroud, vice president of loss prevention at Falvey Insurance, delays are often due to a transportation provider (carrier) conducting its own investigation first, the victimized truck driver not reporting the theft immediately, or uncertainty as to the requirements of the carrier to contact law enforcement and which agency they need to report to. Insurance companies will involve claims, loss prevention, and recovery professionals to assist in the investigation, depending on the size or sensitivity of the loss. Each has its specific task during the claims process. The claims department will handle the mechanics—receiving information from the client, filing the necessary paperwork, and processing the payment. Loss prevention personnel will look for trends and help discover any systemic issues that could account for the loss and share these with their client in order to help prevent future incidents. Recovery teams attempt to find the stolen product through GPS tracking, if available, looking at locations known to store or sell stolen cargo, and working with police.

The insurance company may also send a marine surveyor or adjuster on site to investigate the loss, just as an auto insurance company would send an adjuster. Many insurers have in-house surveyors they send for certain losses based on pre-established criteria or use third-party surveyors from an approved list (vetted surveyor database).

The surveyor's role and scope of assignment are determined by the insurance company, but generally they are there to establish the nature, cause, and extent of the loss. The ultimate goal is full recovery of the stolen goods, but surveyors also look for opportunities to lessen the financial impact of the loss, such as through developing evidence of negligence and thus liability or discovering violation of a policy warranty.

Liability

Insurance companies determine liability (who is to blame) for a cargo theft in a number of ways. Violation of a policy warranty is one. Warranties are specific obligations that the assured must do or not do in order to retain coverage. There are a wide range of possible warranties that a shipper or transportation provider may be required to comply with: for example, using team drivers in order to ensure the load is never left unattended while in transit or not stopping within the first 200 miles from the point of departure (the red zone, where cargo theft incidents are most likely to occur).

The key in this process is determining if a third party, such as the transportation provider, has liability for the theft. In the event that all warranties were followed and all security requirements by the shipper were met, finding liability in the transportation provider will be difficult. However, if during the investigation certain warranties were ignored or in-transit security policies not followed, the insurance company then has the opportunity to develop a case showing negligence on the part of the transportation provider and then potentially offset some of the cost in paying the claim to the product owner. Even in such cases, however, the total cost of the claim is rarely deferred completely due to limits of liability.

Premiums

The loss ratio for an assured is simply the amount of claim payments and associated expenses made over the course of the policy period versus the premium. A 100% loss ratio means that premiums paid equaled the cost of the claims to the insurance company. While the target loss ratio varies between lines of business and companies, if it is too high, insurance rates can be adjusted, warranties issued, or other remedial actions taken so that the insurance company can potentially recoup its losses over time. Insurers will likely factor in historical experience with a client and overall relationship so there is a qualitative component of the decision-making process.

Cargo insurance is required as a condition for the registration and continued operation of motor carriers and freight forwarders, but not for brokers (Augello, 2004, p. 38). 49 U.S. Code 13906 established liability coverage for motor carriers (trucking companies or transportation providers) (BMC-32 Endorsement) and provides insurance coverage even if the carrier refuses to pay a claim for which it has legal liability to pay. As such, the product owner is provided with legal protections in the event of a loss that the transportation providers is responsible for, but refuses to pay, which is significant in cases such as a carrier filing for bankruptcy or closing its doors.

The problem, however, is that for high-value cargo, the motor carrier and its insurance company's liability limits are such that claims paid rarely cover more than 5 to 10% of the shipment value. The motor carrier is also allowed to be "self-insured" if the carrier's financials show an ability to satisfy obligations for bodily injury liability, property damage liability, or cargo liability (Augello, 2004, p. 39). Again, in the case of high-value cargo, however, the motor carrier will contractually limit its liability in the event of a theft, leaving the cargo owner and its insurer to bear the majority of the loss.

The problems do not end there. Fraud, refusal of payment, and other issues can arise during the process of making claims for stolen cargo in which multiple entities are involved. For example, insurers generally issue checks to their insured party (shipper, carrier or intermediary) rather than to a third-party claimant. These proceeds have been embezzled by the carriers, brokers, or freight forwarders and diverted for their personal use. To avoid such losses, shippers should enter into preshipment contractual arrangements with their carriers and intermediaries, requiring that they be named "loss payee" on the carriers' and intermediaries' policies.

In the event that the motor carrier was at fault in a high-value cargo loss, its insurance limits provide for only a small percentage of the total claim. Over time, individual losses such as these affect the entire industry, as insurers raise rates across the board based on statistical data regarding theft losses.

It is similar to auto insurance, in which rates fluctuate based on the volume of claims paid by the insurance company. In this case, drivers who have never filed a claim are paying for the claims of others. The increased costs of insurance premiums are then passed along, from insurance company to customer to supply chain vendors, eroding the revenue along the way, until the cost is ultimately passed down to the consumer through higher prices.

Summary

Multiple variables, in addition to the initial cost of a cargo theft, must be considered to capture the true impact. Just as with the time spent remanufacturing product to replace a stolen load, other business units must spend time reacting to a cargo theft incident. These administrative costs include time reporting the theft incident to management, filing the claim with the insurance company, preparing necessary documentation, and conducting internal investigations.

These costs result in higher retail prices for consumers. Recognizing the true impact of cargo theft is also beneficial in determining the return on investment of security programs. While many executives see security as a nonrevenue-generating function, by highlighting the inherent risk of cargo theft and its impacts on the company's bottom line and name brand, expenditures designed to thwart or prevent cargo theft can be shown to have real cash value.

In determining the need for security programs, companies should consider the full impact felt from a cargo theft, not simply the value of the load or the expense of replacement parts and services. The loss of market share, higher insurance premiums and restrictive policy warranties, and other downstream costs, not to mention corporate/brand reputation and customer loyalty, must be taken into account. The actual cost of cargo theft far exceeds what's spent for necessary, preventive measures.

Key Points

- Cargo theft has significant downstream costs that go far beyond the value of the stolen goods, in some cases 4 to 10 times more.
- These costs, while difficult to quantify, are estimated through a variety of methods and are passed down to the consumer through increased prices.
- Loss of market share presents multiple issues for manufacturers, including the loss of customers, increased sales for competitors, and additional costs to the manufacturer to win back client loyalty.

- Insurance companies play a key role in this process and are highly motivated stakeholders in cargo security, especially as cargo theft is often seen as "an insurance problem" and not a crime.
- The pharmaceutical sector endures an even larger array of downstream costs and liabilities, to include public health concerns, product recalls and destruction, and reputational risk.

DEVELOPING
A SOLUTION

11

DETERMINING RISK

INFORMATION IN THIS CHAPTER:

- How to determine the overall risk of theft in a supply chain
- Methods for conducting risk and security assessments
- Sources of information in determining and managing risk
- Key factors of supply chain operations that create risk

Companies are coming to grips with the fact that it is far more difficult for them to control and understand the risks associated with today's truly global and interconnected and thus increasingly vulnerable supply chain. While the increasing risks to supply chains are becoming more understood, which go beyond cargo theft specifically and include other forms of risk such as supply chain disruptions, delays, and terrorism, it can be extremely difficult to quantify those risks and create standards by which both risk and their methods of mitigation are measured. Supply chain risk varies significantly with even small shifts geographically; cities, regions, and countries experience different rates of cargo theft with organized crime employing different modi operandi, posing added potential for serious disruption. In a multinational supply chain, finding a singular product or service ("silver bullet") that will mitigate every risk encountered is simply not feasible. A layered approach incorporating policies, procedures, and personnel, adding in technology, will be required to shore up security in each phase, but in order for this to occur, the company must first fully understand its risk.

To effectively grasp the supply chain risk that cargo theft presents to a company, logistics and/or security management must understand and anticipate the intentions and operations of cargo thieves, knowing what cargo criminals seek to steal, what methods they use to conduct their crimes, and how other companies have been successful in securing their supply chains. Additionally, logistics and security professionals need to conduct a thorough assessment of each leg in the supply chain and, armed with best practices developed internally and through

151

collaboration with other companies, analyze logistics procedures, transportation policies, and routing all through the lens of a cargo thief to better identify where product is prone to large-scale theft.

A key weakness of many security initiatives is that they focus only on internal operations (Voss, 2009, p. 9), often overlooking external threats, vendor management, and other facets of a supply chain involving numerous entities and people beyond the control of corporate security. Disruptions to the supply chain, including catastrophic losses from cargo theft, are more likely to be caused by forces outside the enterprise, such as cargo theft gangs, whereas internal operations suffer most often from small-scale pilferage (shrinkage).

Supply chain professionals must be aware of cargo criminal activity not only at/near shipping origin points but at destinations and along the expected transport routes. It is imperative that they take advantage of existing technologies and proven loss prevention tactics to create an environment where thieves are more likely to move on to another company to target. To do so, industry professionals must first understand the factors that contribute to their overall risk—the first key step in developing a theft prevention plan.

The Complexity of Assessing Risk

Understanding the downstream effects of supply chain disruption due to cargo theft, natural disasters, damages, fire, labor disputes, and other natural or man-made events can be difficult to translate into time lost or monetary costs, making such endeavors even more necessary. One example often cited was the 10-minute fire at a Philips Electronics wafer fabrication facility in New Mexico, which manufactured cell phone components for both Ericsson and Nokia. The original estimate of the extent of the fire provided some assurance that production output would be essentially unaffected; therefore, Ericsson did nothing.

Taking a more "belt and suspender" philosophy, Nokia decided to immediately find an alternate source for the parts. Although the plant fire had been isolated to one small section of the facility, the smoke and particulates had contaminated much of the building, causing a lengthy shutdown. Ericsson suffered a serious blow to its business and had to delay the launch of a new model. Nokia, however, was able to move on with barely a supply hiccup. Knowledge may be power, but risk management and decisiveness may win the day.

The need to understand, measure, and mitigate supply chain risks has grown in importance for two primary reasons: (1) complex supply chains (global and interconnected with more touch points) are more prone to disruptions and (2) inventory cushions that would dampen any supply shortfall are frankly anathema to today's just-in-time and lean manufacturing practitioners.

Professor Yossi Sheffi of the Massachusetts Institute of Technology uses a two-by-two matrix when characterizing supply chain risk: high probability vs low probability and large impact vs small impact. Sheffi argues that managers should only concern themselves with the quadrants that denote high probability with low impact and large impact but low probability of occurring. In order to accomplish this, the industry as a whole, as well as individual managers, executives, and academics, must be able to predict the risk of disruption and quantify its financial and operational impacts.

One reason for looking at supply chain disruptions in this way is the concept that a small number of accidents constitute the majority of the total supply chain impacts felt in the supply chain. This concept is also seen with natural disasters, where a small number of incidents—hurricanes, for example—cause the majority of all damage due to natural disasters. The same concept can be said about cargo theft, as the major incidents in the United States make up only a small number of the total; however, they have the greatest total impact on operational and logistics disruptions and overall monetary loss.

The other quadrant to be focused on—high predictability and low impact—can be associated with events such as pilferage throughout the supply chain. Even though each incident has a negligible impact on supply chain operations and minimal financial loss or operational setback per incident, when occurring at high frequency, these attritional drains are insidious and can lead to an attitude that factors them into the cost of doing business.

By understanding and applying these concepts into an overall risk analysis for an entire supply chain or even a single transportation lane, the logistics and security professionals of an organization are better prepared to apply accurate return on investment (ROI) metrics when proposing a supply chain or in-transit security program. Without a solid understanding of the risk, money and effort are wasted all too oftentimes, providing either too much security to a low-risk environment or not enough security to a high-risk environment, both of which can have significant downstream consequences.

Product Type and Value

As discussed in Chapter 7: Product Targeting, certain products, such as electronics and food and beverages, are stolen at a substantially higher rate than other theft-attractive commodities such as pharmaceuticals and tobacco. This does not mean that the cargo that experiences less theft is less desirable to cargo criminals. This is an important distinction to make. One thing needs to be remembered: consider the amount (volume) of a product type in transit. While definitive numbers of full truckloads on the road by product type are not available, intuitively we know there are a substantially higher number of food and beverage loads transiting our nation's highway system each year than specific products such as pharmaceuticals, consumer care products, or tobacco. Therefore, the overall risk to certain loads is not directly proportional to the overall number of thefts each year or the comparative percentage of thefts of product types, but rather those data along with their sheer volume.

Through data about theft incidents, interviews with cargo criminals, and other information collected, there is general agreement within the supply chain industry that electronics, pharmaceuticals, tobacco, and consumer care products are the most-sought-after goods. Their pure intrinsic value and ease of movement and sale on the black market make these items the perfect score for cargo gangs.

Aside from the type of product being shipped, the overall value of goods in transit must be taken into account when determining the threat from criminal elements. If a product can be sold easily on the black market, the more expensive the product is will result in a higher return on investment, or margin, for the cargo criminal and the broker, especially considering that fencing most stolen goods brings the seller 10 to 20 cents on the dollar.

Another important factor is the price fluctuation of goods. As demand (and price) goes up for commodities, so does the risk of theft, providing high-value goods to the marketplace at substantially discounted prices. This was shown in a study by Freight-Watch, clearly showing the correlation between the rate of copper theft and the index price of copper. During the study, the theft of copper was analyzed on a quarterly basis and was compared to the average price of copper over the same time period; there was an obvious positive correlation between the two variables.

In a July 20, 2011, *Wall Street Journal* article by Kelly Evans, sales of tablet personal computers (PC) and the impact on the electronics industry were analyzed. Research showed that for every two tablets sold, one PC was taken off the market (Evans,

2011). This shift in buying preference in the consumer electronics industry represented a clear shift in consumer demand. Based on these findings, supply chain security professionals can derive some sense about the risk they face, particularly in companies that produce tablets, smart phones, PCs, and other electronics, and adjust their security protocols accordingly. To understand product demand, and therefore the theft risk, is a powerful predictive tool in the fight against cargo criminals.

Location of Facility

Companies that own, lease, or use cargo facilities in Los Angeles, Dallas/Fort Worth, Miami, Atlanta, Memphis, and other known hotbeds of cargo theft activity have an increased propensity to be victimized by burglaries and robberies. There-fore, operations in high-risk communities must also incorporate a sort of geographic risk along with the product type and value mix, as the mere location (in relation to the region, state, or city) can have a substantial impact on the overall risk faced.

While general crime statistics, such as those provided by local or county law enforcement agencies or services such as CAP Index Inc., can be helpful in determining overall crime rates in areas, to include burglaries, generally these data are more focused on crimes again homes or persons. Because of this, companies seeking to obtain updated information regarding warehouse thefts should contact a local cargo theft task force if one exists in the area, organizations such as FreightWatch, or a regional transportation security council to help determine the overall risk of facility thefts for their area.

Other considerations include a cargo storage facility's prox-imity to wooded areas, low traffic roads, and other variances that can provide criminals with the opportunity to conduct unde-tected surveillance. Ideal targets for criminals are facilities that cannot be seen easily from the road and are located in areas with low traffic volumes with no other nearby facilities but also close enough to a major highway for quick escape. Thieves that target warehouses and similar facilities also have an exit strategy. All of these factors should be taken into consideration during the facility selection process and the site security development phase.

Routing

As with the risk associated with cities or areas where facilities are located, shipment routing can have a substantial impact on the overall risk of catastrophic theft. Transporting valuable cargo through high-risk zones may not affect the potential for loss directly; however, stopping in these areas will. As discussed earlier, the concept of active targeting is predicated on criminals' singular focus on a particular load and stealing it once left unattended, regardless of the area; criminal elements still exist that operate only in certain areas, seeking out goods that can be stolen easily and moved quickly to secured locations for product download and storage.

As with the route taken, the duration of the trip can have a substantial impact on the risk of theft, most notably with the number of stops required while in transit. As over 97% of cargo is stolen when stationary, each stop presents cargo criminals with an opportunity to acquire the load if left unattended during a stop. Of course, countermeasures such as team drivers can be a mitigating factor to this risk, which is discussed more in-depth in this chapter; however, this can often be a point of failure, relying on team drivers to remain with the vehicle at all times, while overlooking other security best practices necessary to ensure the security of the load.

Frequency of Shipments

The total number of loads shipped per week, month, or year has a direct impact on the overall risk of theft through simple laws of probability. The more often an act is performed, the more likelihood of something going wrong increases with each iteration.

If the average person drives his or her car once a week, the probability of being in an accident in that person's lifetime is substantially less than a person who drives his or her car every day. All other things being equal, the same can be seen with high-volume shipping. Companies that ship or transport hundreds of loads each day are more likely to be victims of cargo theft than a company shipping one per week or month.

Mode of Transportation

Mode of transportation is another component of the overall supply chain and cargo theft risk. This factor, coupled with others, such as geographical region or the vendor managing the cargo, can result in significant volatility in risk of theft as well as other supply chain disruptive events such as delay and damage. Each transportation method (road, rail, air, and ocean) presents a different set, and level, of exposure to risk.

Truck transport is the most vulnerable to theft; this is intuitive given the environment. In-transit loaded trucks are often stopped/staged/stored at un- or undersecured locations such as truck stops, rest areas, drop yards, and open access parking lots. There are also meaningful differences in this mode; full-truckload, less than truckload, and even parcel/express cargo traveling over the same roads have unique theft and risk profiles.

Additionally, if modes other than truck are used for transport, such as rail, air, or sea, the risk of theft while in transit must be accounted for, in addition to the inherent risks associated in areas around the major ports of hubs used by these modes, as discussed in Part 1 of this book. Finally, shippers must not discount the inclusion of truck transport associated with other modes, such as air or rail. Despite these other modes serving as the primary method of movement for the majority of a trade lane, undoubtedly in almost every circumstance, the cargo will be moved by truck at some point, bringing the cargo back to a substantially higher level of risk.

In-Transit Policies and Procedures

The breadth and scope of in-transit security policies and procedures vary dramatically among transportation providers. It is imperative that shippers clearly understand the security protocol of their carriers and how effectively this is transmitted to the absolute linchpin and key cargo theft deterrent, the driver. Whether a company establishes its own tailored set of standards or adopts industry best practices, there needs to be rules of the road.

Many transportation providers have little or no security policies. Operational efficiencies, allowing drivers to select their own routes and stopping locations based on fuel prices, often trump proven in-transit security measures. This role is filled most often by the shipper and agreed upon with trucking companies as part of contractual negotiations for pulling high-value cargo for the shipper. Examples would be actions required by drivers when stopped (turning off truck, removing keys from the ignition, and taking them with you; locking doors; using air cuff locks and other vehicle-immobilizing devices; and not leaving the load unattended), prohibiting stops in high-risk zones, prohibiting drivers to depart the destination if delivery was not possible upon arrival, and requiring them to remain on site until the product is offloaded.

Of course the requirements placed on a provider will depend on a wide array of variables, including what cargo is being shipped, origin and destination, mode of shipment, logistics methodology, and more. Methods of implementing an effective in-transit security program in order to combat cargo theft are examined later in this book.

Demographics

The two primary demographic data points to consider when analyzing cargo theft risk are the population of an area and its level/volume of supply chain activity. Cities such as Memphis or Louisville have incredibly high volumes of supply chain activity, serving as major hubs for two of the most prominent integrated transportation companies, as well as being linked to major highway, rail, and ground conduits, with relatively low population densities when compared to other cargo theft hot spots such as Los Angeles or Dallas. Based on data gleaned from real-world cargo crime statistics, it does not appear to matter how many people live in a certain city of metropolitan area; the key differentiator is the amount of cargo pulsing through its logistics networks

Other Factors

A variety of additional factors can affect the overall risk of a facility or in-transit operation. The level of crime in an area, weather, microeconomics, and packaging all play a role. The more these are understood, the better able it is to develop meaningful and actionable measures to deal with them.

Prevailing crime data whether considering in-transit or facility security cannot be overstated. Nevertheless, local rates are often overlooked in the decision-making process when establishing a location for a warehouse or distribution center, but must be accounted for when determining risk.

Another risk factor is weather. Weather can cause significant delays in in-transit operations, produce false alarms in intrusion systems, and increase the overall level of complexity in a supply chain that criminals can exploit. The $76 million warehouse burglary occurred during a large thunderstorm that had emergency services occupied and resulted in numerous false alarms at facilities throughout the area. By anticipating local and seasonal weather patterns, as well as other natural disruptive events, and incorporating emergency preparedness plans into the cargo security programs can actually bolster a company's supply chain resilience.

The use of company names, corporate logos, or other identifying information that can provide clues as to the contents of a shipment should not be on exterior packaging (cartons, crates, and drums). Prudent shippers are increasingly moving to plain packaging, but a struggle still exists between marketing departments that want to promote the brand and security personnel tasked with protecting company assets, whether mobile or in situ. In 2010, several men broke into a public warehouse in Long Island. The facility was used to store high-value products for four clients; three used packaging without any obvious identification but the other used their logo on all six sides of its cartons. The latter cargo was stolen while the rest was left behind.

Security Assessments and Site Surveys

A supply chain security program should be assessed periodically to ensure effectiveness and that costs are in line with the program's stated goals. A program analysis or assessment looks at the supply chain as a whole (suppliers, shippers, transportation providers, and intermediaries, along with facilities and physical and procedural controls) with the goal of determining where risk or security gaps exist. To facilitate this, security surveys must be conducted as well. These assessments can be at the site or trade lane level, where a security expert will assess the infrastructure as well as policies and procedures that are practiced.

Security assessments and site surveys can be conducted by one of two means: (1) internal assessment, conducted by a company's in-house security staff, or (2) bringing in a firm specializing in supply chain risk analysis and security plans. Regardless of the method by which a company chooses to inspect its supply chain security plan, the areas discussed in Chapter 13: Physical Security and Chapter 14: In-Transit Security must be reviewed, analyzed, and updated with respect to changes in threat to a company's supply chain in order to ensure that effective theft mitigation occurs.

Before a security assessment begins, it is critical that the goals are understood by all parties involved. They can be as simple as a single lane analysis or as complicated as a global supply chain assessment, determining every risk, ranging from government regulations to terrorism to piracy to civil unrest. The scope of the assessment and how the results will be addressed are critical components of the assessment planning process.

Once the goals and scope have been established, the method by which the assessment is to be conducted must be determined. Depending on the depth and breadth of the assessment, it generally consists of a combination tabletop risk analysis and on-site security survey. When determining what to assess, the items discussed in Chapter 13: Physical Security and Chapter 14: In-Transit Security provide an excellent framework for identifying key assessment elements.

Another decision point is whether the assessment is going to be conducted by internal personnel or if an outside firm will be brought in. There are pros and cons to either option but one constant remains—qualified individuals are needed to perform the assessment and site surveys. Conducting site surveys is far more complex than simply following a standard checklist, as using this method can overlook critical risk exposures, especially if an inexperienced person is assigned the task.

Another factor in the decision-making process is how the results will be perceived internally. If the results would be better received from an outside "expert," then contracting out the work makes sense. If, however, the company's culture is one of accepting constructive criticism only from within, then an internal, yet qualified, inspector would appear the optimal choice.

Regardless if the resources selected for this work are from internal or external sources, the assessment process must be risk based and conducted in order to establish or improve the company's supply chain security program. Results from the surveys and assessment should be the basis for the supply chain security program and written with the company's business model, established processes, and overall culture in mind.

Results from the surveys and assessment can provide other benefits to both operations (principally supply chain) and corporate management. Metrics such as ROI should measure the effectiveness of the cargo security program once implemented. Recommended security measures do not have to always translate into added costs and should never decrease supply chain efficiency or an increase in costs. In fact, many security best practices regarding supply chain operations can actually increase efficiencies at no cost.

Ultimately, once the results have been analyzed, the company has to take the findings and make a business decision on what new systems or programs will be implemented or existing ones improved. Once the supply chain security program has been implemented or revised based on the security assessment project, reassessments should be scheduled as necessary (commonly approximately 12 months from the project implementation date) to ensure that the program is truly meeting its goals of reducing cargo theft and maintaining supply chain efficiency. Also, the risk to a modern supply chain can be quite fluid, requiring continual evaluation of a program's effectiveness so that plans can be adjusted accordingly.

The environment in which the supply chain operates can be very dynamic. While some threats will remain constant over time, others will appear, disappear, and alter at great frequency, and must be understood, planned for, and security programs adjusted quickly in order to mitigate from these changes to the threat environment. Because of this, supply chain risk assessment should be conducted continually—no less than every 12 months—and supply chain security programs should be written as a living document, being updated constantly to meet threats as they emerge.

Key Points

- Determining the risk of theft to a company and its product is the first step in creating a supply chain security plan.
- Risk is substantially affected by product type and its ability to be sold on the black market. The overall value of the product serves as a motivating factor for criminal gangs.
- The location of a facility plays a role in determining the risk of theft. While less of a factor than product type and value, areas with high crime rates are more likely to be attacked.
- Products shipped through cargo theft hot spots are at increased risk, especially when truck drivers stop and leave their loads unattended.
- Existing contracts with transportation vendors need to be reviewed by analyzing the operational requirements through a security lens and determining what policies (or lack of policies) are placing goods at undue risk. This will provide a starting point for contract discussions with current or prospective service providers when creating and implementing a new supply chain security program that includes in-transit security requirements.
- Experts should be used to conduct supply chain risk assessments and site surveys in order to determine risk and implement or revise security programs.
- Assessments should be conducted periodically and designed to enhance overall security of supply chain operations within the existing parameters of the company's business model and requirements.

12

ROLES AND RESPONSIBILITIES
The Layered Approach

INFORMATION IN THIS CHAPTER:

- Role of the supply chain security manager
- Competing priorities in developing security and supply chain security programs
- Topics to be included in policy development and execution
- Role of insurance companies, law enforcement, and third-party security providers in a supply chain security program

No battle plan survives first contact with the enemy.

Helmuth von Moltke

The 21st-century supply chain is longer, faster, and more complex than ever before, with decreasing product inventory, increasing number of touch points, and more demanding cost constraints. This escalation in complexity comes with the added risk of large-scale theft. Supply chain security has developed significantly since the early 2000s and con\tinues to grow in importance as vulnerabilities are discovered, supply chains are expanded, and risk is increased. Securing a warehouse or distribution center is no longer a sufficient means of protecting a company from theft. "The lengthening of supply chains across international borders and sometimes entire hemispheres has resulted in both cheaper labor and more expensive security measures" (Blanchard, 2006).

Security is becoming a core business function in many companies and is being integrated into all supply chain activities. In the past, corporate security has been an optional part of a company's business makeup, and even companies with security would rarely have it involved in the supply chain. Now, the term "supply chain security" is part of the corporate lexicon—even to the point that firms are creating a management position specifically to bridge the gap between logistics and security.

Advances in this niche industry, however, are not without challenges. Company executives are not always open to increasing security expenditures, as security is commonly seen as

163

a pure cost to operations often without a quantifiable return on investment. Staff, programs, and equipment such as cameras, alarms, and other systems are viewed as necessary evils that are often provided with as little budget as possible to "get by" with. While the implementation of security measures is often expensive, negatively impacting a company's bottom line during initial stages, supply chain security can have a profound monetary benefit over the long term. "Cargo security technology and monitoring solution can provide significant return on investment, and often at bargain prices considering the value of the capital that could be lost by a disruption in the global container shipping" (Blanchard, 2006).

Quantifying savings from security programs, for the most part, relate to the change in cargo theft rates year to year. It can be argued that effective programs provide a number of intangible, but still valuable benefits. They include:

- Reducing loss of goods
- Enhancing overall quality
- Providing corporate peace of mind ("quiet night's sleep")
- Improving reputation and brand equity
- Offering competitive, and at times sustainable, advantage
- Facilitating business acquisition
- Allowing entry into high-hazard markets
- Limiting regulatory burdens
- Lowering noncompliance exposures
- Lessening inspections and delays
- Stabilizing, if not lowering, total cost of risk

It is critical that supply chain security managers have a clear understanding of the return on investment (ROI) that their programs are providing. By providing quantifiable reduction of theft, potentially to the tune of millions of dollars annually, such programs can have a dramatic impact on the direct bottom line, without even including the incredible array of downstream costs that arise with the theft of large quantities of product.

Security of a supply chain, however, is far more complicated than hiring a single manager to run an internal program. Corporate policies and procedures, physical security plans, in-transit security plans, and collaboration (internally, with vendors, with industry, and with law enforcement) are all critical to a successful program and truly secure supply chain. Of course, other stakeholders are involved in wanting to see a company's cargo arrive on time and intact. Insurance companies are the most obvious ones, as a secure supply chain is critical to reducing losses and thus claims.

This layered approach—a combination of personnel, policies, physical components, and technology—is a proven strategy for ensuring that cargo remains secure in a fast-moving, highly adaptable and complex environment.

Corporate Security and Logistics

The ability to prevent cargo theft has a significant impact on a corporation's bottom line, reduces overall costs, and prevents an undue increase in retail prices. In recognition of this fact, companies are increasing budgets and giving more latitude to security and logistics managers to develop security programs in their supply chains and purchase the necessary technologies necessary to assist in the process.

Companies are starting to manage security as a core business function through all supply chain activities, a key change in the overall mind-set in companies regarding security and the ROI that can be achieved through proactive supply chain security programs. Such programs can provide a significant ROI, often at bargain prices, considering the value of the capital that would be lost by a disruption in the global supply chain (Blanchard, 2006).

Supply chain security is driven by the product manufacturer, owner, or shipper (these terms are felt to be interchangeable but shippers will be referred to throughout the rest of the book). The shipper sets the tone for security in the supply chain, providing guidance to third-party logistics, transportation providers, and other vendors on the degree of security to be used in handling, storing, and shipping its product. Because of this, it is imperative that the shipper has written security standards not only for its own companies to follow, but also to be passed on to suppliers and vendors, ensuring that they have and comply with the same security standards that are applicable to the services provided to the shipper. There are numerous terms for such a document, such as freight security requirements or standards of care; no matter what they are called, they should be the single source for security requirements that all companies involved in the shipper's supply chain must comply with.

One difficulty in determining security standards in the supply chain is the gap between logistics and security and who is responsible for fulfilling this role. Some companies have begun assigning a manager who works for logistics but has a dotted line responsibility to the head of security. This is considered by many to be the ideal situation; a person with specific expertise in supply chain security can create and implement security standards under the aegis of logistics. Other companies rely on a combination of security and logistics personnel to work collaboratively.

Regardless of the method used, shippers in today's risk environment are beginning to see this role as imperative to the overall success of not only their supply chain, but also the company as a whole. This position can be used throughout the supply chain, assisting with procurement, vendor vetting, and, of course, the governmental regulatory environment for trade programs such as Customs—Trade Partnership Against Terrorism and Authorized Economic Operator—areas that would fall directly under the supply chain security manager's purview.

Policies and Procedures

After appointing the person who will have responsibility for oversight and execution of a comprehensive supply chain security program, next must come the establishment of the program itself through written policies and procedures.

Informal, unwritten rules exist in many organizations; employees and vendors can point to examples of "that's how things have always been done" or similar reasons for various processes. Personal preference by staff members and management citing "flexibility" with allowing tasks to be performed in a variety of methods can result in dramatically varying protocols at every stage in the supply chain. If this kind of situation is questioned, a shrug, wink and a nod, or other act of dismissiveness is common, particularly if the area under discussion has not resulted in product loss or damage.

Unfortunately, while such scenarios are common, the unwritten policy proves to be no policy at all, especially in a court-room when attempting to determine liability after a large-scale theft. Simply put, if a policy is unwritten, then the policy does not exist and cannot be enforced.

Beyond providing an established document for enforcement, written policies that are thought out and done well can be extremely effective in providing clarity, responsibility, scope, and requirements for the security of cargo from origin to destination.

Supply chain security policies must be both inward and outward looking—applied to both company personnel and external business partners. A supply chain security policy should cover all the components listed in Chapter 13: Physical Security and Chapter 14: In-Transit Security, ensuring that all variances in product flow for each business line are analyzed and accounted for.

A basic policy outline includes:
• Roles and responsibilities
• Authority
• Communications

- Human resources
  - Hiring practices
  - Employee education
  - Background investigations
  - Termination procedures
  - Rehiring practices
- Facility security
  - Perimeter security
  - Physical security
  - Procedures
  - Subcontracting
  - Investigations
  - Law Enforcement contacts
  - Access control
  - Key control
  - Closed-circuit television
  - Intrusion detections (alarms and motion detection)
  - Alarm monitoring
  - Lighting
  - High-value cage
  - Security officers
  - Search procedures
- Fulfillment process
  - Product in storage
  - Product on docks
  - Driver controls
  - Loading process
  - Unloading process
  - Security seal procedures
  - Pick and pack operations
  - Trailer staging
  - Driver instructions
  - Prealerts
- In-transit security
  - Transportation provider selection
  - Vehicle requirements
  - Truck Security
  - Trailer Security
  - Risk Analyses
  - Tracking requirements
  - Tamper alarms
  - Team drivers
  - Stopping procedures
  - No-stop zones
  - Secured parking locations

- Communications
- Routing
- Arrival procedures

A shipper may also want to institute an active monitoring program for high-value shipments. This should be documented and included an appendix to in-transit security or as a stand-alone policy (see Chapter 15: Active Monitoring).

As noted previously, such a policy, if done correctly, can provide substantial benefits to supply chain efficiencies as well as increased security for cargo and bring a clear return on investment through dramatically decreased thefts, damages, and other problems along the supply chain (for additional information on the benefits of an in-transit security plan and using tracking technology to maximize the supply chain, see Chapter 19: Beyond Security).

Collaboration

In order to combat cargo theft and provide a truly secure supply chain, collaboration is critical. This must occur between all links in the supply chain and relevant stakeholders. From collaboration, security best practices can be developed, establishing what works, what does not, and how to implement security procedures most effectively without hindering the efficiency of the supply chain. Security programs that diminish supply chain efficiency will be discarded quickly by executives as its "cost" adds up quickly as the price of logistics increases and efficiency is degraded. Through collaboration and continual improvement, supply chain security can be an easy fit within any logistics program, providing a secure supply chain through procedural changes, technology, and vendor compliance.

Some firms see their liability ending when ownership of their product is transferred to a supply chain partner, thereby eliminating the need for collaboration and cooperation. But as already discussed, cargo theft affects everyone, not only in the supply chain, but consumers as well. A secure supply chain is beneficial to all involved, not just the product owner.

Collaboration is not nearly as complicated or difficult as it can sometimes seem, especially with cargo theft and supply chain risk, which can be very ambiguous or an area where many companies are resistant to sharing information that could highlight failures in their security programs. While this may have been an adequate depiction of cargo theft collaboration in the past, now there are numerous organizations and vast amounts of information available at little or no cost. A list of these organizations and companies is provided in the resource section at the end of this book.

Insurance Companies

The insurance industry plays a critical role in supply chain security and reducing cargo losses. As an insurance company takes on new clients, it goes through an array of processes to determine a potential client's overall risk, necessary and recommended improvements to their security programs, and, of course, the level of coverage and premium offered.

When a new client is proposed, an insurer will perform an assessment of the client company to determine two things: (1) insurability of the potential new client, looking at the overall security of the insured product throughout their supply chain, and (2) willingness to work with the insurance company and make changes to fill the security gaps. The insurance company serves largely in a consultative role, creating a collaborative effort with the ultimate goal of securing the supply chain using carrier selection, physical and procedural measures, and contractual terms with vendors and transportation carriers. After a large loss or a series of smaller systemic ones, this will often result in policy warranties and/or rate changes.

Such changes could include requiring team drivers to be used for more shipments along more lanes, increasing security measures at facilities or during transit, and adjusting terms with motor carriers to increase liability, adjust in-transit behavior, or other terms.

Insurers can also help identify trends not only in a specific client's loss history, but throughout their book of business now and in the past. These historical data, coupled with best practices, can be powerful tools in preventing or minimizing cargo theft. Of course it is the application of this information, which requires a willing client, that is fostered through a collaborative effort/environment by the insurer in order for the risk of cargo to be reduced.

A company's loss history and experience with a particular commodity (scar tissue) can have an impact on whether the insurance company will even provide coverage. One example is cell phones, items that due to their high value and theft attractiveness are hard to underwrite profitably.

Loss control is a value-added service provided by most major insurance companies. According to Alan Spear, director of cargo security with Chartis Insurance, the aim is to prevent thefts from occurring, saving both parties' significant time and money in the long run. Through this role and over time, insurance companies have been able to develop best practices, security recommendations, and process improvements that can be brought to bear in cooperation with clients to identify and fix problems for clients to assist them in reducing losses.

Some of these may be mandatory due to the high risk of cargo theft or the area in which the client operates. Others may be suggested, recommended, or even strongly recommended, with the end goals of shoring up the client's supply chain and mitigating the risk of loss. The goal of this process, essentially, is to fix the problem before it's broken through a cooperative effort between the insurance company and its clients.

Insurance companies can be used by a manufacturer to get vendors to be more compliant with recommended security measures. Seen as an objective source that is looking for best security practices, a vendor that a security manager cannot get to comply but is protected through executive contacts can be moved into compliance with a negative security rating from the insurance carrier.

With the vast data available to insurance companies, they are uniquely positioned to conduct risk analysis for clients—combining this historical record with the various components of risk discussed in Chapter 11: Determining Risk. Many insurers offer these services as a value add-on to their clients in order to assist in reducing risk and preventing losses before they occur.

As best practices are developed, insurance companies play a vital role in proliferating those best practices throughout their client bases, assisting shippers and their logistics providers with adapting their policies, procedures, and equipment to keep stored and in-transit cargo as secure as possible. This role is not only vital to the supply chain industry as a whole, but also has a direct ROI for the insurance companies, as losses—and therefore claims—are reduced.

One final way in which insurance companies play a role in overall supply chain security is motivation for their clients to maintain high levels of security and risk mitigation to deter losses and prevent the negative impacts they cause. Reducing premiums for companies with good loss experience can be a positive motivation and resonate with C-level management.

Third-Party Security Providers

Outside security providers enhance supply chain security in a cost-effective manner. This can be done through a variety of ways, but largely center around physical security (security officers and on-site guard services) and transportation security (i.e., companies that provide human or physical escorts and/or provide covert GPS tracking technologies) providers.

This chapter discusses the role that each player in a supply chain security program plays. Whether or not to use a third-party security provider is covered in the following two chapters (Chapter 13 for physical security guard services and Chapter 14 for in-transit security providers).

It must be completely understood that the company that contracts the services of a security provider is ultimately responsible for shaping the policy. While these providers can help determine how they can best assist at the end of the day, it is that company's responsibility. This means ensuring that adequate documentation is created and that all stakeholders are clear on their respective roles and duties. It is surprising how often this critical step is missing and contracted security companies work without a clear set of instructions, yet alone guidance. This environment can result in significant security gaps that are exploited quickly (and all too easily) by cargo criminals, resulting in devastating loss at both the facility and the in-transit level.

Another critical step in determining the role of a third-party security provider is an analysis of the company's strengths, capabilities, and limitations. While this should obviously be conducted during the selection/vetting process, this analysis is often overlooked when implementing the contracted services into an organization's supply chain.

The role of the security service provider must be tailored to meeting the specific needs of the client. The facility and/or in-transit security provider has to be a good fit—the right fit for the client and the assignment. Their products and services must have enough flexibility to allow them to devise customizable solutions, rather than off-the-shelf programs, that ensure total supply chain security.

Law Enforcement

As with securing one's home or automobile, the role of the police in cargo theft exists largely to respond after an incident has occurred. Theft prevention falls almost entirely on the shoulders of the homeowner or driver. When you park your car at the mall, you don't leave the keys in the car and your wallet on the seat and rely on the police to safeguard your property. Neither should you leave valuable cargo unattended conveniently loaded in a truck that has inherent mobility.

While the police can assist through proactive measures such as additional patrols around industrial areas and other similar programs, it would be impractical to think this type of activity could be offered across the nation's vast highway system and the countless locations where loads are left unattended daily. Any expectation for police to reduce warehouse burglaries or in-transit theft can only be possible after the fact, during investigations, and, hopefully, arrests and successful prosecution. However, it is the goal of the security professional to keep the theft from occurring in the first place, which requires an understanding that prevention lies squarely on the shoulders of those involved in the handling and transportation of cargo. While many of the cargo theft task forces throughout the United States conduct proactive operations such as stings, bait trailers, and undercover operations (for additional information, see Chapter 18: Cargo Theft Task Forces and Organizations), these programs are designed to target thieves for arrest and prosecution and should not be considered a substitute for a sound supply chain security program.

With this in mind, the process of creating security programs for in-transit risk mitigation should certainly include coordination with local, state, regional, and national law enforcement, but primarily as a means for having established relationships and lines of communication for information sharing and rapid response in the event of a theft. Plans that rely on law enforcement as a key piece of their theft prevention plan are destined to fail.

Key Points

- Supply chain operations are becoming far more complex and sophisticated, with more potential for disruption in the event of a theft or other type of loss-causing incident.
- Supply chain security is becoming a core competency within many companies inside their supply chain operations.
- Significant return on investment can be achieved through an effective supply chain security program.
- Corporate security and logistics divisions must work together to develop key policies and procedures to keep cargo secure regardless of where it is in the world.
- Thorough policy development is the first step in ensuring that an effective supply chain security program is implemented.
- Insurance companies and third-party security providers can provide expert guidance and assistance in developing policies and implementing supply chain security programs.

PHYSICAL SECURITY

INFORMATION IN THIS CHAPTER:

- How to take a known risk model and create a security plan for supply chain operations
- Section by section descriptions of topics necessary for a layered security approach
- Additional areas of consideration beyond security, such as company culture, environment, and legal/human resource policies
- How to focus on low- or no-cost solutions to keep security budgets in line with overall company objectives

A physical security plan serves as the basis for supply chain security programs. While cargo moves throughout the world, at no point will there be a large volume of product in one location than when stored inside warehouses and distribution centers, which therefore are in need of thorough security policies and procedures to ensure the product's protection. According to Richard Gigliotti and Ronald Jason in *Handbook of Loss Prevention and Crime Prevention*, there are five levels of security: minimum, low, medium, high, and maximum.

Levels of Security

Minimum Security

This level requires the desire to impede some unauthorized access to a facility or location through a combination of simple locks and physical barriers. (This would be suitable only for facilities that store goods of little or no value to a criminal.)

Low-Level Security

This next higher level of security adds to the existing level of security, along with a measure of detection. Through the use of physical barriers and locking systems designed to delay or impede access to a facility, a facility can add the ability to detect

173

unauthorized access through the addition of lighting and an alarm system. (Similar to the minimum level of security, this level would be appropriate for the same type of facility, but perhaps located in an area of higher crime rates where vandalism and other security issues are of concern.)

Medium-Level Security

In addition to impeding access and unauthorized access detection, this level of security adds an assessment feature that includes activity around the facility, taking into account the normal flow of business, as well as possible criminal activity. By increasing the level of security features from the low level of security, establishing a perimeter barrier, in addition to an existing physical barrier, around the primary area being protected, and using guards or other features enhance deterrence and detection capabilities. (This is used for facilities manufacturing or storing items of moderate value with a small level of desirability for sale on the black market.)

High-Level Security

At the high level of security, existing simple or advanced security features are replaced with state-of-the-art measures, such as closed circuit television (CCTV) systems, perimeter alarms, high-security lighting, access controls to the perimeter and to the facility, formal response plans, and regularly scheduled site surveys and security assessments to determine the overall effectiveness of implemented security measures. This protection is consistent with high-value goods such as electronics, pharmaceuticals (typically over-the-counter and consumer products), high-end clothing, wine and spirits, and tobacco products.

Maximum Security

The pinnacle of security incorporates all the desired attributes of the first four levels, adding the ability to neutralize any unauthorized external or internal activity. This would include sophisticated alarm systems that cannot be defeated by a single individual, on-site response protocols, and 24/7 armed security staff on site. While this level of security is rarely seen in the manufacturing and logistics industries, it is used in military installations, some power plants, nuclear sites, and other critical infrastructures. Sites that store products of extreme value or desirability should consider adoption of some or all of these features.

An assessment of a company's products (their value and theft attractiveness), site location, risk tolerances, and budget will allow a company to determine the right level of security. Also inherent in this is the selection of security policies and procedures to be followed.

During this phase it is crucial that all security countermeasures be analyzed, determining that their capabilities and limitations to ensure optimal placement and deployment and security policies are implemented to ensure coverage, obtaining the desired level of security.

The emphasis of most cargo facility security plans lies in the capabilities of physical aspects (fences, gates, lighting, alarm systems, CCTV, and the like). However, the supply chain adds another dimension, the introduction and removal of goods. The process by which drivers arrive; where they are and are not allowed; counting, verifying, and loading of cargo; and steps to ensure the cargo is secured is absolutely key to a successful program and is often the most overlooked from a security perspective and viewed as a logistics issue.

Note: This chapter is designed to provide an explanation of the variety of security features and measures that should be considered when creating or analyzing a security program. It is not the purpose of this chapter to provide technical details of the technologies presented. These should be assessed based on specific needs.

Administrative Information

Any security policy should have information to ensure anyone reading it understands how it is to be applied to their business unit, why the roles and responsibilities exist, and how it will be enforced. It should also include specific tasks for those identified in the policy as well as references used in the creation of the policy and the responsibilities of those specifically identified within the policy.

The scope statement of any supply chain security or cargo security program should be simple and straightforward. The purpose of this statement is to ensure that the policy is understood within the context of what it is attempting to achieve, who it affects, and, possibly more importantly, what areas it does not apply to.

Authority for policies is generally derived from other policies or executive decisions that give the policy and its author the directive to create and implement a cargo security initiative. Generally citing the directive policy is sufficient for any policy being developed with regards to authority.

Any references used in creating the policy or those that can be used to help clarify certain terms or concepts should be listed either at the beginning of the document or at the end as an appendix. This would also apply to technical definitions used in the plan.

Responsibilities labeled within this section should include all personnel with direct involvement in the program's development, implementation, maintenance, or enforcement. This would include personnel such as the supply chain security manager, logistics or transportation managers, site security staff, procurement, and any others designated with direct authority or responsibility within the policy.

Site Security Management

The size, number of buildings, functions, operational tempo, and geographical location all help determine if a site will have a dedicated security manager. Other factors include product value or desirability, the level of security desired for the site, and the culture of a company with regard to security and budget. A common practice is to give an existing manager the secondary role of security manager.

There is no "one size fits all" answer to the question of whether a dedicated site security manager is needed. Clearly in the interest of maximizing security, having a dedicated site security manager is ideal, but it is recognized that this is not always feasible.

Whether a dedicated site security manager is in place or an existing manager serves in this role, every site should have a single person responsible for all security policies, procedures, and equipment. This includes an integration of lighting to ensure proper functionality of CCTV systems, processing and access of visitors, vendors and truck drivers, and a variety of other daily practices that have potential impact on the overall security of a facility and the people and products held within.

The site security manager should also be trained in the best practices of physical and procedural security. Organizations such as the American Society for Industrial Security (ASIS) offer an array of training and certification curriculums to assist in a security manager's professional development. Continuing education expands one's knowledge base and lets one keep aware of best practices, technology, crime trends, and emerging threats.

Contact Persons

A phone tree or list of designated persons responsible for the security program should be included within the policy, as well as a separate list of those who should be contacted in the event of an incident, cargo theft, or other emergency. This list should be reviewed monthly and revised as needed. It is imperative that the list be accurate to ensure rapid notification of the appropriate personnel in the event of an emergency and that all personnel on the contact list are trained and ready to fulfill their duties once contacted.

Risk Assessments

Supply chain risk assessments and individual site and lane assessments should be required for all locations and lanes used (for additional information, see Chapter 11: Determining Risk). Lane surveys should be updated at least annually, with site surveys conducted every 2 years and supply chain level assessments updated every 3 to 5 years based on outcomes of the lane and site surveys. Other triggers, such as a large-scale loss or increased theft activity can determine if an updated survey or assessment is needed. These triggers should warrant a new survey and/or risk assessment to ensure that the company's supply chain security policy is adequately mitigating risk in that area or business unit.

Components of such a risk assessment should include points of origin and destination (to include general crime around them such as CAP Index reports and the routes used between them), product transported on the lane (to include value and demand on the black market), and the transportation providers used.

These can be performed internally or by a supply chain security consultant if a company does not have the staff or bandwidth to complete these assessments.

Cargo Crime Intelligence

Collecting information and intelligence on cargo crime, emerging risks, and industry best practices is critical for a comprehensive and effective supply chain security program. There are a number of organizations and resources available to industry professionals for them to keep informed of the latest trends, as well as providing in-depth historical analysis and predictive modeling for shifts in supply chain risk.

A member of the supply chain security staff should be designated with finding resources best suited to meet a company's specific needs as well as monitoring the information coming in to analyze incidents and trends applicable to the company's overall supply chain risk.

This section should also cover how information is to be disseminated to appropriate personnel. Acquiring intelligence and conducting analyses will not enhance a supply chain security program unless it is being shared with the right people and used when making security and business decisions.

The Resource section of this book provides information on a wide range of companies that can assist in this area and provide industry professionals with an array of intelligence products from individual theft reports to long-range data analysis.

Applicant and Employee Screening

It is imperative to the success of a corporate security plan that employees act in the best interest of the company. Internal theft, leaking insider information, and other illegal actions by employees can drain a company and render security policies ineffective. While it is impossible to predict someone's actions or know their intentions, certain measures can be taken by a security staff and/or human resources department to assist in the selection of new employees.

The overall purpose of applicant screening is to find the most appropriate person for a particular position (Purpura, 2008, p. 110). Screening methods vary significantly among organizations, but some basic components are the resume and the application form. These documents serve as the primary means to determine if a prospective employee is a good fit with the company. The Port Authority of New York and New Jersey performed an interesting study on fraudulent information during the application process by asking if a person had experience with certain types of equipment. More than one-third claimed to have experience on equipment that did not exist (Purpura, 2008, p. 117). Other forms of screening include commonly used interview process and testing.

Once a viable candidate has been identified and his or her application received, companies should then conduct a thorough background investigation. The purpose of the investigation is twofold: (1) verify all pertinent information in the applicant's resume and application and (2) attempt to discover anything in the applicant's history that would disqualify him or her from employment. The interviewer should ask specific questions about areas that would disqualify a person.

When reviewing applications, some early red flags can be easily recognized:

- Unsigned forms
- Incomplete addresses or post office box numbers

- Conflicting dates of employment, education, or military service
- Gaps in employment
- Change of occupation
- Sketchy employment information
- Social security number variance
- Omission of reason for leaving previous employment (ASIS, 2004)

The background investigation can be handled by the corporate security department or by human resources. It is critical to remember that the purpose behind the investigation is to ensure the right person is hired, not a mechanism to disqualify the candidate. Of course, criminal history, convictions, and other negative information not disclosed in the application process should be analyzed and a decision made as to the person's qualification based on the "whole man" concept.

The whole man concept is designed not to allow a single issue in a person's background to categorically be a barrier to employment. For example, if a pharmaceutical company has a zero drug and alcohol policy, but a 40-year-old applicant has a citation for marijuana possession at the age of 18, the whole man concept would take into account the applicant's age, maturity level at the time of offense, and the fact the applicant has had no further offenses.

Perimeter Security

A perimeter boundary, such as a fence, is the first layer of security that anyone attempting to enter a facility will encounter. Regardless of the level of complexity in perimeter security or the absence of any features, methods used to secure a perimeter must be included in the facility security plan and incorporated into the daily operations of the site. This can have significant implications on how visitors, vendors, and truck drivers are granted access, the process for managing unauthorized access to the site grounds, and the ways by which employees enter and leave for work, impacting each and every person who enters or leaves the site on a daily basis.

The most common perimeter boundary used is a fence. Most often chain link, a fence provides the following:

- Gives notice of the legal boundary of the outermost limits of a facility
- Assists in controlling and screening authorized entries into a secured area by deterring entry elsewhere along the boundary

- Supports surveillance, detection, assessment, and other security functions by providing a zone for installing intrusion detection equipment and CCTV
- Deters casual intruders from penetrating a secured area by presenting a barrier that requires an overt action to enter
- Demonstrates the intent of an intruder by their overt action of gaining entry
- Causes a delay to obtain access to a facility, thereby increasing the possibility of detection
- Creates a psychological deterrent
- Reduces the number of security guards required and frequency of use for each post
- Optimizes the use of security personnel while enhancing the capabilities for detection and apprehension of unauthorized individuals
- Demonstrates a corporate concern for facility security
- Provides a cost-effective method of protecting facilities

The primary objective of a fence or other perimeter barrier is to delay access by potential criminals and funnel traffic to a minimum number of entry and access points. In a maximum security environment, a fence is not the ideal perimeter barrier (a solid wall is preferred) but in most cases, a chain link fence with barbed wire across the top is sufficient for the supply chain industry.

The type of perimeter boundary used will have a significant impact on the policies and procedures for accessing the facility grounds, including access being granted with or without an appointment, if identification will be checked and/or recorded prior to entry being granted, registration of personnel and vehicles at the access point, and so on. While this first step of establishing a perimeter barrier seems to be the simplest, it provides for an array of possibilities and will affect the culture of security at any location.

As fences and perimeter boundaries will generally only provide deterrence and delay capabilities, additional security measures should be included in the planning, installation, and daily procedures of a perimeter security plan. Additionally, stand-off distance and use of terrain must be considered in order to maximize the effectiveness of the perimeter boundary and total system integration.

Physical Security

Standards for high-security facilities are well established, but are not implemented easily. Each and every aspect of physical security must be analyzed, weaknesses determined, and countermeasures put into place to ensure that the highest level of security is reached. These include

- Personnel doors
- Locks
- Dock doors
- Emergency doors
- Walls
- Ram bars
- Roofs
- Windows

Even with the ever-changing criminal threat, the basics of alarms, real-time monitoring, CCTV, and card reader access systems have been in place for years and are still the place to start when creating a cargo facility security program. It is critical, however, that these apparatuses need to be installed not simply because they are necessary, but are deployed in line with how the security manager plans for each measure in order to thwart the efforts of cargo thieves. For example, alarm sensors may be installed on each dock door so that if opened, the alarm monitoring company will be notified of a break-in. This can be defeated by criminals, however, using blow torches to cut a hole in the dock door, sufficiently large enough to load a trailer through, never disturbing the alarm system. Therefore, the security manager should consider redundant security systems such as motion detection devices in order to combat this emerging trend.

In order for physical security features to function properly, security policies and procedures must be in place. A card reader system is immediately made ineffective if employees are propping exterior doors open while they go outside on break or for ventilation purposes. The same is true for personnel ID badges and visitor badges. If they are not required to be worn, and done so in a uniform manner, the ability to recognize who is and is not authorized to be in critical areas of the facility is diminished significantly. Policies and procedures must be in concert with the physical security features and compliance with them audited to ensure that the holistic security system is effective.

One aspect of physical security often overlooked is exterior lighting. Locations with a large amount of exterior lighting have a significantly lower rate of criminal incidents occurring. While this seems to be a common sense issue, it must be noted that lighting is an extremely effective and inexpensive way of preventing theft and other criminal acts. It also makes for a safer environment, especially if cargo/truck operations take place at night.

For a physical security plan to be effective, the functionality and limits of each physical security feature must be known and implemented in a manner that allows for overlap and fluid coverage of all critical points.

Access Control

The basic concept of access control is to permit or deny entry, manage the density of movement within a defined space, and protect an area, property, information, or people from unauthorized observation or removal. When developing an access control program, it is critical that the objectives of the program be clear as this will have significant influence on the type, degree of reliability, and cost of the system (ASIS, 2004).

The key to a successful physical security program is to understand the risk posed based on the criteria discussed in the previous chapter, incorporate applicable security measures that are established as industry-best practices, and understand that the threat is always changing. Because of this, periodic reassessments are vital to ensure not only if your physical security program is well maintained and functional but also if there are any emerging threats or trends that require adjustments to policies or security measures currently in place.

There are a variety of access control techniques ranging from simple lock and key to more sophisticated systems such as coded card access combined with retinal scanners. In its basic form, the access control system is designed to identify the person attempting to gain access, determine if he or she is or is not authorized access, and then grant or deny access. The most common methods used today for this process are

- People—usually a receptionist or guard to check identification and verify access authorization
- Card reader systems—compare the coded card with computer records indicating if access is granted
- Biometric readers—use a person's physical properties for identification and determine if he or she is allowed access

The system used should have functionality beyond simply access to a facility. Access controls should be designed to ensure that only authorized personnel are permitted into areas in which they work or are required to enter as part of their job function. For example, office staff would not need access to the loading dock area, therefore their access badges should restrict access there. Even within a warehouse, there can be only a limited number of personnel allowed to enter high-value cages and vaults.

An electronic access control system should be used throughout a facility, record all entries (even attempts), and be reviewed periodically to check for attempted unauthorized use or suspect behavior (i.e., a single employee exiting the dock area repeatedly within a small time frame with no valid business reason).

Key Control

A single individual should be made responsible for the management of all physical keys used within a facility or site. All lock installation, maintenance, and upgrades should be managed by this person, who is also responsible for issuing, tracking, and retrieving keys to and from authorized personnel.

Keys not in use should be placed in a secure container such as a safe or lock box. All keys should be serial numbered, excess keys should be inventoried monthly, and a log of all issued keys should be maintained and updated for accuracy as changes are made and during the monthly inventory. All keys should be marked stating that duplication is unauthorized. There are some key designs that are more difficult to duplicate so investigation into these seems appropriate.

Management should conduct a periodic audit of the key control system (annually at a minimum), which would require all key holders to present their assigned keys as well as an inspection of the keys kept in storage.

The complexity of the security program will dictate the features in a company's key control program, but the minimum attributes listed earlier are critical to ensuring keys are not provided inadvertently (or, worst-case scenario, purposefully) to people wishing to steal from or otherwise cause harm to a site, its product, or personnel.

Closed Circuit Television

CCTV systems are one of the most frequently used security applications. Reliable and cost-effective, CCTV systems play an integral part of most security programs, along with alarms, fire detection, and access control systems. CCTVs are used in virtually every facility that houses product with any degree of desirability, from electronics to tobacco to clothing. While CCTV systems offer a reliable means for monitoring facilities and allow for detection of unauthorized access and a means for the apprehension of offenders, care must be taken to ensure that the systems are installed properly in order to maximize their full potential.

Although initially met with resistance by employees in the industrial community, CCTV systems today are readily accepted as part of the working environment. As cargo losses have continued to rise throughout the supply chain, cost-effective means have been sought out to mitigate thefts and decrease the overall cost of investigating crimes (and to prevent them from happening in the first place); CCTV plays a definite role and has become a common part of this process.

The greatest potential for CCTV is its integration with other sensor systems (alarms and motion detection), as well as its use to view remote areas with potential security and safety problems. When used to its fullest extent, a CCTV system can serve as a tremendous tool for detecting the presence of unauthorized personnel by alerting security staff monitoring the system. As part of an overall security policy, the reaction of the guards once an unauthorized presence is detected must be established in writing along with management notification procedures.

Beyond detection of unauthorized personnel, CCTV systems can also serve in other roles, such as investigating accidents, employee misconduct, and more. The only way in which a CCTV system can serve as a theft prevention tool is if the system is being monitored by someone who is in a position to respond immediately to a threat. Without a monitoring and reaction/response capability, a CCTV system provides historical data and does not serve in a theft prevention capacity, but remains an integral part of a physical security plan.

In the role of asset protection, a CCTV system can be used to detect unwanted entry into a facility, beginning with access through the perimeter barrier and following the intruder through a series of cameras throughout the interior and exterior of the facility.

Coverage

Adequate CCTV coverage should include the following areas:
- 360 degree exterior perimeter
- Interior and exterior of all entry/exit points
- Interior and exterior of all dock doors
- The shipping yard
- High-value cage/vault
- Goods in storage
- Vehicle entry/exit (capturing license plates and truck driver faces)
- Security room entry point

- Information technology room or location of security systems entry point

As with the overall level of security, the number of cameras used, their capabilities, and the areas covered will be dependent on the product being stored, its desirability by thieves, and the overall potential loss to a company in the event of a catastrophic theft.

Typically, the CCTV system serves as a deterrent to (internal) theft and provides visual evidence of crimes committed (internal theft and warehouse burglaries/robberies). The most common mistakes with CCTV systems are a lack of coverage in critical areas, poor camera positioning, and no active monitoring when staff is available. CCTV systems have to be integrated into the overall facility security program and therefore must be installed properly, designed to provide the desired level of coverage and be monitored by trained personnel.

Positioning

The positioning of cameras is also important. Cameras set too low, too high or covering too large of an area can result in deteriorated images or blocked images altogether. Security managers should ensure that the camera capabilities and coverage requirements are clearly communicated to the provider/installer. Additionally, adjustments must be considered, for example, how the facility will be set up and operated during the day, before installation. While a trailer may not be present when the cameras are installed, if not taken into consideration, the entire field of view could be blocked once a trailer is backed into place.

The ideal camera-to-door ratio for the interior dock area is one camera for every three dock doors with the camera positioned so that the inside of each trailer can be viewed when the doors are open. Cameras positioned along the same wall that is being monitored can view product being loaded or unloaded, but are ineffective at identifying which dock door is being used during the activity being viewed.

The common location for exterior camera installation is on the facility, facing down the wall of the facility and/or out into the parking area facing the facility perimeter. While this method provides a more cost-effective means of installation and provides good coverage of parking lots and other areas, it generally fails to provide adequate coverage of areas closer to the facility, particularly entry/exit points and dock doors.

Storage

Just like high-value goods and other critical components stored within a facility, the CCTV system should also be stored in a secured environment. Too many times criminals escape capture or detection because they were able to access the CCTV system, destroy the DVRs, or disable the monitoring component of the system. Internal rooms with reinforced doors and locking systems are ideal for CCTV system storage, along with limited access and an alarm or motion sensors inside the room for detection of unauthorized access.

System Integration

A CCTV system is most effective when integrated as part of the overall physical security program. As with any layered approach to security, this system combines personnel, procedures, and technology (equipment) in such a way to maximize the use of each individual component. When designing a program or examining additional security features, each element should be assessed to determine how it will contribute to the overall goal of preventing loss of cargo.

Other important features of a CCTV system include continuous recording DVRs (vs. motion only), pan-tilt-zoom cameras (vs. stationary cameras), and infrared capable cameras (vs. those requiring an external light source). It is important that the objectives of the CCTV program are understood when selecting cameras types and their positioning to ensure each camera is utilized to their fullest potential to maximize all systems being used.

Management must understand that a complete CCTV system can be composed of components from several manufacturers; therefore, they need to ensure that all equipment is compatible. Other electronic components can also be tied into the CCTV system to provide overlaps in security coverage, such as alarms and motion detection by zone, as well as access control systems to ensure that any activity within the facility (or on the facility grounds) is covered by CCTV cameras and recorded.

Lighting

Primarily thought of as a tool for detection, a good lighting system can be one of the most potent crime deterrences available. Criminals, as a rule, prefer to conduct their activities under the cover of darkness, clearly with the goal of avoiding detection and capture. Because of this, a site that provides an extremely lit ground and facility creates a difficult environment for success.

According to John Tabor, director of loss prevention at National Retail Systems, a logistics and transportation company that services the retail industry, "If every dime of my security budget had to be spent on one thing, I would spend it all on lighting."

Such statements only highlight the importance of lighting as part of an overall physical security program, yet it remains one of the most commonly overlooked best practices.

Outdoor lighting should be (at a minimum) adequate for both security purposes and safe cargo operations. The spacing between lighting stanchions should be limited to no more than 150 feet in order to ensure consistent illumination throughout the area of coverage. Lighting around the perimeter should be oriented to provide glare in the face of potential intruders and avoid any glare in the face of CCTV systems covering the facility exterior.

As with all other security functions, a backup generator or other power supply should be available and automatically begin providing power in the event of a power outage in the main supply. Additionally, all power feeds to the lighting system should be underground or otherwise protected to prevent intruders from easily cutting the power and disabling the lighting system.

Alarms (Intrusion Detection Systems)

Alarm systems, also referred to as intrusion detection systems, provide companies with the ability to detect the presence of personnel within an established boundary or general area. This can serve to detect the presence of both authorized and unauthorized personnel; however, it is the latter that is often the most commonly considered when designing and implementing an intrusion detection system.

While an alarm system may serve as a deterrent for a would-be intruder, the primary purpose of such a system is detection and should be used as one part of an overall security system and not be relied upon for the total security of a facility.

Alarm systems come in a variety of designs and features tailored to meet specific user needs. There are three primary purposes for alarm systems:
• Perimeter protection
• Area protection
• Object/spot protection

Perimeter Protection

Perimeter protection is the first line of defense for a facility or grounds and can be applied to the entire area in which a facility is located, the facility perimeter itself, or a particular room or set of rooms. The most common locations for sensors to detect intrusion are doors, windows, skylights, or any other opening by which an intruder could gain entry.

Area Protection

Area protection is designed to detect the presence of a person within an interior room or space within a facility. This method is used to detect intruders who were able to bypass the perimeter detection system or for "stay-behind" burglars who set off the perimeter system, but are able to hide within the facility until the all clear is given. This type of detection system should only be provided in addition to a perimeter alarm system and not relied upon solely for intrusion detection.

Object/Spot Protection

The inner-most layer of intrusion detection would be coverage of an individual object or location. Common examples would be things such as safes, vaults, cabinets, or desks. This final level of security is used when the first two levels of intrusion detection fail or are evaded, providing the facility or owner with one last means of detecting the presence of an unauthorized personnel before a theft has occurred.

It is critical to understand that these three methods of intrusion detection are designed to work in combination with each other, with area protection and object/spot protection serving as additional layers to perimeter detection, not sufficient intrusion detection in and of themselves. As with all security measures used, the level of their effectiveness is impacted directly by the quality of equipment used, the methodology for their employment, and the means by which other security components overlap and complement their capabilities and limitations.

High-Value Cage

For sites that have product of particularly high value or desirability, use of a high-value or high-security cage is recommended. These cages can range from a simple chain link fence within a section of a facility to a walled and armored vault.

Regardless of the style of cage that is created for the security of these high-value goods, a few common security features should always be present.

First is a method for ensuring that access is gained by authorized personnel only and that it is limited to a select few personnel within the company, not simply anyone who works on site. This is done mostly through electronic access cards with special entry permissions for the high-value cage gate or door. In addition to the access control system in place, CCTV cameras should be positioned to capture images of personnel entering/exiting the cage from both the interior and the exterior.

Second, a truly effective cage should have a ceiling/roof and ideally not use an exterior wall as one of its sides. If an exterior wall is going to be used, anti-ram bars or other physical barriers should be placed to defend against attempts to access the high value cage by ramming the exterior wall with a vehicle or other means. Essentially, the high-value cage should be fully contained with minimal opportunities for access without delay or detection.

This brings the author to the third point, which is to ensure that adequate intrusion detection systems are in place on the exterior and interior of the cage. As outlined in the alarm section of this chapter, use of a layered alarm system approach is necessary for the full security of a high-value cage by using perimeter, area, and potentially object/spot security systems.

Security Officers

The decision whether to use on-site security officers is based primarily on the level of security that a company thinks is required to ensure that their product (and personnel) is kept safe. If the decision is made to use security personnel, the follow-up question is whether the officers should be armed, which again goes back to the level of security required at a facility. Of course, to reach this decision, all the various factors relating to the necessary level of security are considered, with additional factors such as budget, company culture, and operational impacts being considered.

Other considerations to having a security service on site include other duties/roles that the service can fulfill. Visitor control, driver control, cargo load verification, seal application, and trash collection supervision are just a few examples of roles vital to having a secured facility and can be performed by a contract security company rather than having in-house managers fulfill these roles.

Regardless of the roles performed by contracted security companies, the duties for each security officer on site must be established in writing as postorders and made available to the management staff to ensure that each security officer is performing as required.

Trash Collection and Disposal

Theft facilitated through the trash collection and removal process is one of the older but still commonly used methods of employee theft. Product is hidden inside trash, collected, and removed by an employee and placed in a dumpster or other trash receptacle and then later recovered by the dishonest employee. While this method involves theft at very small quantities per instance, over time it can become a significant problem and one that can be avoided with relative ease.

Trash collection should be performed by designated personnel only. All trash should also be screened for any product prior to being removed from a facility, ideally being by a supervisor or above or by a member of the security staff. Additionally, the personnel removing trash should not have to leave the facility to dispose of the trash or, at a minimum, only have to walk a few feet away. Any path that requires personnel to walk by or near vehicles or other areas in which they could off-load legitimate product while delivering trash to a compactor or dumpster should be changed.

Compactors are an ideal solution for reducing the risk of theft through the trash removal process. Compactors loaded directly from the facility floor and placed into operation once loaded prevent product from being hidden within the trash, placed in a dumpster, and later recovered.

In cases where extremely high-value product is very small, such as computer chips and components and pharmaceuticals, such measures are absolutely imperative in preventing rampant employee theft through this simple and time-proven method.

Shipping and Receiving

Security of products during the shipping and receiving process is important, as these are operations where goods are vulnerable to theft. The high level of activity in the dock area, coupled with loading, unloading, and staging of cargo, makes for a dynamic environment and, depending on the size and complexity of an operation, can be extremely difficult in safeguarding goods.

While barriers, restricted areas, cameras, locks, and other security features discussed previously in this chapter are important factors in keeping a dock area secure, is the processes and procedures that will have the greatest impact on the cargo integrity through the shipping and receiving processes.

Another vital aspect of dock security is to ensure that all dock doors are closed (ideally locked or latched) when not in use. Often hot weather is cited for keeping some or all dock doors open while the facility is in operation. Scissor gates or other forms of screens can be fitted easily into the dock door and allow for airflow while providing an effective barrier to entry.

The use of these systems is crucial for deterring and preventing both opportunistic thieves and preplanned theft schemes from stealing cargo in the dock area successfully.

Other aspects of security around this part of a company's operation, such as driver control, documentation, and use of lock and seals on trailers, are included in the next chapter, which covers in-transit security.

Trailer Storage/Yard Security

Whether or not trailers are kept on site for loading purposes, it is imperative that the yard area around the docks be secured from unauthorized access. While not always the easiest thing to do depending on the facility being used, its proximity to the street, if it is part of a shared facility, and multiple other factors involved, the simple fact remains, however, that when warehouse burglaries occur, the theft gang almost always uses a tractor–trailer and the dock area to load cargo and remove it from the facility. If adequate detection security measures are not in place in this area, criminals will have that much easier of a time stealing large volumes of cargo successfully.

Securing a yard involves the basic tenants of security, including deterrence, delay, and detection. This area should be encompassed by the facility's standalone perimeter barrier or fence, most commonly a chain linked fence. Lighting should also be a priority in this area for both deterrence and detection purposes.

CCTV cameras should be focused on the gate (entry/exit) as well as the exterior of the docks and along the fence lines to capture/detect personnel attempting to gain entry to the yard.

For empty trailers stored in this area (storing/staging loaded trailers is *never* recommended), trailers should be parked in a manner that does not inhibit the proper functionality of security measures (and vice versa, security measures should be installed so that parked trailers will not inhibit their functionality). Trailers should also be parked a minimum of 6 feet from the fence line and parked with at least 3 feet between each other to allow for viewing/CCTV coverage between trailers.

A security guard should control entry and exit to the yard, allowing only authorized personnel that are expected through a prenotification system. All drivers arriving must be required to present ID that matches with the information provided in the prenotification system. Guards should also check the yard itself periodically for potential intrusion or attempts at intrusion.

All outbound trailers must be inspected to ensure that the driver is taking the load assigned to him and that the seal (if present) is the correct seal and affixed properly.

Maintenance and Services

Maintenance is a key component to the successful operation of a security system. If one component fails, it needs to be repaired or replaced quickly. An out-of-service system provides no protection. Near continuous operation is accomplished by the direct replacement methods through immediate maintenance by an in-house service organization or (more commonly) by having a quick response service arrangement from the installer or a contracted maintenance company.

Preventative maintenance is critical in decreasing opportunities for system failure and minimizing system down time. General inspection, cleaning, and maintenance should be conducted at a minimum in the CCTV system no less than on a quarterly basis, with a full system check and maintenance performed by the installer or contracted service company annually.

Regardless of the method of service used, it is critical to ensure that the right service company is selected. The company selected needs to understand emerging technologies and their benefits, be customer oriented, and be able to inform the user on how new equipment and products can benefit their overall security program.

Key Points

- First understand your risk and determine the level of security necessary. Not all products need the same level of security, as geography can have a dramatic effect on the required level.
- Have a written plan and cover every possible aspect of security necessary to achieve the desired level of security. The plan should be a living document that is updated constantly.

- Ensure that security measures are strategically implemented, providing overlap and redundancy so that no single point of failure leaves a facility vulnerable.
- Remember that there is more to securing a facility than preventing theft—workplace violence, outside threats, and other security concerns should be recognized and accounted for in the security plan.
- A company's culture has a dramatic effect on the acceptable level of security in place and its level of intrusiveness—changing this culture to be more security oriented cannot be done overnight.
- Do not forget about lighting, trash, or the dock area, as each of these, if addressed properly, can potentially have the greatest impact on theft reduction possible.
- Security improvements do not always require capital. There are numerous no- or low-cost measures that can provide significant enhancement simply through creation of, or changes in, processes at zero cost to the company.

IN-TRANSIT SECURITY

INFORMATION IN THIS CHAPTER:

- How to create an in-transit security plan that is customizable to an ever-changing logistics environment
- A breakdown of the topics required for a comprehensive in-transit security plan and methods for assessing in-transit security risk
- How to apply a layered security approach to a multitier, multivendor distribution model
- Use of technology in logistics and transportation security programs

Envision a company that manufactures and distributes cargo considered by any measure to be high value and theft-attractive. The company fully understands the desire by criminals to steal its product and has a state-of-the-art security program at its facilities.

In place are towering perimeter barriers, armed guards, surveillance cameras surrounding each site, key card access monitored by a 24/7 security staff, and motion detection throughout the facility, including all offices and product in storage. The company spared no expense in assembling their security program, taking every reasonable measure to ensure that unauthorized persons are kept out and product is kept in.

Now imagine this same company using a third-party truck or freight broker service for transportation providers. A load is ready for pickup, at which time the broker arranges for a trucker the company doesn't know, a driver arrives they have never met, his identification is not checked or employment verified, he does not sign in any log book, and yet his trailer is loaded and a company logo security seal is placed on the trailer.

Also, the driver and his dispatcher are responsible for scheduling the delivery appointment because that would require another staff member for the shipper company, something they do not want to do. So the driver makes the appointment for Friday afternoon but leaves the facility on Tuesday for the 10-hour drive to the destination.

So a driver whose ID was not retained by the shipper, who may or may not actually work for the company he claimed to, has a load valued in the millions of dollars, and 4 days to make a 10-hour trip.

Additionally, the company doesn't use any form of covert tracking devices so the moment that tractor–trailer left their facility, the company had no idea where its cargo was any more.

Ludicrous? It happens every single day in America's supply chain. Every day.

Amazingly, when this complete lack of transit security is laid out to a company, particularly a company that is very "security conscious," the reasons quickly come to the front.

"We are measured on how fast we get product out the door." "We don't have staff to schedule appointments." "We don't have staff to place tracking devices in loads or have them monitored." "We've never had a loss before." All ring hollow when a load is stolen because it sat in an empty parking lot, unattended.

The need for a robust in-transit security policy, one focused on loss prevention, has never been more necessary than today.

With available policy templates, tracking technologies, vehicle immobilizers, locking systems, security seals, and other proven tools at our disposal, it is critical that security and logistics professionals are well versed in the systems they employ, understand their uses and limitations, and ensure their programs are robust, redundant, and limit single points of failure.

Driver Controls

On August 23, 2011, a driver for a transportation provider arrived at a distribution center in Ontario, California. The driver obtained the contract for the load through an Internet-based platform where shippers can place information on loads needing transportation and allows carriers to bid for the work. The driver arrived, the trailer was loaded, and he departed, never to be seen or heard from again.

The driver's identity was false and the transportation company was fake. It's hard enough to deal with a stolen load despite the best policies and procedures in place, but when a company hands cargo over to a criminal willingly, literally loading it in his truck for him, that is a tough pill to swallow. While this particular incident occurred in California, this happens throughout the United States and in 2011 at unprecedented levels.

Luckily there are simple, proven steps that can prevent this from happening. The first step lies in the selection process for transportation providers and what companies can and cannot pull high-value cargo from a shipper. This is covered in detail in the next subsection of this chapter.

Next is making sure the person who arrives to pick up the cargo is indeed the authorized driver from the preselected transportation provider. This can be accomplished through the following measures (or a combination of them):

- Have the transportation provider send the driver's name before his arrival.
- Provide the trucking company with a pickup number that the driver must provide to be allowed on site and receive the load.
- Check the driver's ID and ensure that it matches with the name provided ahead of time.

CASE STUDY: GIVING CARGO AWAY

Cargo theft is a multibillion dollar per year problem that plagues our global supply chain. From small-scale pilferage to full-truckload theft and warehouse burglaries, criminal enterprises are continually seeking methods to successfully steal, transport, and sell legitimate goods on the black and gray markets for profit. While shippers are armed with knowledge, security countermeasures, and budgets to prevent thefts from occurring, criminals have the experience, desire, and, maybe most importantly, the creativity necessary to successfully conduct their crimes and leave the victims behind to pick up the pieces.

Cargo criminals can be very creative in acquiring goods illegally— and modi operandi (MOs) can vary significantly from country to country or region to region. That being said, however, there are only so many ways for criminals to steal loads. There are partial load thefts, full trailer/ container thefts, warehouse burglaries/robberies, and so on. As such, many MOs have been seen around the world as they are utilized successfully by cargo criminals.

Even rarely seen MOs can be repeated in other parts of the world with no seemingly obvious connection. For example, the method of stealing cargo from a moving truck by off-loading it into a trailer vehicle was seen a couple of years ago in China and then later seen being done successfully in both Germany in 2009 and in Spain in 2010.

Possibly the most frustrating way for any company in the supply chain to lose a load is through the MO of fictitious pickup: when the company responsible for the care of the product willingly (albeit unknowingly) gives the cargo to the criminal, most of the time loading it into his trailer for him, and watches as the cargo criminal drives away, only to find out hours or days later that the driver was not a driver, but a crook, and their cargo will never be seen again.

Whether referred to as a fictitious pickup, deceptive pickup, fraudulent documentation, or other various names, the general concept is the same. A fictitious pickup occurs when a criminal presents him- or herself as a legitimate transportation provider to the load point of origin. Once believed to be the legitimate carrier for that shipment, the facility loads the cargo and the load is released into the care of the criminal.

Hard to imagine this happening? It occurs all the time.

In the spring of 2011, almost a dozen incidents of fictitious pickups occurred in the United States. One scam used the same company name and took eight loads of food products all from the same victim until the scam was realized. As a result, dozens of warning emails and alerts were published by various organizations and law enforcement agencies, attempting to notify and educate the industry of this criminal technique, but it was barely slowed, with reports continuing into June regarding additional fictitious pickups—losses occurring with the literal assistance of the victims.

Fictitious pickups are nothing new, particularly in Europe. This criminal MO has been used for over a decade in various forms, often with drivers posing as working for legitimate transportation providers, relying on the legitimacy of their paperwork's appearance to entice loads to be released to them. This method of theft accounted for over 10% of recorded thefts in the first quarter of 2011.

The primary methods used to complete a fictitious pickup successfully are:

- Creation of a fake transportation company
- Impersonation of a real/legitimate transportation company
- Fraudulent pickup—having fake paperwork, but not an actual company set up

In the United States, a method for acquiring bids for transportation services is to broker loads through the Internet. Shippers post loads needing to be shipped (origin and destination) to which transportation providers respond with competitive bids, from which the shipper selects a transportation provider and awards the load. Unfortunately, this method is ripe with criminal enterprises posing as transportation providers, bidding on loads with the sole intent to steal them, and it is only a matter of time before they are awarded loads and drive away successfully with their target.

Of course, a company does not have to be victimized by this growing trend. In fact, prevention can be relatively simple, but it does require effort on the part of the shipper, and may mean that the lowest cost bidder might not be the selected carrier.

One of the most successful ways of preventing a fictitious pickup from occurring is using only a preselected list of transportation providers for all movements and by providing a pickup number to the selected carrier for each and every shipment. When the driver arrives on site for the shipment, the driver must provide the pickup number or else be turned away. This ensures the company being used is legitimate and the driver that arrives on site is the authorized representative of that transportation company.

For companies that choose to not limit themselves to a predetermined list of carriers, they need to ensure that they are performing all necessary due diligence on companies before awarding bids. This goes beyond Department of Transportation checks to include company history records and referrals from other shippers. If a company was created a month ago and has no clients that will attest to their legitimacy, shippers are better off moving on to another transportation provider, even one that might be quoting a higher price.

In the end, it is incumbent upon the shipper or whomever is contracting transportation services to ensure that only reputable providers are used and that thorough screening of all companies and drivers are performed in advance of the load's departure time to ensure that safe, efficient, and, most importantly, secure transportation services are utilized.

Transportation Provider Selection

Companies are rethinking the way vendors are selected. While cost and efficiency remain critical features of a supplier's package, security is playing an increasingly significant role in the vendor selection process. Carriers are not chosen strictly on price and ability to make on-time deliveries, but security protocols, background checks on drivers, GPS tracking systems, and other security-oriented measures are being used to determine a carrier's suitability to transport a company's product.

Additionally, shippers contracting for the movement of high-value goods are moving away from a brokering model, where any company has the ability to bid for individual loads. Instead, they are using a pre-established carrier base large enough to fulfill the shipper's needs, while small enough for management and quality control. While the use of online sites bidding for loads (via electronic load boards at truck stops, for example) is a common practice in the logistics industry, it is harder to vet trucking companies and drivers; the facilitation the process provides further removes the shipper from the carrier and is not an acceptable trade-off, especially when goods of any real value are involved.

This system is essentially composed of websites in which shippers or their logistics intermediaries, with loads that need to be moved, are made available to transportation providers for competitive bid. Trucking companies can access these sites, see the details of the shipment, and then bid on the business. Shippers can then filter through the received bids and select a carrier for the shipment.

While this system is extremely effective in matching carriers with companies that have transportation needs, it leaves for a lot of ambiguity and uncertainty in the selection process, particularly with regard to quality of service, overall security, and the ability to comply with shipper in-transit policies. Compliance is certainly a difficulty, as these "one off" loads do not provide carriers with the motivation to develop a strong relationship with the shipper as they likely have limited promise of future business.

Background Investigations

Note: this section is intended to provide recommendations and guidance for the use of background investigations during the pre-employment process. While a vital step in vetting personnel who will ultimately be hired to handle, secure, and transport cargo, background investigations and decisions made based on information derived from them are highly regulated on a state-by-state basis. Recommendations in this section should be used within the scope of what is allowable by state law and your company's human resources policies. Please seek clarification on any points from your human resources department.

As part of the transportation provider selection process, background investigations of all drivers authorized to move your cargo should be required. While the information derived from these investigations should not be provided to the shipper, the overall scope, depth, and means by which they are performed should be so they can be audited by the shipper. The depth of an investigation—how far into a person's history it should go and what in a person's history might disqualify him from being an authorized driver—can vary; however, the basics of a background investigation should include the following:

- Go back a minimum of 7 years.
- Include records down to the county level.
- Have a predetermined list of offenses that would make a person unemployable.
- Be consistent with the "whole man" concept.

The importance of thorough background investigations cannot be overemphasized. While it is unclear how often insider information is used by criminals to successfully break into a warehouse or steal cargo while in transit, inserting gang members into the work force or obtaining information from employees is a well-known and well-documented MO that must be taken seriously during the hiring process.

Security Awareness Training

Creating a security culture in business can often be a difficult task. While many companies have security policies and procedures, these are often considered something for the security staff to worry about and often are never given a second thought by other employees. Because of this, the security manager is tasked with not only ensuring that security is considered when business decisions are made, but also getting employees to recognize security as an important part of their daily activities.

One means of accomplishing this is through security awareness training. Effective programs involve, at a minimum, annual training where employees meet with the security staff for refreshers on current policies and procedures and any new ones to be discussed and clarified.

While a shipper may require security awareness training for all drivers working for a motor carrier moving their goods, this does not preclude the shipper from conducting pretrip interviews and providing each driver with an abbreviated form of a security awareness training session prior to being released with the load. In fact, this practice is quite common as the driver's information is being collected and entered into online tracking systems.

Preloaded and Staged Trailers

As discussed in Part I of this book, the absolute most common element in cargo theft within the United States is a loaded trailer left unattended. With the countless variations of theft MOs, this single factor occurs in over 95% of all incidents.

A prime example is the practice of a shipper staging loaded trailers in its yard, a location that anyone can find, with product inside the facility that can be determined easily; if cargo thieves are seeking the shipper's cargo, preloaded and staged trailers are essentially gift wrapped for criminals to take with virtually no effort on their part.

At no time should loads, particularly high-value goods, ever be left unattended for any extended period of time at a facility or distribution center. This is especially true overnight. While distribution and transportation models vary, this cargo would ideally be live loaded with the driver and the tractor–trailer departing immediately upon completion, the security seal being affixed, driver interview conducted, and all documentation verified.

That said, some companies will still choose to preload and stage trailers. This often occurs due to a conflict of shipping/ loading schedules with delivery times or transportation provider schedules. If this process is absolutely necessary for the conduct of business, a number of security measures should be instituted to assist in deterring and preventing loads from being stolen while staged.

First, all staged trailers should be confined to a single secured area of the yard or lot. Ideally, the area should be fenced, at least 8 feet high with barbed wire or concertina wire at the top. The area should also be lighted during hours of poor visibility. Lighting should be substantial, ensuring that any potential intruders are deterred due to an increased potential for detection.

This area should be within direct eyesight of a security officer who is on duty 24/7 at the facility. If this is not possible, the area should have adequate closed circuit television (CCTV) coverage, ensuring that every side of the secured area is captured by the installed cameras. Without the presence of a security officer on site, it is strongly recommended that the CCTV system be monitored continuously by a control center, especially when high-value loads are involved. Some remote monitoring systems consist of motion-activated CCTV cameras, along with an alert message via a wireless software package.

On the trailers themselves, the use of king pin (fifth wheel) locks or other similar immobilization is strongly recommended in order to slow any attempt to steal them. Also, each door of the trailer (both left and right sides) should be secured with high-security locks or seals. Placing a high-security lock on the right side alone is not sufficient for ensuring the trailer is not easily accessible; thieves may simply open that door to identify the nature of the cargo. If the trailer has an inspection door, that too needs to be locked. Additionally, the use of sensor technologies, such as those that can detect motion on trailer doors, is prudent.

Finally, each staged and loaded trailer should have a tracking device embedded within the cargo and a geofence established around the perimeter of the secured yard. It is recommended that the load be monitored actively or that alerts in the event of a geofence break be sent to an offsite monitoring service in addition to the shipper's point of contact in order to expedite the escalation and recovery process in the event that a theft has occurred.

These recommendations are designed to mitigate the chance that a cargo criminal will attempt to steal a staged trailer and limit the time between any theft and detection to facilitate a quick and full recovery. By using the methodology described in this section, the time between the theft occurring and detection can literally be within seconds—a decisive advantage when attempting to recover stolen cargo and capture the perpetrators.

Routing

The most ignored component of supply chain security in the United States is routing based on risk of theft. Shippers almost always give free reign to carriers, and sometimes they, in turn, to their drivers to select the routes, often basing routes on what truck stops accept the gas card used by the carrier. This can be a recipe for disaster, especially if drivers stop in areas known for extremely high rates of cargo theft, leaving high-value (and highly sought after) product unattended, only to find their tractor–trailer gone.

A common claim regarding routing is that (a) drivers know how to do their job and (b) introducing security into the routing process will decrease the efficiency of the trip and increase costs. While it is true that drivers do know how to do their jobs, it must be remembered that drivers are trained to get from origin to destination; however, they are not always aware of the inherent risk of theft to certain commodities or how to keep goods safe from aggressive cargo thieves. It must also be remembered that drivers transport a wide variety of loads. Today it may be empty bottles, tomorrow computers. Without explicit instructions, drivers may handle each load the same.

The introduction of security into the routing process can be minimally invasive. The primary focus is in determining where drivers should and, more importantly, should not stop while in transit. Tools such as county level risk mapping can be used to designate certain areas known for extremely high rates of cargo theft as "off limits" or "no stop" zones. It is often unreasonable to avoid traveling through these areas, as they represent some of the major thoroughfares in the nation, but preventing loads from stopping and being left unattended there can significantly reduce the chances of becoming another victim.

Trip Duration

One of the most significant risks that in-transit high value loads face is when the load is dropped for any period of time. While long stops, such as for dinner or a shower, can present a significant risk, when the trailer is dropped in an open lot, parking lot, or other unsecured location, the potential for that load to be stolen increases even more. In most cases, the main reason a driver is able to drop his load is because the time allotted between pick-up and the scheduled delivery is much longer than the actual time it would take for the trip to be completed. If the destination only receives shipments by appointment, then the driver has no reason to arrive early and will drop the load until he can comfortably make the prearranged time slot. Couple this with other risk factors, such as the manufacturer's name or logo being stamped on the security seal or plastered on the sides of the trailer or the load being followed by cargo thieves, and the potential for theft rises sharply.

In order to mitigate this risk, shippers should take a more proactive role in the process, working with their customers and carriers to establish delivery appointments that make sense. Once a time is established, the shipper can work backward and account for the distance to be covered, weather conditions, potential traffic and construction, and other issues that transportation provider may be aware of. Based on this information, in conjunction with input from the carrier, the shipper should establish a window when the load can be picked up by the transportation provider that provides enough time to reach the destination, but not so much time that the driver will be able to drop the load and leave it unattended. A 3-day window to make a 10-hour drive is a simple way to lose high-value cargo and can be eliminated easily through proper planning.

Security Seals

For all the attention that seals receive in the shipping community, they essentially serve two basic purposes: it keeps honest people honest and it notifies the consignee if a truck/ocean container or other transport conveyance has been opened while en route. A seal is not a theft prevention tool as much as it is a theft indicator. If a person wants to see what is inside a trailer or container, a seal will not prevent him from opening the doors. Even high-security bolt and cable (designed to loop around the vertical locking bars and require two cuts to remove) seals are a simple bolt cutter away from being removed. And certainly a seal will not prevent a thief from driving off with the entire trailer. That said, seals are a security tool and should not be left out of any cargo protection plan. They provide shippers and consignees with a high degree of certainty in product integrity and are a vital layer of supply chain security; not to mention a requisite for Customs–Trade Partnership Against Terrorism certification.

Cargo within sealed trailers and ocean containers is vulnerable to tampering and many thieves know how to defeat seals without touching them. Methods such as opening the left side door by prying back the right side door, drilling out rivets in the door to open the hasp, and other techniques have all been used with great success by cargo thieves. This method is often used when thieves do not want to alert the victims that the product has been stolen, providing them with significantly more time before any law enforcement involvement.

New and advanced security seals, such as those available commercially from Sealock and other seal manufacturers and vendors, are not only more difficult to defeat but provide far more evidence of tampering. Shippers should use seals that meet the physical specifications per ISO PAS 17712. These seals provide security on both doors of a container, preventing the container from being opened without the seal being destroyed. While either can be removed and will offer little defense if someone steals an entire trailer or container, they certainly afford a higher level of protection than the traditional plastic or tin-plated strap seal. (For additional information on locks and seals for trailers and ocean containers, see In-Transit Security Hardware in this chapter.)

Stopping Procedures

One of the key components of any in-transit security plan is detailed driver procedures for stopping en route. Ideally, loaded trailers should never stop, but of course that is only feasible if traveling over short distances. In today's complex supply chain, long haul shipments involve multiple stops en route, dropped trailers, transshipments, and other logistical nuances that increase the need for thorough in-transit security requirements and a higher degree of supply chain/asset visibility.

Several requirements should be required of drivers when they are stopping with cargo while in transit. The first, and perhaps simplest, action to be taken is for drivers to lock the tractor when stopped and turn off the engine. This simple step could be the difference in a theft occurring by simply slowing down the theft gang just enough to be detected, especially if all other recommendations in this section are followed. Additionally, use of an air cuff or other comparable locking devices to help slow a theft attempt can be vital in preventing a theft from occurring.

If dual drivers are being used, one of the drivers must be required to stay with the vehicle at all times. While this requirement may seem obvious, there are numerous instances in which both drivers went inside, often to have a meal, only to return to find their tractor–trailer gone, along with its cargo. One of the common modi operandi of thieves targeting loads at truck stops is to prey upon married couples that are driving together, knowing they are very likely to take their meals together. This may be one reason not to hire husband and wife driver teams (the same rationale could be applied to father–son and brother–brother combinations).

For solo drivers, the time spent inside the truck stop or facility during the stop should be kept to a minimum. The least amount of time that the trailer is left unattended, the less opportunity thieves will have before criminals are able to steal the cargo. Additionally, the tractor–trailer should be parked so that the driver can see it as much as possible while inside the facility.

When available, the trailer should also be backed to a hardened surface in order to prevent access to the doors while stopped.

For shipments under an active monitoring or other tracking program, use of a geofence around the truck stop can be an excellent way of detecting a theft within seconds of occurring. With the ease of establishing geofences through improved technologies, these can be done quickly and ensure that loads (or, more accurately, the embedded tracking device) are detected leaving the facility before the driver has returned and communicated to his dispatch that he is resuming his trip.

Whether under a monitoring program or not, it is also recommended that drivers contact their dispatch prior to stopping and then contacting dispatch a second time prior to resuming the trip. While a good practice for any shipment, this is vital for using geofences successfully around loads while stopped.

Finally, before resuming the trip, drivers should conduct a thorough inspection of the tractor and trailer, looking for evidence of tampering, to include the integrity of the seal and lock and any other compartments or access panels to the vehicle and that all tires and other equipment appear to be in good working order.

Overnight Stops/Drop Trailer

For loads that must be dropped over a long period of time, particularly overnight, there are several optimal ways in which security can be applied to ensure that the cargo remains safe until picked up by an authorized driver. Of course, never leaving loads unattended is the ideal way to ensure their security and is the only method for complete assurance that loads will not be stolen by traditional nonviolent cargo theft gangs; however, this obviously is not always possible.

The first step for securing loads to be left unattended for long periods of time is selection of a secure lot or location to leave the loaded trailer. Many factors go into this process, including the area of the country the drop will occur in, the product being transported, the level of desired security (or risk tolerance), and budget. These facilities should be protected by fences, lighting and other perimeter security features, guarded by on-site staff 24/7 and/or monitored via electronic security measures (such as motion detection, CCTV, and alarms), and other business models available by companies offering such services.

Next is the application of appropriate locking devices to delay access to the doors and prevent tractors from hooking up to the trailer. While such devices cannot prevent a theft from occurring, they can certainly deter or delay a theft to the point that criminals will move to another load due to fear of being detected while attempting to bypass the security measures in place.

Finally, the use of covert cargo tracking devices can be the most effective means of ensuring that cargo is not lost in the event of a theft and that detection occurs immediately once a theft occurs. In the event that the secured lot and locking systems emplaced fail to keep a load from being stolen, by emplacing a geofence (or electronic boundary) around the stationary load, the user or a control center can be notified immediately when the load begins to move and crosses the electronic boundary, which allows for an immediate response protocol, which can enhance the chances for recovery exponentially.

Transportation Provider Compliance

Along with selection of a transportation provider, shippers need to work with their carriers to ensure that requirements for cargo handling and security will be followed by the vendors' drivers after shipments have departed. All aspects of a supply chain security program are often outside of the shipper's control (and for many, outside their visibility as well), leaving the product's security solely at the discretion of the driver. Shipper requirements, ideally written as a standards of care document, would ideally be included in contractual agreements with the transportation provider and include, at a minimum, the security requirements discussed in this chapter.

Compliance can be spot checked both on a scheduled and a random basis. Assessments or audits can be performed through a variety of methods, including interviews, on-site inspections, following actual loads, or checking GPS tracking systems in real time or through historical reports. Often shippers will use a combination of the aforementioned methods and other creative means to ensure that their cargo remains secure throughout the due course of transit, including incidental times at rest.

Supply Chain Security Company Selection

Even with the most qualified supply chain security staff, the time, effort, and expense demands of a robust supply chain security program make performing all of the duties in-house difficult at best. Because of this, most companies outsource some or its entire supply chain security program to a third party. When considering a supply chain security vendor, a company should evaluate the vendor's program with regards to operational impact, sophistication of technology, and, of course, price.

While the service offerings, at least in writing, may all seem the same, the manner in which the discrete functions are performed will make the difference. Look for experience in the transportation space along with references, most importantly previous and existing clients.

For more information on supply chain security companies, see the Resource section of this book.

Physical Escorts

A common method for over the road cargo security is the use of physical (human) escorts to follow loads and ensure they arrive at the destination safely and on time. The typical way in which this is performed in the United States is for an escort company to provide one or two employees who will follow a tractor–trailer via a rental or company car. They begin at the point of origin and stay with the load until received by the consignee.

Prior to departure, the escorts should discuss with the driver planned stops, actions while stopped (i.e., one escort stays with the load at all times), actions upon breakdown or other emergencies, and other administrative details that need to be worked out before transit begins. The escorts follow the load to the destination and remain on site until received by the consignee. This process can vary from shipment to shipment, ending when the security seal is broken, after the product is unloaded, or upon cargo count and condition verification. Whatever the method used, it should be understood by all parties what constitutes the end of a shipment and when the escorts will no longer be responsible for the security of the product.

It is also important that everyone understands the role the escort plays in the event that a theft, or theft attempt, occurs. As discussed previously in this book, the majority of cargo theft incidents in the United States are nonconfrontational and nonviolent, which translates into gangs not attempting to steal loads that are attended. That is not to say, however, that escorted loads are never targeted by theft gangs and that an aggressive gang will not make an attempt to steal the load. The role of the escort and expectations must be established in writing. Generally, escorts are there to ensure that the criminal is aware that the load is being watched and then observe any move on the load so they can report to their client and law enforcement.

Studies have shown that the use of physical escorts is the most effective way to decrease the risk of theft, with losses occurring in less than 1% of escorted shipments. This degree of security comes with a high price tag and an array of other drawbacks that can make this method of loss reduction less attractive. For example, cost is often a large issue. A person in a car following a load is not scalable. Because an escort cannot follow two loads heading in opposite directions, the expense cannot be spread across multiple projects or shipments. Another is the liability of the escort company. Putting millions of miles on the road every year increases opportunities for mechanical breakdowns, flat tires, accidents, and other events that can impact not only the escort's performance and ability to meet contractual obligations, but also the potential direct liability of the escort company if the driver is involved in an accident with another vehicle.

Even with the 99% success rate, other methods of in-transit security have shown to have nearly the same level of success with substantially reduced costs and without the wide array of disadvantages. The concept of active monitoring, discussed in Chapter 15, is an emerging risk mitigation technique and game changer, shown to be 97.5% effective and attainable at a fraction of the costs of physical escorts. It is also scalable, with monitoring centers capable of tracking hundreds of shipments at a time.

Electronic Escorts and Monitoring

GPS tracking, often referred to as an electronic escort, is another emerging method for tracking cargo shipments. There are two primary forms of tracking that provide entirely different levels of security and transparency and need to be differentiated.

The first is onboard GPS tracking that is provided by the transportation company. This refers to installed GPS tracking systems on the tractor–trailer. Attached most commonly to the cab of the truck, these external tracking devices are the most common in the transportation industry and provide trucking companies with a method for knowing a truck's location, relaying messages to the driver, and fleet management needs.

The second is covert or embedded GPS tracking devices. These devices are designed to be placed inside the cargo itself and provide the shipper (or whomever is managing the tracking system) with the ability to see where the cargo is at any given time, even if separated from the tractor–trailer. While many of these devices do not use actual global positioning systems technology but are a combination of GPS and cellular with the GPS secondary for them to work, they need an "eye to the sky" and that by design should not be feasible inside a trailer, they still are loosely referred to using the term.

When analyzing each of these types of tracking systems, their utility and drawbacks will show how each design serves different purposes. Onboard GPS systems are ubiquitous; it seems as if every truck is equipped with a device. These devices are marketed as providing shipment visibility, providing peace of mind to the cargo owner. The downside to these GPS devices is that cargo thieves, particularly the more professional gangs out of Florida, New York/New Jersey, and Los Angeles, know what to look for and will quickly disable onboard GPS systems installed through standard means. Consequently, such GPS tracking systems do not fare well once a truck has been stolen, providing little or no assistance in actually finding the cargo. Couple this with the modus operandi of swapping out a tractor and replacing it with one brought by the criminals, which further cripples recovery efforts.

For shippers just interested in tracking cargo and not concerned with monitoring the transportations provider's equipment, embedded tracking devices are a better fit. These small devices are relatively inexpensive, are compatible with a variety of technologies, and, most importantly, are covert so while someone can retain visibility of the cargo, thieves will not (or should not) know they are inside the load. A list of devices and technologies available in the market are included in the Resources section of this book.

While having a tracking device embedded in the cargo and the ability to see where the shipment is at any given time are great tools for supply chain visibility and control, they provide little theft mitigation (actually stopping thefts from occurring) and can be slow to provide recovery assistance in the event that a theft occurs. The next chapter discusses the concept of active monitoring and how it can be used to help prevent thefts from occurring and provides recovery of stolen loads in near real time.

In-Transit Security Hardware

Before discussing the variety of physical and electronic security hardware available, it must be understood that this is a rapidly evolving field, with new entrants and equipment, updated and improved infrastructure, and developing techniques to thwart theft. The information contained within this section should be considered more as a snapshot in time and merely a sampling of what is available, how it can be used, and how to maximize its use in order to develop the most comprehensive in-transit security program possible.

Tracking Systems/Devices

There are generally three different types of tracking systems available for shippers and those wishing to know where their cargo (or anything for that matter) is. For the sake of simplicity, these will be referred to as overt, covert, and embedded models.

Overt tracking refers to tracking systems mounted to the exterior of a truck, trailer, or ocean container (rarely done). The device can see the sky, and be seen by everybody, as it is affixed to the vehicle or trailer/container shell. These come in a tremendous variety of forms, including the well-known Qualcomm dome, Skybitz, and trackable locking devices for security trailer or container doors.

Qualcomm is one of the most recognized names in tracking systems in the supply chain. Since 1988, the Qualcomm Enterprise Services division has been providing integrated trucking and logistics wireless systems and services to trucking companies around the world. Backed by a global, 24/7, and world-class technology infrastructure, Qualcomm Enterprise Services provides service to more than 2500 clients today. Qualcomm's first wireless products and services included the OmniTRACS satellite locating and messaging service, used by long-haul trucking companies, developed from a product called Omninet. The OmniTRACS mobile information system was introduced in 1988 and proved to be an innovative force in enterprise mobility.

Covert and embedded tracking refers to use of a tracking device placed within the shipment, most often within the trailer or container, and, depending on the depth to which the device can be placed and still maintain a strong signal, determines if the device is covert (simply placed within the trailer/container, but not placed inside the cargo itself) or embedded (the device can be placed as deep within the cargo as desired, making it more difficult for thieves to find if the load is stolen).

The two most common technologies used in cargo security are CDMA and GSM/GPRS. Both are cellular-based technologies, with CDMA functional exclusively in the United States and Canada, while GSM/GPRS devices will generally work anywhere in the world there is a cellular signal, provided the correct SIM card is in place. Despite the global reach of GSM/GPRS technologies, there are advantages to using CDMA-driven devices for domestic loads or import/export with Canada, which are discussed further in this section.

There are strengths and weaknesses to overt tracking (satellite-based tracking) vs. cellular-based tracking (covert and embedded tracking). For overt (satellite) tracking, shipments can be tracked nearly anywhere in the world, to include crossing oceans. This ability to roam seamlessly can be very beneficial in knowing where cargo is at all times without having to worry about various cellular networks and the services they provide. Weaknesses to using such systems, however, include potentially weak signals that require line of sight (can be blocked as the shipment goes under structures, etc.), they can be quite costly, and possibly the largest weakness—they can be seen by anyone, particularly cargo criminals. Theft gangs well versed in overt tracking systems can recognize them and defeat them easily.

For strengths and weaknesses of cellular-based technologies, let's look at CDMA and GSM/GPRS separately. As discussed previously, CDMA technology-based tracking devices only work in the United States and Canada. Despite that limitation, CDMA tracking devices are the most popular for cargo tracking in the United States. CDMA tracking devices support cellular location-based services, which provide a strong signal strength, allowing devices to be placed deep within the cargo (embedded) and receive strong reliable position locations.

GSM/GPRS devices are deployable with near global roaming, providing shippers with a far wider spectrum for tracking capabilities. The weakness, however, in contrast to the CDMA, is that GSM/GPRS devices support few cellular location-based services, which does not allow these devices to be placed deep within the cargo, therefore making them covert but not exactly embedded.

Manufacturers of covert and embedded devices include companies such as the aforementioned Qualcomm, Enfora, and Sendum.

Locks

A very wide variety of locks are used in the supply chain industry, ranging from off-the-shelf padlocks to high-end GPS trackable locks such as the SLM discussed previously. What follow are some additional locking systems and hardware used commonly by shippers of high-value cargo to keep their goods secured while in transit.

Sealock: Sealock hybrid devices combine the tamper evidence functionality of security seals with the theft deterrence and delay of locks. Such devices are referred to as hybrid devices that perform multiple functions simultaneously. Sealock designs provide a robust tamper-evident physical deterrent, as well as tamper-evident sealing device. They are all designed to address the vulnerabilities and flaws inherent in the design and manufacturing of ocean containers and over the road trailers (Figure 14.1). For more information, see http://www.sealock.com.

ENFORCER adjustable lock: Made of 10-gauge, chrome-plated spring steel, it is placed around the vertical locking bars of trailers or ocean container doors, thereby securing both. A cast steel block protects the ABLOY padlock from physical attack. This lock secures both trailer doors rather than just

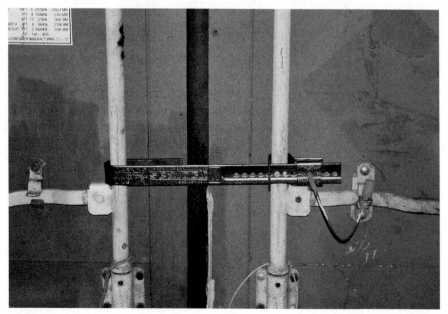

Figure 14.1 Sealock.

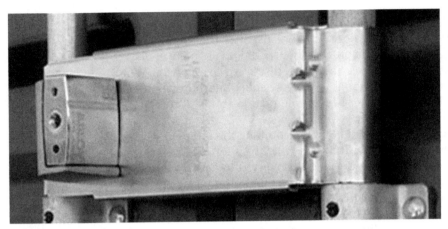

Figure 14.2 ENFORCER adjustable lock.

one. The ABLOY cylinder allows for a number of keying combinations and allows for maximum key control as keys can only be cut by the manufacturer, Transport Security, Inc. (Figure 14.2).

ENFORCER landing gear lock: Easily installed heavy-gauge high carbon steel lock box covers and locks the landing gear handle on the trailer. Once locked in position, the handle cannot raise or lower the landing gear of the trailer. The unit comes with a high-security ABLOY 341/25 padlock (chrome-plated, rotating disc, case-hardened steel, pick-proof design). Many trucking companies also utilize these as a preventative measure and lock in the up position when connecting to the tractor power unit; they prevent the driver from unhooking from the trailer and dropping a trailer (Figure 14.3).

King pin lock: The king pin lock prevents coupling with any fifth wheel. Perhaps the most commonly used security device on the market, this kind of lock has a unique conical cast aluminum alloy design. The internal capture slide uses an ABLOY high-security locking cylinder with internal tumblers like a safe. Only 1 of 360 million keyed combinations will open it. This king pin lock is utilized typically at distribution centers and terminals where other security features are in place as an added security layer (Figure 14.4).

Seal Guard Lock: Portable, easy-to-install steel cover for cargo seals on trailers and containers. The sleeve and pin slide through the lever hasp to protect the back and sides. Adding the cover and lock ensures that only the driver controls access to the seal for the entire cargo delivery run. Choose from

Figure 14.3 ENFORCER landing gear lock.

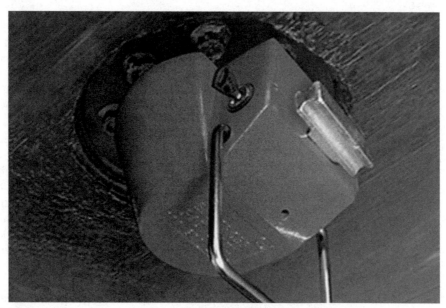

Figure 14.4 King pin lock.

Figure 14.5 Seal Guard lock.

a unique hex keyed bolt (5800) or traditional keyed cylinder (5850) locking system. Many trucking customers have been having issues with seal tampering and unauthorized removal, causing refusal of loads, etc. The Seal Guard lock secures the trailer door as well as prevents unauthorized access to the trailer seal (Figure 14.5).

ENFORCER air cuff lock: Constructed of thermoformed, high-impact resistant polycarbonate material, the air cuff completely covers and locks the dash-mounted air valve levers to prevent the truck and trailer brakes from being released. The unit is portable and easy to install with no drilling or permanent installation parts required. The lock takes only a few seconds to place and secure. The air cuff lock is cited as a successful deterrence device used throughout transit and is believed to have prevented a large number of truck thefts over the years (Figure 14.6).

Casings and accessories: Rugged, lightweight vinyl case holds the locks and seals necessary for complete over the road

Figure 14.6 ENFORCER air cuff lock.

tractor and trailer security. Drivers appreciate these tools for confidence and peace of mind when dealing with the responsibilities of cargo delivery. Owner operators treat these as tools of the trade, and companies implementing a security kit program have reduced the number of truck and trailer thefts within their operations.

Information on locking systems and images was provided by Transport Security. For additional information, see the Resource section of this book or www.transportsecurity.com.

Security Hardware Uses and Limitations

While security hardware is a critical component for ensuring that cargo remains secure while in transit, it is critical that users understand their uses, effectiveness, and also limitations.

Understanding what security systems a company wants to use and the uses for each piece of hardware is critical for a well-thought-out and overlapping supply chain security program. Just as important, however, is understanding each security feature's limitations and realizing what they are and are not designed to do.

Too often people rely on equipment to perform functions they simply were not designed to do or were incapable of doing.

A classic example is the use of security seals for over the road shipments. Simply put, seals were designed to provide shippers and transportation providers with the ability to identify if a trailer or container had been opened. All too often though, seals are thought to provide shipments with a theft prevention measure, while in reality they provide nothing of the sort. With a large majority of cargo theft in the United States categorized as full truckload or full container thefts, seals affixed to a stolen trailer or container would literally serve no purpose.

The same is true for locks; however, locks do provide at least a slightly higher level of theft deterrence and delay at least to the casual criminal. The presence of a high-security lock in the case of casual criminals may provide just enough of a reason for them to move on to the next trailer—one without security devices applied—preventing the targeted load from being victimized. The professional cargo theft gang, however, will not be fazed by the use of a lock—even a high-security one. In most cases, they do not even open the trailer doors until the entire load is well down the road where they can operate without fear of being detected.

This is not to say that seals and locks should not be used. Quite the opposite, these best practices are absolutely vital to a robust supply chain security program in ensuring that cargo arrives at its destination intact and unmolested. The point, however, is to ensure that utilization of the devices is done so with full knowledge of their limitations so that adequate policies, procedures, and other systems can be layered to prevent thefts from occurring, detect thefts that do occur, and/or recover stolen cargo quickly if a theft transpires.

Key Points

- In-transit security plans are often overlooked in logistics operations.
- Transportation provider selection and their compliance with security policies are paramount to successfully keeping cargo secure.
- For theft prevention, a layered approach (people, policies, and technology) must be used to prevent a single point of failure from leaving high-value cargo susceptible to theft.
- Covert tracking technologies are becoming incredibly commonplace in high-value cargo shipments and are considered

by many to be the most cost-effective means of providing security.

- A variety of security hardware is available that should not be relied on solely but rather as part of an overall in-transit security plan.

ACTIVE MONITORING

INFORMATION IN THIS CHAPTER:

- How an active monitoring program works and why it may be right for a company's supply chain
- How to get the most from an active monitoring program
- Methods for customizing programs to meet a company's supply chain needs
- Impact of an active monitoring program on overall supply chain security

"Out of intense complexities intense simplicities emerge."
Winston Churchill

A few minutes before 10 a.m. on Thursday, September 29, 2011, a pharmaceutical delivery driver emerged from a pharmacy in Detroit, Michigan, after making a delivery to find two men who had broken into his van and were rummaging through the variety of pharmaceuticals contained within. When the driver confronted the men, they ran off, climbing into a white panel van and driving away, taking with them several totes filled with pharmaceuticals.

Fortunately for the driver and his company, and less fortunately for the thieves, one of the totes stolen had an embedded tracking device, and the FreightWatch command and control center was alerted to the theft.

The control center contacted the Detroit Police Department and, at 10:30 a.m., the police arrived at a residence where the tracking device was sending locates from. At the residence, police found the van and one of the suspects inside the van, who was subsequently arrested.

Upon entering the residence, the police found the totes, the pharmaceuticals, and the tracking device—all of which were returned to the pharmaceutical delivery company. The second suspected was found hiding inside the residence, who was also arrested. All of this occurred in less than 45 minutes.

Supply chain security complexities can sometimes seem overwhelming to those tasked with securing goods in transit, ensuring vendor compliance, and attempting to gain transparency throughout the process. To accomplish all these while keeping costs and manpower requirements within a reasonable budget is no easy chore. Often, the result is to focus on areas where and when cargo is most at risk and the mitigation technique used will result in the greatest reduction of loss.

One solution is the concept of active monitoring. While used primarily for high-value loads that are in transit via over the road transportation, this concept is simple and effective enough to be used throughout the supply chain.

Active monitoring is the use of covert electronic tracking devices placed within the cargo and monitored remotely by an internal, or contracted, control center. This process provides a method of checking the location of loads at predetermined intervals (e.g., every 15 minutes, 30 minutes, hour) and also monitors the compliance of in-transit security requirements, such as stopping only in authorized areas, on-time delivery, and loads remaining on the preapproved route.

Implementation of an active monitoring program can be met with negativity or pushback, particularly if being emplaced with the existing fleet of transportation providers. The use of turn-by-turn directions, additional requirements around stopping, reporting and other administrative tasks, and receiving resistance from transportation companies and their drivers, at least in the beginning, are quite common; however, over time the result is actually an extremely beneficial and mutually supportive relationship between carriers and the monitoring center. During the research conducted for this book, multiple examples were found of drivers calling the control center out of habit, even for loads that were not being actively monitored, as well as drivers calling in suspicious activity and stating they feel more secure on the road when being actively monitored while hauling loads of extreme value and desirability by cargo thieves.

The absolutely most critical feature that active monitoring provides is the positive impact on driver behavior while transporting high-value cargo. The last line of security for an in-transit security plan is the driver and compliance with established protocols while on the road. While examining in excess of 190,000 actively monitored loads, in almost every example, as programs were implemented, the rate of protocol infractions by drivers was high while the volume of shipments tracked remained low. However, after a few weeks or a month, the infraction rate decreased dramatically, leading to transportation providers receiving an increased number of contracted loads of high-value goods because of their compliance.

Origin and Destination

The first step in establishing an active monitoring program is determining the routes to be transited, starting with the origin and destination. As origins and destinations are entered into the online tracking system, geofences are placed around each location to prevent unauthorized departures from points of origin and notification, beyond the required phone call from drivers, when loads arrive at the destination.

Shipments being tracked by an active monitoring program are identified as such by the shipper, and an array of administrative data must be entered into the online tracking software, which is discussed in additional detail later in this chapter. Once data are entered and the load is ready for departure, the driver must contact the control center with notification of his departure, which begins the active monitoring activity.

This notification is absolutely critical for a variety of reasons. First, without notification, the control probably thinks that the load has been stolen (due to the geofence around the facility being broken when the load departs), resulting in activation of the theft recovery protocol. Second, loads have to be monitored on a preset schedule (i.e., every 15 minutes, 30 minutes, or other preestablished timeline), and without notification that a shipment has begun, the active monitoring program cannot commence.

Notification of a load's arrival at the destination is likewise important and for more than simply knowing when to discontinue the monitoring process. One of the critical risks for cargo occurs when a driver arrives at the destination and is unable to deliver the load and decides to depart the facility and wait for a delivery time. This often coincides with stops for breakfast or dinner, as drivers relax from a long journey, frequently leaving loads unattended, not realizing the opportunity this lapse gives criminals.

Routing

Along with the origin and destination of each lane, the carrier must provide the active monitoring company with turn-by-turn directions for each lane, sometimes including three or four variations for the same lane, accounting for the types of trucks used, road restrictions, weather, and other contingencies. Directions are the basis for the georoutes to be placed in the tracking software. A break in a georoute begins a protocol for infractions, generally starting with a call to the driver or his dispatch and escalating as needed.

Additional items to consider when creating turn-by-turn directions is trip duration, number of stops likely during the shipment, and high-risk zones transited. During this process, getting assistance from a company or persons knowledgeable about high-risk zones can significantly alleviate the risk of theft by ensuring that these areas are designated as "no stop" zones and/or bypassed altogether; use of a different route can alleviate a significant threat. The monitoring company can then ensure compliance with the created protocol, for example, ensuring loads do not stop where they are prohibited.

Administrative Processes

The entry of administrative data into the tracking system is paramount but often one of the first points of failure. Transportation provider details, driver name and contact information, driver's license information, and tractor–trailer license plates number and other markings, as well as trailer license plate and trailer number/markings, are all critical pieces of information necessary to ensure that monitoring is performed correctly and that, in the case of a theft, recovery is made efficiently.

In addition to the information obtained and loaded into the tracking system prior to loads being released, a few administrative tasks must be completed as well. The most common of these includes the use of a driver interview, typically in writing with a checklist that covers the "rules of the road" for the driver. Additionally, drivers are provided with an active monitoring card that highlights key points to remember during the route, including the control center's phone number and other critical information pertaining to the shipper and route.

It is the process that surrounds the gathering, entering, and relaying of this information to all parties involved that ensures every scenarios can be covered in an efficient manner and truly begins to enact behavioral change.

Geofences and Georoutes

The use of electronic barriers, essentially establishing routes for shipments to move within and provide immediate notification of a deviation or breach, is critical to the success of a monitoring program. Geofences are established around facilities, drop lots, truck stops, or any other place that a monitored truck is at rest and requires a phone notification before movement can begin without triggering a recovery protocol. Depending on the tracking software used, geofences can be placed on the exact barriers of a facility or yard, providing an extremely precise and timely notification that a load is in motion (regardless of whether it's authorized or unauthorized).

Georoutes are similar to a geofence, but are placed along the route a load is to transit, generally with a 1-mile space on each side of the route, allowing the driver some flexibility off his route for stopping, traffic, etc.

Beyond Location Tracking

The concept and execution of an active monitoring program are relatively simple, effectively composed of collecting all necessary data for the shipment, pre-establishing geofences and georoutes, and having a protocol in place for infractions and a theft in progress. By having an active monitoring program, however, the shipper is able to obtain a variety of additional benefits beyond the simple tracking of loads from origin to destination.

Shippers are able to emplace and monitor the compliance of transportation providers for detailed in-transit security requirements, such as authorized and unauthorized stopping zones, duration of stops, and actions to be taken at the destination if immediate unloading is not possible.

Through the use of an active monitoring program, the shipper or product owner has the ability to know his product is not only being tracked 24/7 as it moves across the country, but also can log-in and see any load's location at any time from his computer. Additionally, through the use of marrying technologies, such as an array of sensor technologies in addition to the covert tracking device, shippers can know the temperature of loads at any time while in transit, whether an unacceptable level of shock or drop has occurred, or even if the level of lighting is increased substantially (i.e., if someone opened the trailer doors).

Immediate Notification of Route Deviation or Theft

As with virtually any other crime that involves the unlawful acquisition of property, the faster the theft is reported to police, the higher the likelihood of successful recovery. Even with a tracking device being embedded in the cargo, if given enough time, criminals will eventually discover the device and discard it. With an active monitoring program, realization that a theft has occurred can often happen even before the driver knows his load has been stolen, and the recovery process can begin immediately.

For this to occur, the shipper's protocols must be established in writing and known to all players in load movement and monitoring. This will be the basis for the monitoring center to know when the shipment is on track, or if its movement is outside of what would be considered normal, and entice a response by the control center and the recovery process to be activated.

The most common ways a control center can be made aware that a load has potentially been stolen include
- Loads moving off course
- Loads reversing direction
- Loads departing from a stop too early

In the case of a load reversing direction or having been stolen while the driver has stopped but the thieves keeping the load on the same highway that the georoute is set for, there will be no electronic notification of the load being off course. Because of this, the active monitoring feature of the program (i.e., a control center representative checking the load's status every 15 to 30 minutes and being aware of estimated stopping times and other intricacies of the movement) is vital to recognizing a theft in progress, even without phone notification from the driver.

Recovery Process

The recovery process must be documented in writing and practiced frequently by the monitoring company along with the shipper and transportation provider. Because several things have to happen to recover a stolen shipment successfully, each party must understand what is required of them. Key factors for ensuring the quick recovery of a load include
- Quick reporting of the theft by the truck driver
- Contacting the law enforcement agency having jurisdiction where the load is located (identified by the embedded cargo tracking device)
- Ensuring that all descriptive information is readily available for law enforcement (license plate numbers, truck and trailer numbers/markings, load contents and descriptions, etc.)
- Contacting the cargo theft task force (if one exists in the area that the load is located) to assist in coordination with multiple law enforcement agencies as required

If these steps are known, understood, and executed promptly by the parties involved, the likelihood of a prompt and full recovery increases substantially. While the process seems simple, it may only be needed once over the course of a year; therefore, making a process that is unnatural and unfamiliar to the parties can only seem natural and familiar with practice.

Impact on Driver Behavior

The greatest benefit of an active monitoring program is the positive impact on driver behavior with regards to ensuring that shippers' in-transit policies are complied with and the cargo remains secure.

Data from transportation providers that begin active monitoring programs show a dramatic decrease in the number of route deviations and policy violations in a very short period of time. As routes, policies, and security requirements become more routine for drivers, companies also see increased efficiency on the road, better delivery times, and a clearer sense of what is happening with high-value cargo while in transit.

While such a program is often seen as intrusive or a burden to drivers while they are on the road, the long-term results are quite the opposite, with drivers often making statements such as feeling more secure while on the road with high-value cargo. With a cooperative program that provides assistance to drivers and ensures that loads remain secured from origin to destination, an active monitoring program is by far the most cost-effective means of reaching the highest level of security for in-transit goods.

Key Points

- Active monitoring is a key method for shippers to keep track of their cargo and be able to react in real time to supply chain disruptions and recover cargo in the event of a theft.
- In order to achieve proper coverage through an active monitoring program, several points have to be recorded and kept on file in order to identify the associated load with the tracking device providing locates.
- Electronic borders around lanes and specific locations can provide instance notification that a load is off course or moving when supposed to be stationary.
- Active monitoring can provide information on a variety of metrics beyond simple location that can improve supply chain efficiency, vendor compliance, temperature maintenance and control, and more.
- The primary benefit of active monitoring is the impact on driver behavior, which can ensure compliance and provide immediate response in the event of a theft.

16

AIR CARGO SECURITY

INFORMATION IN THIS CHAPTER:

- How shipping cargo affects overall security for in-transit cargo
- Nuances to air cargo that increase risk and decrease visibility
- Impact of government attention to air cargo on loss prevention and overall supply chain security
- Methods for ensuring proper supply chain security compliance in air cargo

The nation's economy relies on fast and on-time cargo delivery. Air plays a critical component, facilitating deliveries of high demand (and often high value) cargo across the country in timelines measured in hours as opposed to days or weeks. In 2008, U.S. air carriers carried about 4.4 million tons of international air cargo, accounting for 18% of the 25 million tons transported globally in international service. U.S. air carriers' international cargo traffic generated 33 billion revenue ton-kilometers, accounting for 25% of about 131 billion revenue ton-kilometers of global international air cargo traffic. Since 2005, the U.S. share of world air cargo tonnage and ton-kilometers has declined as the annual growth rates of Asia's air cargo markets increased (Figure 16.1).

The critical nature of a fast and efficient supply chain is only enhanced through just-in-time manufacturing, lean processes that call for little or no excess product in storage, and shipment departure times that leave little room for delay to make on-time deliveries.

When comparing air shipments versus other modes of transportation, air clearly provides the smallest amount of cargo transported when analyzed by weight. In 2008, the air cargo industry moved 11.8 million metric tons of cargo according to the North American Transportation Statistics database, compared to 1754 million metric tons via rail. When analyzing cargo moved via air in terms of value, however, the critical nature of the air component becomes clear. While moving just 0.08% of total freight tonnage in the United States, the air cargo sector moves

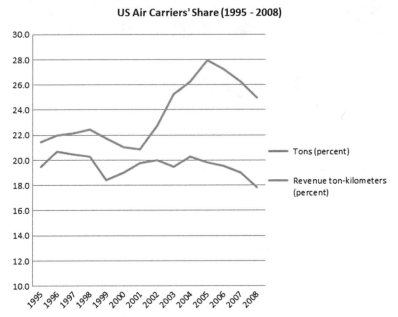

US Air Carriers' Share (1995 - 2008)

Tons (percent)

Revenue ton-kilometers (percent)

Figure 16.1 Source: Bureau of Transportation statistics.

28% of total cargo by value, according to the U.S. Department of Transportation.

Since 1980, the growth in freight mileage for air cargo, measured in terms of ton-miles transported on an annual basis, has far outpaced growth in any other transportation mode. While domestic growth in the volume of air cargo shipments has been relatively, and somewhat unexpectedly, flat over the past few years, it is estimated that domestic air cargo shipments, expressed in terms of revenue ton miles, will continue their historic growth trends and increase another 58% by FY2020 compared to FY2006 levels, according to the Congressional Research Service.

When analyzing air cargo shipments, virtually all loads are labeled as either import or export, with domestic flights occurring in between—either from the import hub to a domestic location or from a domestic location to an export hub. This system requires a complex array of cargo-handling companies, freight forwarders, airlines, government oversight, and customers themselves, ensuring that cargo is packaged, labeled, configured, loaded, and shipped without incident or error—a daunting challenge when considering the billions of pieces of freight moved every year this way.

When analyzing various roles, two key figures in this process are the freight forwarders and customers. Both of these take on direct responsibility for cargo collection and preparation prior to being its delivery to the airport for shipment. The freight forwarders and/or customer will collect the cargo and build them on pallets—referred to as ULDs—or send the cargo loose to the airline. The airline accepts, verifies, and builds the ULD if necessary or loads the previously built ULD onto the aircraft.

Very few airlines actually have their own cargo-handling units, but rather subcontract the work to companies such as Menzies Aviation and Swissport International. This operation transfers the responsibility of the cargo from the customer or freight forwarder to the airline and is a key point in which potential losses can occur.

Additional risks exist within this system that might not be readily apparent to shippers using air cargo for their method of shipping. For domestic shipments, portions of the shipments may actually be shipped via ground even though it was tagged for air. For example, a cargo load from Shanghai through LAX destined for Las Vegas, after being off-loaded at LAX and cleared by Customs, may be loaded onto a truck within the airline's business (owned or contracted by the airline) and shipped to Las Vegas via ground. Not hidden by the airlines (if a customer asks what mode was used for the last leg of the shipment, the airline will provide the information—but no one ever asks), and the cargo arrives at the destination on time; it was moved, however, by a much riskier mode of transportation, especially when dealing with high-value products, which is the typical cargo label for those shipped via air.

Cargo Theft and the Air Industry

Cargo theft and the air industry constitutes probably the most complex area of loss prevention and the supply chain with simply being able to identify losses that are associated with air cargo versus standard ground, over the road, or facility thefts. For obvious reasons, losses virtually never occur once cargo is being loaded onto the aircraft, is in flight, or is being off-loaded. When losses generally do occur it is while in cargo-handling facilities, storage at the airport, or in transit to or from the airport or the aforementioned facilities.

Because of this, the majority of theft associated with the air cargo industry is pilferage. Small-scale theft occurring on a frequent basis, leaving shipments "short" as opposed to being stolen in their entirety, is a constant problem that companies must deal with when shipping via air, but does not result in crippling losses that can occur when fully loaded trailers or containers are stolen. The cargo is really at risk once the loads are placed into trucks and leave via ground according to Bob Ghan, security director for the Western States and Southern U.S. Border with DHL. Many thefts of cargo designated for shipment via air, which end up stolen, were done so when outside the purview of the air cargo industry (i.e., after it was loaded and shipped via ground) and are associated with ground in-transit thefts.

When analyzing cargo theft trends in the air cargo industry and looking for hot spots of theft activity, theft rates remain relatively consistent from airport to airport. Of course the total volume of losses is higher at an airport with more robust cargo programs simply due to the volume of theft, with losses occurring almost exclusively as pilferage, it is often difficult to determine where in the supply chain the cargo was stolen or if the shortage was due to mishandling or cargo being lost while en route.

Of course losses occur in other ways and not simply through theft. Misplaced and mis-shipped cargo is a common occurrence and a regular headache for freight forwarders. As companies rely heavily on electronic inventory systems, cargo can arrive at a facility, be off-loaded, not be scanned, and therefore be missing—all while sitting inside the very warehouse that it is supposed to be in. When asked about the cargo's location, a manager will check the automated system, see the cargo was never scanned in, and therefore believe it never arrived and report the cargo as not present.

Of course, even with the high levels of security around airports and associated buildings with the air cargo industry, these facilities are not immune from being victimized by criminals. In early 2007, a recently terminated driver for a logistics provider managed to steal a company truck. Using his uniform and familiarity with the air cargo terminal at Miami International Airport, he was able to pick up a regularly scheduled load of cell phones, making off with over $1,000,000 in product.

The suspect did not have a company badge or documentation authorizing him to pick up the shipment, but because of complacency and familiarity, those involved in the shipping process failed to realize he was not the authorized transporter and willingly gave him the cargo—very similar to the fictitious pickup schemes discussed in Chapter 2: Cargo Theft Defined.

Government Regulation and Air Cargo

Security for the U.S. airline industry is almost entirely regulated by the Transportation Security Administration (TSA). After September 11, 2001, security and screening at airports were almost exclusively for people boarding aircraft. Since then, however, cargo screening has become an increasingly hot topic, with government mandates requiring 100% screening of all cargo. In October 2011, the TSA announced that it would miss the December 31, 2011, deadline for 100% of all international cargo to be screened, stating that the expected date for implementation would be some time in 2013.

The TSA's security regimen for air cargo is divided into two distinctive program areas: (1) the Transportation Sector Network Management air cargo division charged with the strategic development of programs and (2) the Office of Security Operations charged with program compliance. The air cargo division is responsible for working across TSA, Department of Homeland Security, and other governmental agencies, domestic and international, to develop air cargo regulations, technological solutions, and policies that continuously enhance the security of the air cargo supply chain while maintaining TSA's commitment to ensure the flow of commerce.

According to the TSA website, in response to possible threats to air cargo security, the TSA uses a multilayered approach that includes

- Vetting companies that ship and transport cargo on passenger planes to ensure they meet TSA security standards.
- Establishing a system to enable certified cargo screening facilities to physically screen cargo using approved screening methods and technologies.
- Employing random and risk-based assessments to identify high-risk cargo that requires increased scrutiny.
- Inspecting industry compliance with security regulations through the deployment of TSA inspectors.

As discussed in Chapter 1: Cargo Theft 101, government security programs around the transportation sector are not designed for purposes of loss prevention, but rather to prevent terrorism or any other ways by which the supply chain can be used for illicit purposes. However, because so many security features overlap with loss prevention programs, in the case of air cargo, the increased security around airports and cargo terminals provides significant levels of security that assist in mitigating the risk of theft for cargo while inside the purview of an airport or carrier's facility.

Security Considerations and the Air Industry

The risk of theft and pilferage of air cargo ramps up once goods leave the airport via ground. This requires shippers and their logistics providers to ensure that their planning and security preparations are done with more than the air cargo portion of the shipment in mind. How cargo will be collected, moved to the airport, handled, loaded, off-loaded, cleared through Customs, if applicable, moved to storage, and eventually taken to the end destination must all be planned for appropriately. This high level of understanding and detail must be translated in a comprehensive security plan that allows for the various levels of security necessary at each stage of the shipment.

The next critical factor in keeping air cargo secure is thorough vendor vetting, with the high number of touch points in this mode of transportation with a wide spectrum of companies ranging from internationally recognized names to local "mom and pop" firms. Prior to use, they must be thoroughly vetted.

First and foremost, the company must be a legitimate business, having met necessary licensing, insurance, and other regulatory requirements. Second, the company has a good reputation within the industry and is known for providing professional services with a good loss history. Third, personnel within the company should be screened with background investigations and trained thoroughly in cargo handling and theft prevention best practices. Finally, the company is compliant with all shipper physical and in-transit security requirements as applicable.

In order to be successful in this process, a company must focus on reducing the number of suppliers between itself and who is actually handling the cargo. Every time a logistics function is brokered to another provider, another layer is applied between the shipper and the cargo, significantly reducing the shipper's supply chain visibility, reducing the clarity of security requirements for storage and in-transit cargo, and substantially increasing the likelihood of loss or theft.

Key Points

- While cargo shipped via air is quite safe during the air transport process, the ambiguity and multiple touch points around the process of getting cargo to and from air terminals create a significant risk for shippers.
- Cargo being shipped by air will still be moved by ground. Not only will cargo be moved to and from the airport via truck, but even the air carrier itself may move the cargo along one leg of the route via ground if necessary and more cost-effective.

- While new restrictions and security parameters around air cargo have paid dividends in the overall security of cargo at airports, thefts continue in this mode of transportation, primarily targeting cargo being moved to and from air cargo-handling facilities—via ground.
- With every additional layer of service providers between the shipper and the cargo, an additional risk of loss or theft is created.

17

RAIL AND PIPELINE SECURITY

INFORMATION IN THIS CHAPTER:

- Targeting by criminals of the railroad and what they steal
- Components of the railroad system that leave cargo vulnerable to theft
- Methods for keeping cargo secure while being shipped via rail and intermodal transportation
- Security issues beyond loss prevention with pipelines in the United States

The nation's railroad system hauls as much as 45% of our country's freight measured in ton miles. Competing with other modes of transportation—maritime, air, and road—the railroad continues to remain a critical piece of the supply chain, ideal for moving bulk products and commodities such as coal, ore, and chemicals.

In 2002, the rail system in the United States moved 1.5 trillion ton miles, generating $36.9 billion in revenue.

Bulk items, especially chemicals, and the cross-country (land bridge) as well as international movement of intermodal containers quickly led to discussions of national security and terrorism. In 2002, a member of Al Qaeda was found inside a shipping container in Gioia Tauro, Italy. The Egyptian man was found inside a container equipped for a comfortable ride to his intended destination of Halifax, Canada.

The discovery served as an alarm for the international shipping nature of intermodal containers, many of which are moved via rail and ground across borders. The scope of this book, however, is loss prevention and the supply chain security measures necessary to reduce in-transit losses. As discussed in Chapter 1, a program designed to prevent terrorism or smuggling does not necessarily equate to an adequate loss prevention program and vice versa. While there is a significant amount of overlap, the goals of each program are truly different from each other and should not be used as a means of accomplishing another's goals.

Cargo Theft and the Rail System

Cargo theft and the railroad has its roots firmly planted in the 19th century, as legendary characters such as Butch Cassidy and the Sundance Kid robbed trains while fighting off Pinkerton men in gun battles made for the movies. Today, passenger trains targeted by robbers from the Wild West have been replaced with cargo trains targeted by both organized gangs and opportunistic thieves hoping to make a quick buck.

Strings of rail cars, often loaded with intermodal containers and trailers of electronics, cars, cigarettes, tires, and a myriad of other high-value products, serve as a tempting "moving" target for criminals. Organized gangs often utilize inside information to assist in locating cargo worth stealing, while leaving low-value or unmovable product alone.

Organized theft groups are generally associated with larger incidents, where the criminals clearly knew what they were targeting, leaving trailers or containers alone while successfully stealing six-figure loads. Their frequency of activity, however, is generally far less than that of opportunistic criminals, who jump on slow-moving trains in hit-and-run-style theft attempts, seeking to off-load anything that they can sell. Theft today—largely pilferage from stopped or slowed trains and full container thefts from rail facilities and yards servicing the rail industry—presents a substantial problem for the rail system through economic loss as well as security vulnerabilities.

From 1992 through 2003, the Conrail Boyz (CBR) wreaked havoc on the railroads in New Jersey. They, the CBR, are considered by many to be the more prolific train robbers of all time, responsible for stealing millions of dollars in lucrative goods, especially electronics and high-end clothing from freight cars (Thomas, 2010).

The leader of the gang, 28-year-old Edward Mongon, began stealing small cartons of cargo from stationary freight trains at rail yards in the late 1980s. By living in an apartment adjacent to the rail yards in Newark, Mongon learned the schedule of train arrivals and departures, as well as the times inspections were made by security guards and local police. Additionally, Mongon acquired a radio that received transmissions from the trains and dispatchers. Through this, Mongon was able to get invaluable information, including departure times, train routes, locations, and destinations (Sweet, 2006).

As he developed systematic means for selling cargo on the black market, Mongon began to recruit additional members and soon had a gang of thieves that became experts in robbing trains.

In the beginning they only stole cargo from strings of trains at rest; however, as the gang evolved, they started to target moving trains.

The Conrail Boyz became efficient in deceiving security measures utilized by the railroad companies. For secured rail yards, the gang would break the electricity in the fences to allow for undetected access. For moving trains, the gang would find desolate areas along the routes, remote intercept points, and areas of sparse population as opportunities to attack and jump onto the rail cars (Zambito, 2009).

Equipment used by the gang included items such as bolt cutters to open the containers on moving trains and infrared binoculars to keep watch for police at night. Gang members on the trains would break into the containers, remove the cargo, and toss the goods to members waiting on the ground, who would then load the cargo into prepositioned trucks and transport the merchandise to their storage facilities (Thomas, 2010).

Experts estimate that the Conrail Boyz stole in excess of $20 million in cargo from trains over an 11-year period. The gang pulled off countless rail heists, two of which generated some significant media attention. One was a theft of Sony PlayStations valued in excess of $5 million, and the other was a load of Tommy Hilfiger clothing worth more than $200,000. The Hilfiger theft was estimated to have taken the gang less than 8 minutes to perform.

An intense police investigation began in December 2001 of the Conrail Boyz and their theft activity. New Jersey police used helicopters and strict surveillance on areas where the Conrail Boyz were believed to be off-loading stolen cargo. During the investigation, one of the gang members was arrested, and during his interrogation he revealed important information about the gang, including modi operandi and additional areas of operation. Police also found out that Mongon had never held a legitimate job and that all his revenue came strictly from his cargo theft activity (Hyslop, 2003).

In 2003, 24 members of the Conrail Boyz gang were arrested and received sentences ranging from 10 to 12 years in prison. The leader, Edward Mongon, was charged with racketeering and money laundering and received a 13-year sentence in prison (Zambito, 2009).

Organized theft gangs such as the Conrail Boyz continue to target the rail system, requiring intense efforts by railroad police and logistics professionals to secure in-transit cargo in this mode of transportation. The task of monitoring trains, however, is no simple matter. It is difficult for train engineers to see the entire train due to their enormous length, often snaking more than

150 cars long, and the seemingly endless miles of track are filled with areas of sparse population difficult to monitor. Additionally, organized criminals with inside information can move quickly, targeting rail cars, containers, and trailers with the desired product, wasting no time searching through containers of unwanted products, off-loading their goods, and escaping—often without detection until the train arrives at its destination.

Cargo criminals are becoming increasingly innovative and creative in their craft. Understanding train schedules and routes, they can have trucks waiting for the criminals to hit during a stop and off-load the cargo right into a vehicle for a quick escape.

As with over the road cargo theft, the rate of theft in the rail system is statistically very low; however, the impact is clear, with an estimated direct product loss of $12 to $20 million annually. This direct product loss does not take into account the entire array of downstream costs associated with cargo theft discussed in Chapter 10: The True Impact of Cargo Theft.

Product Targeting

Bulk products and commodities are the not the only items being shipped via rail in today's supply chain. Electronics, automobiles and auto parts, tobacco products, clothing, and numerous other goods are moved daily through the railroad system. Organized criminal groups go to great lengths to acquire information necessary to successfully hit the car or containers loaded with their targeted products and not waste time searching through containers with things they cannot move or sell. The ability to hit the right containers, at a time when the train is stopped or slowed to allow for easy off-load at a known location where the gang can have transportation assets and personnel assembled and ready for the product, is a combination that is extremely difficult for the railroads and shippers to combat.

The rate of theft within the rail infrastructure is on par with national levels of cargo theft, as electronics, building materials, and household goods are all stolen most frequently from the rail system.

Hot Spots

In 1995, dozens of armed gunmen attacked a train outside of El Paso—just steps away from the Mexican border. Accomplices, who had boarded the train at an unknown time and location, tripped the train's emergency braking system by popping the air hose. Then, the gunmen came out of their hiding in the nearby steep ravines and surrounded the train.

While the train was stopped, the on-board suspects began dumping product—televisions and clothing—from the cargo containers onto the Mexican side of the train. When U.S. Border patrol agents arrived at the distressed train, the thieves held the agents off with gunfire. Mexican police notified by phone arrived at the chaotic scene as well. Eventually a dozen suspects were arrested, although numerous others escaped, along with 32 televisions.

Since then, numerous security improvements have been put in place to deter Mexican theft gangs from crossing the border and attacking the rail system outside of El Paso, but theft in this mode of transportation is far from gone. In 2002, the rail system around El Paso experienced 122 robberies in a 9-month period, showing that the issue of cargo theft and the rail system is not an easily solvable problem.

Today, cargo theft in the rail system is spread across the United States in a manner similar to over the road theft, with areas of concentrated activity occurring around major logistics hubs and major rail hubs such as Los Angeles, Chicago, St. Louis, and Memphis.

In 2008, the Chicago-based cargo theft task force investigated over 100 cases with regards to railroads theft, recovered $6.2 million in merchandise, and made 31 arrests.

With the complexity of such enormous hubs such as Chicago, containers are moved frequently, being placed in various locations waiting to be reloaded onto another train or be picked up for movement via truck. This complexity is ideal for the cargo criminal, who can use this to his advantage to steal entire containers and be hundreds of miles away before the containers (and the product inside them) are even discovered missing.

Security Considerations and the Rail Industry

Systems used for transit cargo security for other modes also apply to the rail industry. Loading/unloading procedures, locking devices, and GPS tracking are all applicable for cargo being moved by train, although the usages of these systems must be amended in order to meet the particular requirements (and risks) associated with rail cargo. The classic layered approach of ensuring that the right people are involved and trained, appropriate policies and procedures are in place, and the use of technology and hardware is applied appropriately are just as necessary for a secured supply chain, regardless of the transit mode of choice.

An additional layer of security within the rail industry is the existence of railroad police organizations. Railroad police officers are employed by every major rail company and provide an additional level of security for the rail system as a whole and the cargo being moved.

With their roots in the mid-1800s with Pinkerton's, the approximately 1000 railroad police officers in the United States are tasked with securing both freight lines and passenger lines. The duties of today's railroad police officer often involve routine uniform or plainclothes patrol of rail yards, depots, and railroad property either by foot or by car, conducting complex investigations involving cargo theft, theft of equipment, arson, and even investigate assault and murders that may spill over onto railroad property.

Trespassing is a common crime that railroad police handle, not only for the security of the rail system, but the safety of those trespassing. Although most trespass for the sake of catching a ride on a freight car or simply passing through railroad property, there is no lack of criminals entering railroad property with the intent to steal. While most are petty thieves, some are organized criminals that steal high-value merchandise from trains, sometimes using very sophisticated methods to commit their crimes, such as countersurveillance against railroad police, portable radios and cell phones to communicate, and rental or stolen vehicles to load the stolen merchandise.

The supply chain involves numerous modes of transportation, each of which must be protected in order to prevent further downstream impacts from being felt. One breach of supply chain security may result in the denial of service or product delivery, causing a cascade of events for other transportation, manufacturing, or distribution mechanisms. This is true for theft incidents just as much as infrastructure or other potential points of failure. Rail or highway bridges can become single points of failure for the supply chain in a particular region. Because of this, the impacts of theft or other supply chain disruptions can wreak substantial havoc on the supply chain system as a whole.

Additional tools that shippers can use for enhancing security for rail shipments include:

- Better security locks and seals, such as the ENFORCER or Sealock. While they can be defeated, they take longer to break and in rail theft, timing is often of the essence.
- If on a stack train, positioning adjacent containers or trailers so that their doors are facing each other, making it hard to gain access, let alone opening up doors and getting cargo out.

- Using deep well rail cars so that part of the bottom container is below the rail car top, preventing doors from opening, at least not very far, so suspects cannot enter the container and cargo cannot be removed.

Pipeline Security

Pipelines are considered a specialized means of transportation, used since the 19th century to move gases, petroleum, chemicals, coal, wood, and a variety of liquids such as milk and water. One of the primary uses of pipelines in the United States today is the movement of liquid fuels and natural gases. Most pipelines today are a combination of underground (buried) and aboveground (exposed) systems.

Pipelines by their very nature are vulnerable targets. Their distances make them virtually impossible to protect.

When analyzing security strategies for pipelines, the following data points should be gathered and analyzed as part of the process:

- Age of the pipeline system
- Distances
- Presence of civil unrest (generally not applicable for pipelines in the United States, but should not be ignored for those transiting multiple international boundaries)
- Maintenance records
- Historical loss records (experience from both quantity and quality standpoints)
- Percentage of pipeline that is land based vs over water (land-based spills are easier to contain and clean up)
- Presence of existing remote-sensing equipment along the pipeline (pressure changes, leaks, etc.)

There are approximately 493,000 miles of pipeline in the United States today with approximately one-third moving petroleum products while the remainder is a conduit for natural gas. Growth in the pipeline sector has been limited as they are expensive to build with significant upfront investment requirements and the lack of apparent needs for expansion due to current demands being met by existing infrastructure.

The protection of pipelines from terrorism, illegal tapping, and sabotage became an even greater priority after 2001. Similar to air and rail cargo, discussion regarding security in the pipeline industry led quickly to terrorism prevention strategy. The Transportation Security Administration (TSA) even has a pipeline security division within their Office of Transportation Sector Network Management. In the case of pipelines, protection of the transportation mode itself is just as critical as preventing illegal tapping or theft from the system. Damage to a pipeline can cause significant loss and delays.

Theft and the Pipeline System

Theft from pipelines is far more common in the international arena than in the United States. Reports of petroleum theft from pipelines in countries such as China, Nigeria, and Egypt are almost commonplace, while comparable reports in the United States are sparse at best.

According to the pipeline security division of TSA, theft of products from pipelines is not a common occurrence in the United States. Pipeline theft is more common in Africa, where deeply impoverished populations live near the pipelines. Pipeline theft in Africa is done out of desperation for fuel by the impoverished populations. The amount of product that is stolen is usually minimal, but many people are injured or killed during these thefts.

Product theft directly from the pipeline is rare in the United States because of the nature of the economy. Populations are not extremely impoverished as in Africa, and criminal organizations are not as aggressive as in Mexico. Pipeline theft is not impossible, but it is far from routine in the United States. Product theft from pipelines occasionally occurs when natural gas or other commodity providers bypass reading the gas meter and customers do not pay for the entire product they received. One product in particular that is sometimes stolen from pipelines is anhydrous ammonia, which is used to make methamphetamine. This is not usually stolen in large quantities.

Ways in which product is stolen from pipelines is by tapping into the line or siphoning from a valve. Groups that pose potential threats for pipeline theft include terrorist groups, such as Al Qaeda, and environmental extremist groups. U.S. companies do not take much action to prevent theft because it is such an insignificant issue (Figure 17.1).

In Mexico, pipelines are common targets for criminals as well as leftist and other extremist political groups, with theft and pipeline damage through sabotage occurring endlessly. According to Dow Jones, PEMEX, the state oil company in Mexico, suffered more theft of fuel from its pipeline system in the first 4 months of 2011 than it did in all of 2010. From January through April it lost more than 22,000 barrels more, in terms of volume ($25 million more in value), than the previous year.

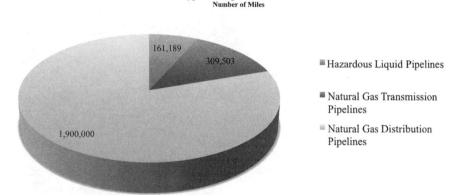

Figure 17.1 Courtesy of FreightWatch.

As fuel prices continue to be a point of financial strain, the threat of criminals stealing petroleum in the United States through theft from the pipeline system is all the more real.

Key Points

- While over the road cargo is the preferred choice for criminals seeking high-value goods, railroads still move ample volumes of merchandise that traditional cargo theft gangs will target.
- The extreme length of trains and numerous urban areas transited make securing cargo in transit a very difficult job for both railroad police agencies and shippers.
- Security best practices used for truck transportation can and should also be applied (albeit in a slightly different manner) to cargo being shipped via rail.
- While theft from pipelines continues to be a substantial issue for companies in other parts of the world, theft from pipelines is becoming an increasingly rare event in the United States.
- Theft of equipment from the pipeline industry is the most common theft issue faced by companies, while securing pipelines continues to be a primary concern for other reasons, such as terrorism and extremists groups possibly targeting the pipelines for political or idealistic purposes.

CARGO THEFT TASK FORCES AND ORGANIZATIONS

INFORMATION IN THIS CHAPTER:

- Locations and major functions of cargo theft task forces
- Difficulties and constraints of law enforcement agencies while investigating cargo theft
- Industry groups dedicated to combating cargo theft
- Public—private sector collaborative efforts to reduce cargo theft

Cargo theft task forces are located in several areas of the United States known for extreme rates of cargo theft, including Miami, Memphis, Los Angeles, and Chicago (Gonzalez, 2009). The Miami-Dade Tactical Operations Multi-Agency Cargo Anti-Theft Squad (TOMCATS) is the forerunner in cargo theft investigations, making arrests on a weekly basis and conducting numerous investigations of cargo thefts occurring around the country as the majority of the loads are destined for Miami for sale or export. The California Highway Patrol's (CHP) Cargo Theft Interdiction Program (CTIPs) investigated 773 cases, made 164 arrests, recovered 546 commercial vehicles, and recovered $21.6 million in stolen goods (Gonzalez, 2009).

Even with the increasing exposure that cargo theft is receiving, funding for specialized law enforcement is becoming scarce, particularly from federal sources. The task force in Memphis was disbanded recently, and while Memphis detectives still work cargo theft cases, they are doing so as part of an auto-theft group. The Federal Bureau of Investigation (FBI) has left the Miami TOMCATs, taking their funding and vehicles with them, dealing a huge blow to the TOMCATS unit and a tremendous opportunity for local cargo thieves. So while government officials are paying more "attention" to cargo theft, when it comes down to what is important (money and manpower), their priorities are elsewhere, just as they have always been.

Miami is a hub for stolen cargo—arguably *the* hub for stolen cargo, with an incredible volume of stolen cargo being moved into the Miami area on a daily basis for sale on the black market or loading and exportation to Latin America out of the Port of Miami.

These tasks forces are not immune from the budgetary issues experienced by law enforcement agencies throughout the country during economic downturns. In fact, with cargo theft largely being a nonpriority crime for most police agencies, funding for these task forces is often in jeopardy as precious few resources are spread even more thinly. Because of this, many cargo theft task forces rely on support from their own agencies driven by priorities from industry and the communities, state and federal support through joint operations, and industry support.

Miami-Dade Tactical Operations Multi-Agency Cargo Anti-Theft Squad

When first organized, the TOMCATS was composed of local, state, and federal law enforcement agencies, including the Miami-Dade Police Department, the FBI, the U.S. Customs and Border Protection, the Florida Department of Law Enforcement (FDLE), the Florida Highway Patrol (FHP), and the Florida Department of Transportation (FDOT). According to their website, the cargo crimes section (CCS) of the Miami-Dade Police department's robbery bureau is tasked with the responsibility of stemming the rising theft of cargo from warehouse and transportation facilities throughout Miami-Dade County. These losses can have a negative impact on the community's economy through negative media exposure and the threat of the loss of major shippers who are relocating to "safer" ports and taking hundreds of jobs and millions of dollars with them. Due to the significant increase of organized commercial cargo theft in Miami-Dade County and its negative impact on commerce, the CSS took a leadership role and joined with the FBI, the U.S. Customs and Border Protection, the FDLE, the FHP, and the FDOT to form a South Florida cargo theft task force called the Tactical Operations Multi-Agency Cargo Anti-Theft Squad. The task force is housed within the offices of the robbery bureau, cargo crimes section. This facility is used as the central clearinghouse for the collection and dissemination of all cargo theft information in the South Florida area.

As of the date this book went to print, the Miami TOMCATS was undergoing some organizational changes and restructuring due to budgetary issues. The result of those changes was the disbanding of the TOMCATS as a unit, while some detectives continue to investigate cargo theft under other divisions within the department.

The TOMCATS conducted focused investigations into organized groups, individuals, businesses, and other enterprises engaged in continuing criminal conspiracies pertaining to the theft, distribution, and exportation of stolen cargo. Detectives use a large variety of techniques to infiltrate criminal organizations, gather evidence, make arrests, and recover high-value stolen cargo shipments. All truck hijackings that occur in unincorporated Miami-Dade County are assigned to the task force for investigation.

"In Miami-Dade, however, the 22-member TOMCATS unit is truly a collaborative effort. Several Miami-Dade detectives, as well as a U.S. Customs agent, a criminal analyst, a U.S. Department of Transportation (DOT) officer, one Florida Highway Patrol trooper and a detective from Broward County Sheriff's Office work jointly with FBI agents to investigate the crimes" (Morasch, 2008).

The TOMCATS frequently offers advice and guides industry personnel in keeping their cargo secure. With the sheer volume of cargo theft occurring around the country, and such a high percentage of these incidents being tied to South Florida, the TOMCATS has no shortage of work on its hands.

"Hijackers don't like crowds. Don't stop in deserted areas while waiting to make deliveries," according to Lieutenant Twan Uptgrow, commander of the TOMCATS. "Try to stop at reputable truck stops along the route, and maybe try not to stop at the same location each time." The TOMCATS frequently offers advice and guidance on cargo security to the industry. Among other things, it urges truckers to call local police if they're suspicious about another vehicle following them. Drivers pulled over by an unmarked police car should call 9-1-1 to verify. TOMCATS officers advise truckers to plan ahead when possible and park in secure areas. It's best to find rest stops and other spots where other truck drivers will see them. Watch for cars or vehicles following your truck when you leave the highway. Team drivers also stand a much-improved chance of protecting their loads. Company drivers working alone should have regular communication with their dispatchers.

"A few hijackings have occurred in which persons have pretended to be police officers in unmarked cars," Uptgrow said. "Try to pull over in a well-lit area where someone else can witness what's going on" (Morasch, 2008).

California Cargo Theft Task Forces

With the incredible volume of cargo theft experience in the Los Angeles Basin, and in California as a whole, it is little surprise that the state has three multijurisdictional task forces dedicated to combating this problem. Two are centered in the Los Angeles area: LA County Sheriff's Department and the LAPD. The other task force is run by the California Highway Patrol, referred to as CTIPs.

Los Angeles County Cargo Cats

In January 1990, the Los Angeles County Sheriff's Department formed a new investigative unit with the mission to investigate cargo theft. Named the Cargo CATs (Criminal Apprehension Team), the new unit fell under the major crimes bureau of the department's detective division.

Similar to other task forces, the Cargo CATs are multijurisdictional, capable of investigating the transient nature of cargo theft as county and state lines are crossed.

The unit's website touts over $213.5 million in stolen property recovered and 1275 arrests.

According to the Cargo CATs, the unit's objectives are:

- Increase arrest, prosecution, and conviction of cargo thieves and their receivers.
- Establish a close working relationship with the cargo, transportation, warehousing, and insurance industries.
- Recover and return stolen cargo to owners.
- Reduce cargo theft property crimes.
- Reduce court costs and time by gathering quality evidence to ensure guilty pleas.
- Develop intelligence information about the stolen cargo redistribution system.
- Act as a resource for cargo theft prevention information.
- Establish a statistical reporting system to reflect the cargo theft situation accurately.
- Enhance coordination and cooperation among federal, state, and local law enforcement agencies, as well as cooperation and coordination among prosecutors, law enforcement, and victims.
- Support the enactment of mandatory cargo theft-reporting laws, along with development of a statewide cargo theft database.

California Highway Patrol: Cargo Theft Interdiction Program

According to the CHP, cargo theft in the state amounts to an estimated $10 billion annually with the trucking industry, insurance companies, and railroads the major victims. However, no financial total can adequately quantify the actual total cost of cargo theft-related losses, which include job site downtime, replacement of stolen commercial vehicles, time spent on additional paperwork, and increased insurance costs.

Prior to 1990, no proactive enforcement specifically directed at cargo theft-related crimes existed in California. In the state, consequently, the criminal element determined that the level of profit derived from the theft of cargo loads far surpassed the risk of apprehension. What quickly became apparent was that profits from the stolen cargo were substantial and tax free. Thefts of sought-after commodities, such as televisions, camcorders, VCRs, and computers, could fetch margins as high as 80 cents on the dollar. For example, a gang with several reliable buyers that stole a load of computers valued at one million dollars conceivably could earn as much as $800,000 from the sale of the commodity.

In response to concerns by the California Trucking Association over this rising problem, Assembly Bill 1683 was enacted. This legislation created funding for the enhancement of cargo theft enforcement statewide, and designated the CHP to coordinate and implement the program. As a result, the Cargo Theft Interdiction Program was established in 1995.

In a state as large and diverse as California, each geographic region is unique as to the extent and type of cargo theft experienced. In some areas, efforts were already under way to address the cargo theft problem; in others, virtually nothing was being done, at least in any coordinated manner. Because of these factors, the approach taken in each region may be different; however, the CTIP strived to establish regional teams that can provide a proactive response to this type of crime. The following is a list of areas where CTIP teams are actively conducting investigations:

- Los Angeles—Southern Team
- San Diego—Border Team
- Bay Area/Central Valley—Golden Gate Team

In 2007, the CTIP handled 540 investigations statewide, arrested 91 people, found 438 commercial vehicles (tractors, trailers, and box trucks), and recovered $14.29 million worth of stolen merchandise (Gonzalez, 2009).

New Jersey State Police

The New Jersey State Police (NJSP) filled the headlines in January 2011 with a string of arrests and seizures resulting in recovery of more than $10 million in stolen goods and a number of people charged with a variety of crimes. One warehouse entered by the task force, led by Lieutenant Mike McDonnell, contained stolen product from seven different theft incidents.

The NJSP cargo theft unit is responsible for conducting criminal investigations and supporting the regional intelligence collection plan by collecting, evaluating, and disseminating intelligence data regarding cargo theft activity that affects and is related to the state of New Jersey. The cargo theft unit responds to calls for assistance from other law enforcement agencies throughout the state and investigates individuals and groups engaged in cargo theft activity.

Memphis TAMCATs

With the Memphis area serving as a major hub for logistics operations in the United States, at the crossroads of the Mississippi River and Interstates 40 and 55, almost every major logistics company in the country, along with countless manufacturers, has logistics operations in Memphis, to include the global headquarters of Federal Express. With this tremendous amount of cargo activity also comes an accompanying amount of cargo theft, with Memphis having the highest per capita rate of cargo theft anywhere in the United States. Because of this, it is little surprise that the Memphis area hosts a multiagency task force with the sole mission of combating cargo theft.

The Memphis Auto/Cargo Theft Task Force (ACTF) was formed in 1998 to address a significant crime problem involving the interstate transportation of stolen property, including motor vehicles, and major thefts from interstate shipments. The ACTF is currently composed of officers and special agents of the FBI, Memphis Police Department, Shelby County Sheriff's Office, the U.S. Customs Service, and the National Insurance Crime Bureau. The primary objective of this task force is to reduce the number of automobile, as well as cargo thefts, by the successful prosecution of known career criminals and their associates.

Midwest Cargo Theft Unit

In 2006 and early 2007, the auto theft task force in Illinois kept running into cargo theft cases, resulting in a handful of arrests and recoveries. The unit was later advised by their policy board, however, that the unit's funding was derived from the insurance claims and recoveries and other revenue sources that came from auto theft only—not in the recovery of cargo. Because of this, the unit was only allowed to work auto theft cases, and cargo claims were not investigated.

From that situation, however, was derived the idea for an enforcement initiative. The Illinois State Police formed a group of investigators to pursue cargo theft cases, and in northern Illinois there was no shortage of work for them. From this effort the Midwest Cargo Theft Unit emerged in October 2007 that had a memorandum of understanding (MOU) with the Chicago FBI office in order to expand the group's investigative powers beyond state lines and pursue criminals at a federal level.

The Midwest Cargo Theft Unit is made up of six Illinois State Police personnel and one Norfolk Southern railroad investigator. Other agencies involved in cargo theft investigations that support this unit, as necessary, include the FBI, National Insurance Crime Bureau (NICB), Chicago Police, Immigration and Customs Enforcement, railroad police, local police, and local auto theft units.

The mission statement of the Midwest Cargo Theft Unit is dedicated to cargo crime reduction throughout Illinois and neighboring states through a cooperative effort between law enforcement and the private sector.

The unit has had several key initiatives since its inception and continues to push forward with high payoff cargo theft investigations. The first key initiative of the unit was acquiring the MOU with the FBI in 2007, allowing the unit to chase criminals outside the state of Illinois and investigate federal crimes. The unit is currently developing a number of cases with the FBI to prosecute federally. Additional actions include use of a bait trailer that is in the process of being upgraded with the most advanced technology available. This tactic can prove incredibly beneficial in ensuring that cargo theft gangs are caught and charged at the highest level possible. The unit is also working with state legislators to devise a law exclusively for cargo theft in Illinois with the ability to seize the criminal's assets.

Since its inception, this unit has had a number of high profile successes in arresting and prosecuting cargo theft gangs. After a 6-month investigation the cargo theft unit was able to arrest and recover several million dollars' worth of merchandise. This investigation resulted in the arrest of a major cargo thief in the Chicago area who was the person responsible for the largest fencing operation at that time. After the arrests, the number of thefts reduced dramatically for several months in the Chicago area. The unit recovered merchandise from four different warehouses that involved numerous companies and insurance claims.

Additionally, the Midwest Cargo Theft Unit provides annual training seminars for industry and law enforcement personnel, covering cargo theft topics, loss prevention, and supply chain security methodologies.

Georgia Bureau of Investigations

Georgia's cargo theft task force began with a single detective, Keith Lewis, from the DeKalb county Sheriff's Department investigating cargo theft cases. Through the process of his investigations, and over 20 years' experience in the transportation industry, Detective Lewis was intimately aware of the intercounty and interstate nature of cargo theft and knew that a single detective investigating this criminal enterprise in a single county was not going to be sufficient.

Detective Lewis approached the Georgia Motor Trucking Association with his idea for a state-wide cargo theft task force. The organization embraced the idea and took it to the governor for funding. With the FBI and Georgia State Police uninterested in tackling this largely unknown crime, the Georgia Bureau of Investigation (GBI) was the logical entity to house the new unit, and in 2009 the major theft unit was created.

With statewide jurisdiction, the major theft unit of the GBI has had significant success targeting cargo theft gangs that made Georgia one of the riskiest states in the country for over the road cargo. The unit investigates enterprise-type cases, going after multioffender gangs with connections to millions of dollars in losses annually. They have been responsible for the recovery of $26 million in stolen goods and 91 arrests, with many arrested being suspected of involvement in numerous cargo theft cases.

On Wednesday, June 2, 2010, John Raymond Smith Jr., referred to as Johnny Ray Smith, pled guilty to his part in attempting to sell stolen cargo valued at $3 million in Georgia. Operating Smith Sales Company out of warehouses in Mableton and Hiram, Georgia, the 48-year-old Smith conspired with others to buy, receive, and possess stolen cargo from nearly two dozen interstate tractor—trailer thefts throughout Georgia and surrounding states, including Alabama, South Carolina, and Tennessee. Items recovered during the arrest of Johnny Ray Smith included televisions, computers, consumer electronics, cigarettes, sewing machines, food, and clothing.

The GBI major theft unit continues to run proactive cargo theft initiatives, targeting organized theft gangs, using the Racketeer Influenced and Corrupt Organizations Actand other tools at their disposal to arrest and prosecute gangs targeting cargo moving throughout the state of Georgia.

The unit is composed of four Georgia Bureau of Investigations agents, one member of the Motor Carrier Compliance Department, and Detective Lewis with the DeKalb County Police.

Technology Asset Protection Association

TAPA began in the 1990s as the Technology Asset Protection Association, whose goal was to reduce cargo theft rates in the high-tech industry. With the explosion of new technologies, creating smaller, faster, and better components and finished consumer electronics, cargo criminals targeting these products increased at virtually the same rate.

Seeing the intersection of cargo crime and virtually all high-value, theft-attractive goods, TAPA changed its name to Transported Asset Protection Association, reflecting the group's expansion to include other commodities, such as pharmaceuticals, but maintaining its main charter, to prevent cargo theft from occurring for product while in transit or in storage.

TAPA has three chapters currently: TAPA Americas, TAPA EMEA (Europe, Middle East, and Africa), and TAPA Asia.

According to their website, the vision of TAPA Americas is to bring together manufacturers, shippers, logistics providers, carriers, insurers, service providers, law enforcement, and government agencies to reduce risks of criminal activity in the transportation supply chain. The group's mission is to protect high-value, theft-targeted assets in the transportation supply chain by

- Collecting and exchanging data and intelligence information on a global basis
- Cooperating on preventative supply chain security within industry and with government organizations
- Setting and promulgating best-in-class standards for facility security and transport
- Working as parallel organizations under the TAPA worldwide umbrella

TAPA created its own certification process through which facilities and transportation providers can be audited and become "TAPA certified," showing their compliance with the organization's security standards.

For more information, see www.tapaonline.org.

Nation Cargo Theft Task Force

The National Insurance Crime Bureau is headquartered in Des Plains, Illinois. The NICB is a nonprofit organization designed to detect and investigate insurance fraud and vehicle theft through information analysis, investigations, training, and legislative advocacy. The NICB is widely supported within the insurance industry. According to their website it is sponsored by over 1100 insurance companies and self-insured entities. According to the NICB, member companies wrote more than $317 billion in insurance premiums in 2010—an estimated 80% of the nation's property and casualty insurance.

The National Cargo Theft Task Force and NICB work in cooperation with private industry, insurance, and federal, state, and local governments in order to combat the continued threat posed by cargo theft perpetrators to the economy, the American citizens, and the national security of the United States according to the group.

Pharmaceutical Cargo Security Coalition

A more recently minted organization, the Pharmaceutical Cargo Security Coalition (PCSC), has made great strides in combating cargo theft, particularly in the pharmaceutical and consumer health markets. Two sizeable pharmaceutical theft incidents occurred in 2005—both of which occurred in New Jersey, involving two different companies and millions of dollars' worth of products, which jumpstarted this group's formation. The thefts occurred essentially a week or two apart, along roughly the same stretch of highway; however, neither company knew of the other's loss.

In March 2006, two men, Ken Obriot from Wyeth and Bob Montero from Pfizer, decided to call for a meeting to discuss these large-scale losses. That first meeting, hosted by Pfizer in New Jersey, had approximately 36 invited guests. Most were manufacturers; however, there were a few law enforcement people as well.

Initially, no one wanted to open up and discuss losses they may have suffered. Eventually, however, the walls came down and several cases were talked about. What was learned was that the methodology of the criminals in each instance was essentially the same. The group agreed to begin to keep closer tabs on this type of illicit activity, as well as to share intelligence about these crimes and those that committed them. Hence the group became more formalized but, at that point, didn't have an official name.

Chuck Forsaith of Purdue Pharmaceuticals volunteered to become the "clearinghouse" for all of this information and began a methodical process of collecting data, cataloging it, and sharing it with others within the industry through periodic "alerts" disseminated to all relevant parties.

The group also decided to hold educational seminars at least annually to discuss and expose the group's progress. It was agreed that each meeting would be sponsored by a different pharmaceutical company. The group also agreed there would never be a cost associated with membership or to any of the meetings/conferences/seminars that are held. The group also decided not to have an elected hierarchy. Finally, there would never be any type of a budget. The group would always try to do as much as possible, with as little a monetary investment as possible. As unusual as that may sound, it remains true even to this day.

The name "Pharmaceutical Cargo Security Coalition" wasn't created until late 2009—somewhat reluctantly due to the fact that the group wanted to maintain the simplest form of organization. The demand for information became so great that naming the organization, as well as providing a website for members to be able to utilize, was ultimately inevitable.

Today the group has over 800 members from a number of different disciplines—pharmaceutical manufacturers, wholesalers and retailers; pharmaceutical industry organizations; local, state, and federal law enforcement agencies and task forces; insurers; carriers; freight forwarders; and risk management firms. The PCSC is now aligned with over 20 other industry organizations (representing commodities other than pharmaceuticals) that either combat or monitor cargo theft activity all over the world. More information on PCSC can be found at http://www.pcscpharma.com.

CargoNet

A member of the Verisk Analytics family of companies, CargoNet is a public company designed to collect cargo theft data through industry resources in order to help prevent cargo theft and improve recovery rates using secured and controlled information sharing among theft victims, their business partners, and law enforcement. CargoNet is centered on a national database and information-sharing system managed by crime analysts and subject-matter experts.

According to the company, CargoNet offers integrated databases, a theft alert system, task force and investigations support, a tractor–trailer theft deterrence program, and the TruckStop-Watch program. CargoNet also provides driver education and incentives, secondary-market monitoring and interdictions, crime trend analysis and loss control services, and training. More information on CargoNet can be found at www.cargonet.com.

Supply Chain—Information Sharing and Analysis Center

The Supply Chain—Information Sharing and Analysis Center (SC-ISAC) is part of the National Council of ISAC, an industry–government initiative to gather information from industry and government sources for the purpose of increased security and industry awareness.

The mission of the ISAC Council is to advance the physical and cyber security of the critical infrastructures of North America by establishing and maintaining a framework for valuable interaction between and among the ISACs and with government. The National Council of ISACs, formerly known as the ISAC Council, was formed in 2003 when a volunteer group of ISAC representatives decided to meet monthly to develop trusted relationships among the sectors and to address common issues and concerns. The National Council of ISACs activities include drills and exercises, hosting a private sector liaison at the Department of Homeland Security National Infrastructure Coordinating Center during incidents of national significance, emergency classified briefings, and real-time sector threat-level reporting. The group also sponsors an annual Critical Infrastructure Protection Congress to bring together the critical infrastructure community for networking, learning, and addressing issues of concern to Critical Infrastructure and Key Structures stakeholders.

Members of the SC-ISAC receive quarterly and annual reports on cargo theft, as well as information on emerging threats, individual thefts, and open source media articles. The organization's website says that members are kept informed and are prepared to act on threats to our global supply chain and, in turn, their own industry interests.

According to the organization's website, the mission of the SC-ISAC is to:
- Facilitate communication among supply chain-dependent industry stakeholders
- Foster a partnership between private and public sectors to share critical information
- Collect, analyze, and disseminate actionable intelligence to help secure the global supply chain
- Provide an international perspective through private sector subject matter experts
- Help protect the critical infrastructure of the United States

For more information, see https://secure.sc-investigate.net/SC-ISAC/.

Transportation Security Councils

As of publication, there are four transportation security councils in the United States covering the northeast, southeast, southwest, and west coast. While each council is managed somewhat differently, the general mission of each is to provide a centralized means for collecting cargo theft data, typically from its membership and from other affiliated organizations, and then alerting the membership of recent thefts, emerging trends, or recently published reports, generally through email distribution.

The Eastern Region Transportation Security Council is one of the oldest, if not the first, transportation security council in the United States. It was started in the late 1980s by a number of former law enforcement officers and security managers working in the transportation field.

The group's original name was "The New York/New Jersey Motor Carrier Security Council." These individuals discovered that they were all experiencing the same types of problems, yet had no way of sharing information. They made cold-call inquires to one another and determined there was a need to band together in a collaborative way in order to safeguard their respective businesses and their customers.

The council has changed over the years, as only one or two of the original members are still active, yet they still meet about once a month along with communicating via emails, blasts on thefts, hijackings, and educational opportunities involving the transportation, manufacturing, and cargo world. Although the turnout for meetings varies (typically 25–30 members and guests), the group has approximately 325 active members from the private sector as well as the law enforcement community. Law enforcement partners include, but are not limited to, state police from New Jersey, New York, Pennsylvania, Illinois, Louisiana, Virginia, Georgia, and Florida. Additionally, the group has participants from U.S. Customs, the FBI, the Waterfront Commission, and several local police departments.

For contact information for regional transportation security councils, see the Resources section of this book.

Key Points

- Regional cargo theft task forces often serve as the best law enforcement contact for a stolen load or warehouse burglary.
- These units are located strategically throughout the country and work cargo theft cases exclusively—increasing their

effectiveness in locating stolen loads, recovering the goods, and making arrests.

- Budget cuts faced by numerous federal, state, and local agencies have created significant pressures on cargo theft units for size reduction or elimination altogether.
- Other organizations exist to assist industry professionals in information sharing, training in best practices, and keeping up to date on emerging trends.
- Groups such as regional transportation security councils are excellent examples of private–public sector collaboration in the area of cargo theft and its prevention.

BEYOND SECURITY

INFORMATION IN THIS CHAPTER:

* Increasing operational efficiencies through low-cost technology
* Monitoring vendor compliance
* Reducing damage/spoilage with same products used for security purposes
* Allowing logistics needs drive the use of tracking systems and budget with security as the secondary benefit

The benefits of a secure supply chain go beyond reduction in cargo theft losses. While covert tracking devices, trackable locks, and other electronic equipment are tremendous assets to protect in-transit cargo, that is only one of numerous functions they can perform. By using this same technology as a logistics management tool, shippers and their logistics providers can gain incredible insight into the functionality of their supply chains, with visibility and previously unattainable control of their cargo movements.

This concept, if used to its full potential, can quickly result in the following benefits to a supply chain:

* Increased productivity
* Improved inventory management
* Improved customer relations
* Increased supply chain visibility
* Higher profits through theft prevention
* Product and consumer safety
* Reduction in transit times

The following feedback is from a major manufacturer and their usage of covert tracking devices and the multitude of downstream positive impacts (due to the sensitive nature of their business, the company's name was omitted).

The company has 3500 truckloads annually in the United States that transport cargo to their 19 regional warehouses with an average wholesale value of $3 million.

In 2006, the company began purchasing embeddable tracking devices (specifically the FreightWatch tracking devices—the PT-200 and the F1) and monitors loads from end to end.

Since 2006, the company has had four loads stolen, but all were recovered intact and ultimately made an on-time delivery.

One was even more critical to the company, the variety of other benefits that the tracking devices and their monitoring has brought, which include:

- Carriers are held accountable for the location of the cargo at all times because the company can track them 24/7.
- The company can correct problems immediately before they cause supply chain disruptions.
- They have established a virtual warehouse concept in which they are able to receipt cargo while still in transit.
- The company has been able to lower their deployed inventory, saving them $100 million over the past 5 years.
- They have improved customer service by not losing cargo in transit and making on-time deliveries: 1 late delivery in 2009, 0 later deliveries in 2010, compared to 44 in 2004 and 25 in 2005.
- The costs of logistics have been lowered substantially.
- They have become a preferred company to do business with.
- They have experienced zero stockouts.
- They have inventory accuracy of 99.99994% with less than three cases of product unaccounted for.
- They have increased inventory turns from 34.8 to 52.6 per year.
- Their total delivered cost per pound of product is 19 cents.
  The bottom line for the company is:
- Outperform their competitors
- Turn their inventory faster
- Sell fresher product
- Have fewer late deliveries
- Have higher level of inventory accuracy
- Get preferential treatment from suppliers (carriers and warehouses)
- Are growing market share in a declining industry

Standards of care, predictability, and supply chain optimization are concepts that every logistician wishes to maximize and can now be accomplished through simple monitoring combined with in-transit security and operational plans that will improve profitability and customer satisfaction.

The use of tracking devices throughout the supply chain for monitoring and optimization can ensure that companies are provided with real-time information at the granular level, providing previously unimaginable details on supply chain disruptions, policy compliance, and in-transit milestones to predict delivery times and cargo disposition upon arrival. Through this, the supply chain manager is able to take control of his cargo regardless of where it is in the world and turn data into action in real time (Greene, 2010).

Delays, temperature excursions, route deviations, and theft—all of these remove efficiency from the supply chain and result in late deliveries, refused cargo, and, in the end, increased costs. By seeing delays as they occur, downstream transportation providers can be made aware and adjust their operations accordingly. Clients can be notified and arrangements can be made to fulfill short-term needs until the delays are sorted out. Temperature-controlled cargo can be intercepted and trans-ferred into a working "reefer" trailer or nearby cold storage facility, as opposed to relying on temperature recorders showing the cargo went out of tolerance; useful information but not actionable—helpful in preventing loss.

And of course this is in addition to the security implication of the tracking devices and software, ensuring that cargo is on the approved routes, on time, and, when deviations occur, trained personnel can respond with a predetermined escalation proce-dure to ensure that the cargo is secure or, in the event of theft, is recovered promptly.

Operational Efficiencies

Data provided by cargo tracking technology enable the development of real-time supply chain performance, allowing for more precise information, which leads to better decision making and customer service. This will enable the concept of standards of care to take on a whole new dimension with the visibility provided by the tracking system coupled with operational metrics such as

- On-time performance
- Unauthorized stops/delays/routes
- Unauthorized transshipment locations
- Identifying unauthorized carriers
- Identifying unauthorized modes of transportation
- Monitoring handling to include temperature, humidity, and shock/impact

By having this information readily available for every ship-ment, mangers have a powerful tool for supply chain predict-ability and optimization. Days of product in inventory, cycle times, transit times, and unplanned delays are a few of the metrics that translate into direct costs.

By optimizing the supply chain through more pinpoint performance metrics, management can refine operations to the minute rather than hours or days by having access to

- Actual departure times
- Actual arrival times
- Alerts prior to arrival
- Transit time measurements
- Inventory on hand
- Achieved in-transit milestones

This capability, combined with real-time information surrounding unplanned events, places tremendous power in the hands of the supply chain manager and his or her ability to ensure optimal efficiency at every step in the operation. By using the tracking technologies already available today, shippers can weigh whether they are receiving what they pay for in their supply chain vendor management process, can ensure optimization throughout their operations, and can create methods for supply chain flexibility while maintaining maximum security and efficiency.

Key Points

- Operational efficiencies can be substantially expanded upon and improved by being able to track cargo end to end.
- Supplier compliance will increase as supply chain disruptions decrease.
- Benefits also include decreasing logistics costs combined with more accurate inventories.
- The addition of sensor technologies coupled with remote tracking services (such as temperature monitoring and shock/ drop) can allow shippers to reroute or stop damaged/spoiled goods in transit and dispatch new product in a more timely manner.
- Cargo tracking devices allow a company to gain positive control and visibility of a company's supply chain from end to end.

RESOURCES

Cargo theft data and risk analysis:
  FreightWatch International: www.freightwatchintl.com
  Transported Asset Protection Association (TAPA): www.tapaonline.org
  CargoNet: www.cargonet.com
  Chubb Group of Insurance Companies: www.chubb.com
  Eastern Region Transportation Security Council: 201-330-3681
  Southeastern Transportation Security Council: info@ GaCargoTheft.com
  Southwest Transportation Security Council: www.swtsc.org
  Western States Transportation Security Council: 562-404-3317
  Supply Chain — ISAC: https://secure.sc-investigate.net/ SC-ISAC/

Cargo tracking device technologies:
  Please note that while almost any cargo tracking technology can be purchased from the device manufacturer, many of these do not come with associated tracking software, an obvious prerequisite if your intent is to track cargo on the move. The companies and websites that follow are excellent resources to learn more about devices and their capabilities; however, in order to purchase devices for the purposes of tracking cargo, please see Cargo Track Solutions.

Cargo tracking solutions:
  FreightWatch International — www.freightwatchintl.com
  Track What Matters — www.trackwhatmatters.com
  OnAsset — www.onasset.com
  Lojack SC Integrity — www.lojacksci.com
  FedEx SenseAware — www.fedex.com

Cargo security hardware:
  Transport Security — www.transportsecurity.com
  Sealock — www.sealock.com
  Carrier Security — www.carriersecurity.com
  TydenBrooks — http://www.tydenbrooks.com/

Truck tracking solutions:
  Qualcomm — www.qualcomm.com
  Skybitz — www.skybitz.com

Sendum — www.sendum.com

Enfora — www.enfora.com

Cargo theft task forces:

Miami TOMCATS (Miami, Florida): 305-471-2142

LA County Sheriff's Department (CargoCats): 310-603-3137

California Highway Patrol (CTIPs): soctip@chp.ca.gov

New Jersey State Police: 732-548-7153

Midwest Cargo Theft Unit: cargo_theft@isp.state.il.us

Georgia Bureau of Investigations: info@GaCargoTheft.com

Security manuals and technical information:

"ASIS Protection of Assets Manual" (www.asisonline.org)

"Effective Security Management," Fifth Edition, by Charles Sennewald (Butterworth-Heinemann, 2011)

"Handbook of Loss Prevention and Crime Prevention," Fourth Edition, by Lawrence J. Fennelly (Elsevier, 2004)

Transported Asset Protection Association (TAPA) Freight Security Requirements (FSR) document (www.tapaonline.org/)

Transported Asset Protection Association (TAPA) Transportation Security Requirements (TSR) document (www.tapaonline.org/)

GLOSSARY

Access controls Systems and barriers designed to ensure that only authorized personnel have access to an area or facility or sections within.

Active monitoring Process of remotely monitoring shipments through an online platform that receives a signal from some form of electronic transmitter.

Break glass sensors Motion detection sensors designed specifically to detect when glass has been broken.

Brokering When a transportation provider contracts with another transportation provider to move a load they were asked to move.

Cargo seal A serialized single-use device inserted onto the control door hasp of the cargo space of an ocean container, rail car, or other cargo conveyance. The cargo seal is designed to detect signs of tampering or unauthorized entry.

Carrier Company contracted to transport product from point A to point B with no responsibility for breaking down product, conducting inventory, or any storage or distribution.

Catastrophic loss A large-scale cargo theft incident, generally used when referring to a full truckload theft or warehouse burglary scenario with loss of a substantial quantity of high-value goods.

Closed circuit television (CCTV) System composed of video cameras positioned throughout the interior and exterior of a facility. The term CCTV also refers to the digital video recorder (DVR) or other system used to record and store the images.

Contract security guard Use of a third-party security company to provide on-site (human) security presence. Also known as manguarding.

Corrective actions Recommendations from FreightWatch that McKesson should implement in an effort to mitigate the observed risk.

Covert tracking Method of tracking in-transit shipments so that if stolen, the tracking device is not located readily by the criminals, providing an increased opportunity for recovery.

Covert tracking device A battery-powered electronic device that emits a signal through either cellular towers and/or GPS satellites. This device is embedded in the cargo being shipped.

Driver departure interview A documented briefing given to the driver outlining all in-transit security actions that should be taken while in possession of a shipment.

Driver pickup process A standardized procedure by which a driver is required to produce predetermined information, such as a government issued identification and bill of lading number, to ensure the individual is authorized to pick up the intended shipment.

Egress Movement of personnel or vehicles from a facility or its associated grounds.

Embedded When a covert tracking device is placed inside packaging that makes it appear to be the same as the other product assembled and palletized for shipment.

Exit searches Process by which personnel are inspected prior to exiting the warehouse floor or facility. There are a wide variety of ways by which exit searches can be conducted, pending local law regulations.

Freight forwarder Company that specializes in storage and distribution of goods including, at times, handling logistics and carrier selection.

Freight security requirements Requirements that a company places on its vendors regarding how product is to be handled, stored, or transported. The requirements are specific to the security protocols established by the shipper.

Full truckload, also referred to as truckload A dedicated trailer for a single shipment from origin to destination.

Fulfillment Process by which product is selected, staged, prepared, and loaded.

Geofence An electronic barrier established around a single location to trigger a notification when a mobile asset travels outside predetermined parameters.

Georoute Turn-by-turn directions between two directions that has an electronic fence (same concept as a geofence) that will alert a control center when a device deviates outside of the allowable boundary around the route.

Global positioning system (GPS) An onboard tracking system used for asset management, and ancillary, purposes by transportation providers.

High-value cage/vault An interior room within a storage facility that has additional security measures such as reinforced walls, full floor-to-ceiling metal fencing, access control measures, and CCTV for the storage of high-value goods, controlled substances, and other products more prone to theft.

In transit Term used when a shipment has left the origin but has not yet reached its destination.

In-transit lanes The highway route a transportation provider uses to move product from the origin to the destination.

Ingress Movement of personnel or vehicles into the facility or its associated grounds.

Key control Policy or procedure by which all keys (hard keys/electronic keys) within a facility or other business unit are assigned by serial number, logged, and secured when not in use or in the possession of authorized personnel.

Load/shipment brokering The act of a transportation provider using a third party to transport a client's shipment.

Local/howler alarm Audible alarm designed to let personnel within the facility know that a barrier, such as emergency exit door, has been breached.

LTL Less than truckload carriers collect partial shipments from various shippers and consolidate them into a single trailer for line haul to the delivering terminal or to a hub terminal where the cargo will be sorted, consolidated, and trucked locally to final destination.

Minimum security requirements Established corporate security requirements that must be met by all facilities or business units within a given organization. Generally written at a high level, from which more specific security policies can be tailored to each business unit.

Motion detection An array of sensors designed to detect the presence of a person within the area of coverage and alert a central monitoring station.

Overt tracking Method of tracking in-transit shipments either by personnel (in a trail vehicle) or through electronic means that can be identified readily (e.g., a GPS antenna on top of a tractor or trailer).

Perimeter security A combination of physical barriers and access control measures designed to prevent unauthorized access to a facility's grounds.

Physical security Used to describe barriers, walls, fencing, and other items that provide a physical boundary designed to delay the access of unauthorized personnel.

Ping rate Rate at which a covert tracking device sends a signal detailing its location.

Prealerts Transmittal of shipment information to the intended destination, including information on the driver, security seal numbers, product/inventory, and estimated arrival time.

Proactive monitoring See Active monitoring

Procedural security Method for securing an area or facility through policies and procedures, such as not allowing unescorted personnel within a facility.

Red zone The first 200 miles traveled from the point of origin ("red zone").

Security assessment Site-specific analysis of existing security measures in place and their effectiveness against the threat of break-in, burglary, and internal theft.

Security awareness training Formalized training provided by an employer to staff covering the security policies and procedures of a given organization.

Security countermeasure Policies, procedures, personnel, and equipment in place to delay, detect, and prevent unauthorized access, theft, and other criminal activity within a designated area or facility.

Security escort The act of physically driving behind a shipment to provide security oversight.

Security patrols Security method designed to inspect the interior/exterior of a facility to ensure the physical integrity of all doors, windows, and other points of entry.

Security requirements Requirements that a company places on its logistics service providers regarding how their product is to be handled, stored, and transported, specifically relating to the security protocols that the shipper requires them to implement.

Shipper Company that owns the product being shipped. Typically, this is the manufacturer that receives orders from a customer base that they fulfill through a distribution chain.

Shipping area Area of a facility where product is introduced into a trailer/container.

Site security manager Designated member of the staff tasked with developing and enforcing all security policies and procedures.

Staging Process of placing product in an area (e.g., loading docks) in order to expedite loading or movement. Term is often used with trailers loaded prior to the driver's arrival and then left in a parking area waiting for pickup.

Stopping procedures Part of an in-transit security plan; stopping procedures outlining authorized stopping points en route, as well as all actions that should be taken by the driver while stopped with product aboard.

Supply chain security Use of security countermeasures throughout an organization's supply chain to include all facilities and conveyances (including third-party conveyances) designed to ensure the safety and integrity of product through customer delivery.

Team drivers Having two drivers transport a load in lieu of a single, or solo, driver. Theoretically, this is designed to provide virtual nonstop transport from origin to destination and ensure that one of the team will be with the truck at all times. The last point is key, which is why consideration should be given to prohibiting the use of husband–wife, father–son, or other relative team drivers.

Transportation providers Third-party provider that manages or provides the transportation of products for a shipper.

Unmanned facility Term used when a facility is left unattended by associates for any period of time.

FREIGHTWATCH INTERNATIONAL 2011 U.S. CARGO THEFT REPORT

January 19, 2012

Introduction

FreightWatch International actively tracks and records cargo theft activity around the globe, categorizing stolen loads under 11 different commodity types, and tracking by date, location, modus operandi (MO), and specific product. This report summarizes U.S. theft data collected in 2011 and analyzes trends derived from database content, law enforcement information, and industry personnel. It also draws on observations by personnel in the field.

Summary

FreightWatch recorded 974 cargo theft incidents throughout the United States in 2011—an 8.3% increase over 2010. This represents the highest number of theft incidents per year on record.

With an average of 81.2 cargo theft incidents per month, the U.S. supply chain sustained large-scale theft incidents (e.g., full-truckload/container thefts, warehouse burglaries, driver thefts) at a rate of 2.67 incidents per day.

Of the 974 cargo thefts recorded, 853 (87.5%) were full-truckload or container thefts and 34 (3.4%) were facility burglaries. The year 2011 also saw a rash of pickups by deception (fictitious), with 38 recorded for the year. The 38 thefts accounted for 4% of all incidents. Violence remained an insignificant statistical proportion of cargo theft incidents in the United States, accounting for only 1% of the total incidents recorded for the year.

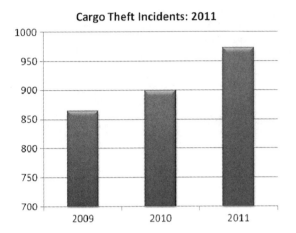

Major Trends

One of the most noticeable trends in 2011 was the continued decline in cargo theft incidents targeting the electronics sector. In 2006, this sector comprised 38% of all recorded supply chain theft incidents in the United States, while in 2011 it recorded just 17%. The most commonly targeted product type for the second year in a row was food/drinks at 22%, followed by electronics at 17% and building/industrial products at 14%.

Deceptive pickups continued to rise in 2011, increasing to 29 on the year, up from 24 in 2010. From April 20 through May 5, eight deceptive pickups occurred across Indiana, Ohio, Kentucky, and New York, involving goods across four different product types. This is just one example of organized criminal gangs' effective use of ambiguity in the supply chain process to obtain product—and in this case have the victims literally hand over the cargo to them.

While the rate of cargo theft has continued to climb annually, the average value per incident dropped substantially in 2011, decreasing by 31% for the year. While numerous factors contribute to the decline in the average loss value, the largest factors include a lack of multiple $1 million-plus incidents, a dramatic decrease in the average value of pharmaceutical thefts, and an increase in theft of lower-valued product types, specifically from the food/drinks industry.

By State

The rate of incidents grew in the top six states for cargo theft in 2011. California, Florida, New Jersey, Texas, Georgia, and Illinois

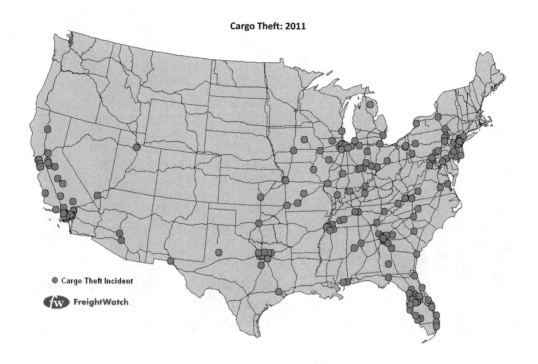

Cargo Theft: 2011

all saw increases in the total recorded number of incidents for the year. The rate of theft for these six states combined grew by 13.7% in 2011.

The top six states for cargo theft in the United States accounted for 75% of all recorded incidents. California, which recorded 254 cargo thefts in 2011, claimed 26% of the nation's cargo theft incidents.

Illinois, which saw an increase from 33 theft incidents in 2010 to 53 incidents in 2011, overtook Tennessee as the sixth most active state for cargo theft in the country.

State	2010	2011
California	229	254
Florida	117	135
New Jersey	121	124
Texas	84	104
Georgia	58	60
Illinois	33	53

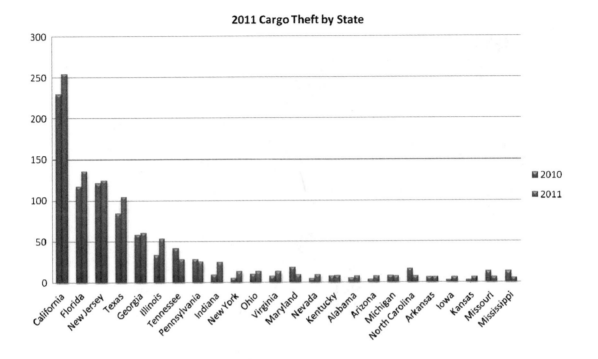

2011 Cargo Theft by State

By Value

The average value per incident has continued to decline since 2009, when it peaked at $591,000 per cargo theft.

The average value per incident in 2011 was $319,000, down 31% from the average 2010 value of $468,500.

The year 2011 also marked the first year on record that the pharmaceutical industry did not have the highest value per theft incident. Instead, the electronics industry averaged just under $1 million per theft for the year, while pharmaceuticals averaged only $585,000.

In fact, as mentioned before, the substantial decline in the total value of pharmaceuticals stolen for the year is a significant contributing factor to the overall decrease in the loss value per incident. In previous years, the average loss per pharmaceutical theft averaged between $3.5 and $4 million, but thefts in 2011 come in at just over a quarter of those figures.

Warehouse and facility burglaries/robberies in 2011 netted criminal gangs an average of $2.92 million per incident. The largest facility robbery occurred in Fremont, California, where armed thieves made off with $37 million in microchips. The largest facility

Product Type	2010	2011
Alcohol	$243,000	$203,000
Auto/Parts	$99,000	$98,000
Building/Industrial	$172,000	$195,000
Clothing/Shoes	$286,000	$190,000
Consumer Care Products	$280,000	$286,000
Electronics	$512,000	$998,000
Food/Drinks	$125,000	$109,000
Home/Garden	$104,000	$88,000
Miscellaneous	$135,000	$99,000
Pharmaceuticals	$3,780,000	$585,000
Tobacco	$1,263,000	$400,000

Number of Incidents vs. Average Value

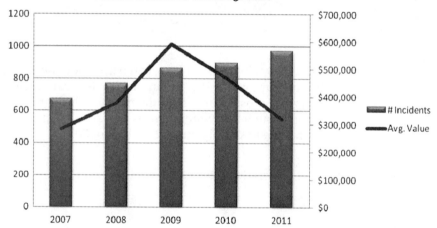

burglary took place in Orlando, Florida, on January 16, when criminals stole an estimated $10 million in mobile phones.

By Date

August and October recorded the highest number of theft incidents in 2011, with 104 and 98 incidents, respectively. This remains true to historical cargo theft trends, with spikes in activity common in mid- to late summer and the month of October. Over the past 6 years, October has consistently been the month with the highest or second highest rate of theft year after year.

Cargo Theft by Month

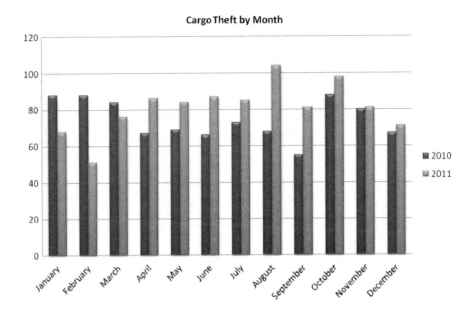

As shown in the chart here, cargo theft rates on average were in decline throughout 2010 (even though the year finished with 899 thefts, the most on record at the time), with the rate of theft flat-lining through the winter months into 2011. Thefts then began to rise relatively sharply into Q2 and Q3 of 2011.

Cargo Theft: 2010 - 2011

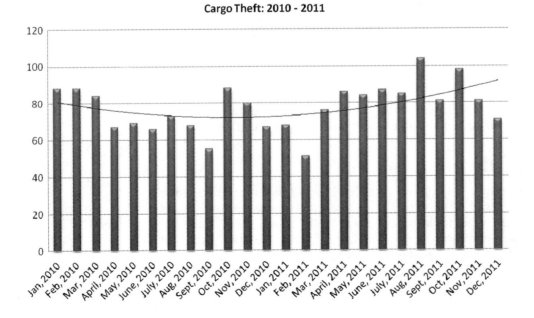

Over the 2011 holiday periods, cargo thefts increased from 2.67 thefts per day to 4.3 thefts per day—a 61% increase. As for previous reports, FreightWatch analyzed the theft rate for each of the major U.S. holidays and their associated weekends (days off). Holidays assessed were:

- New Year's Day
- Memorial Day
- Fourth of July
- Labor Day
- Thanksgiving
- Christmas
- New Year's Eve

Labor Day accounted for 13 theft incidents, Thanksgiving had 12, and the Fourth of July recorded 11, which is comparable to theft rates over these same holidays in previous years.

Day	# Thefts
Sunday	163
Monday	146
Tuesday	103
Wednesday	124
Thursday	107
Friday	154
Saturday	177

As cargo continues to be stolen while parked (or otherwise stationary) and unattended, the predominant trend of weekend cargo theft continues. As illustrated in the chart here, cargo theft in the United States is largely centered around weekend periods, with thefts discovered on Sunday evenings and Monday mornings.

The same is true for facility burglaries, as criminals generally take advantage of weekends to have additional time to move the stolen goods before the theft is discovered. In 2011, 24 of the 35 (69%) facility burglaries recorded occurred over a weekend.

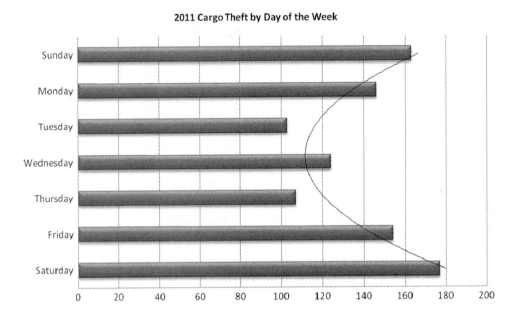

2011 Cargo Theft by Day of the Week

By Product Type

Food and beverages were the most sought-after product type for the second year in a row in 2011, accounting for 23%, or 221 of the 974 recorded incidents. Electronics was second at 17%, while building/industrial was third at 14%.

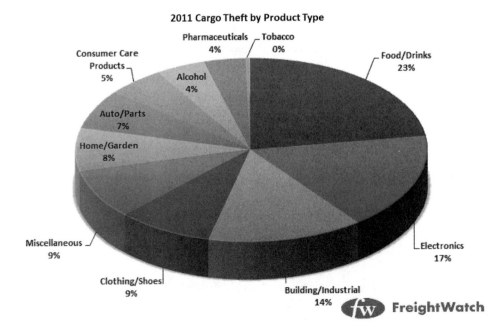

2011 Cargo Theft by Product Type

It should be noted that recorded thefts targeting building/industrial products increased from 86 in 2010 to 137 in 2011, a 59% jump. Forty-three of the 137 (31%) thefts recorded in this product type for 2011 occurred in the state of Texas, specifically in the Dallas/Fort Worth metroplex.

Electronics

As mentioned previously, the rate of theft in the electronics industry has declined as a total percentage of general cargo theft, coming in at 17% in 2011, the lowest rate on record. At the same time, however, the average loss per incident in the electronics sector surged in 2011, increasing 95% from $512,000 per incident in 2010 to $998,000 per incident in 2011.

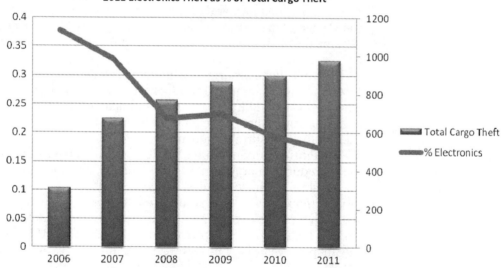

2011 Electronics Theft as % of Total Cargo Theft

Of the 166 recorded cargo thefts for the electronics sector in 2011, 63 occurred in the state of California, 22 in Florida, 17 in New Jersey, and 12 in Georgia.

The most targeted items in the electronics sector were televisions, consumer electronics, and cellular telephones.

Pharmaceuticals

One of the most notable trends for 2011 was not only the decrease in the overall number of cargo theft incidents involving pharmaceuticals (49 in 2010 vs 36 in 2011), but also the dramatic decrease in the average value per incident within the sector ($3.78 million in 2010 vs $585,000 in 2011). With only two thefts valued at more than $1 million, 2011 recorded the lowest overall value of pharmaceutical thefts in the FreightWatch database dating back to 2006.

Of the 35 pharmaceutical theft incidents, Indiana and Florida tied for the most, with six each; Tennessee recorded five, while Pennsylvania, Michigan, California, and New York all had two thefts each.

Theft of trailer accounted for 28 of the theft incidents, with two deceptive pickups and two facility burglaries.

Foods/Drinks

The food/drinks industry has surged among cargo theft gangs as the most predominantly targeted and stolen product type in the United States. Accounting for just 13% in 2007, food/drinks became the most stolen product type in 2010, at 21%, and grew to 23% in 2011.

Fifty-two thefts occurred in the state of Florida (accounting for 24% of all incidents in the product type), 47 in California, 27 in New Jersey, and 20 in Texas. These four states (also the top four states for cargo theft in general) accounted for 66% of all cargo theft in the food/drinks industry.

The most commonly stolen products in this category included meat products, energy drinks, cheese, candy, and sodas, with an average loss per incident of $110,000.

The map shown here is an interactive map showing cargo theft divided into four main categories: general cargo, electronics, food/drinks, and pharmaceuticals. Click the URL below the map to view in your browser and interact with the data points.

(To view the interactive map, go to http://batchgeo.com/ map/c6c1b4bd5b40f95c26c4b02fb11b8b14)

By Theft Type and Location

Cargo thieves in the United States continue to predominantly target loaded trailers and containers that are stationary and left unattended. Approximately 85% of all recorded thefts fell into this category in 2011.

Deceptive pickups increased dramatically in 2011. In the spring of 2011 more than eight deceptive pickups were recorded in just over a week. While the thefts were related by MO, the locations were spread out across the Midwest and Eastern seaboard, with widely varying types of products targeted.

2011 Cargo Theft by Type

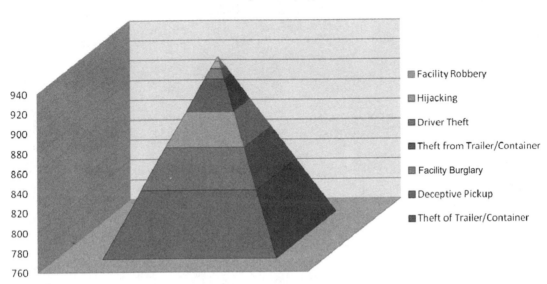

In 2011, 63% of all cargo theft incidents with a known location occurred in unsecured parking areas. The major locations of this type of theft were truck stops (33%), public parking (18%), drop lots (11.5%), and facility lots (8.6%).

Theft from secured lots decreased from 23% of known locations in 2010 to 15% of known locations in 2011.

*There is no general consensus within the industry on the definition of "secured lot," and this designation is assigned when a theft report indicates that the location was a secured parking area.

Contact
Dan Burges
Senior Director, Intelligence
512.532.0159
dan.burges@freightwatchintl.com

FREIGHTWATCH INTERNATIONAL GLOBAL THREAT ASSESSMENT

March 12, 2012

Global Cargo Theft Risk

Global cargo theft risks as shown on the map vary greatly from country to country. Even within individual countries, risks can vary from region to region. On a country-by-country basis, cargo theft threats, as other criminal activity, typically are rooted in social, economic, and cultural conditions. The prevention of cargo theft on a global scale requires intimate knowledge of incident trends on a regional basis, as security programs and mitigation techniques do not always transfer successfully from region to region.

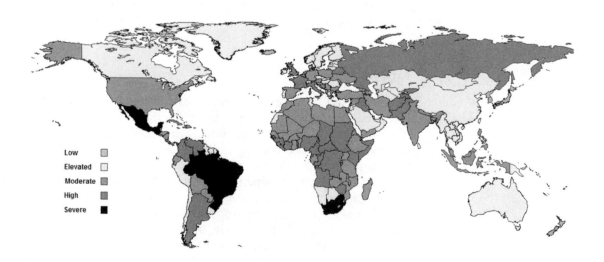

Organizations must diligently gather intelligence and adapt their anti-theft programs to address local threats. The purpose of this report is to outline the risk of cargo theft on a global level, highlighting significant countries in the global supply chain, to assist industry decision makers in determining their supply chain security needs.

According to data collected by FreightWatch International, Mexico, Brazil, South Africa, the United States, Russia, India, and the United Kingdom are the countries most at risk for cargo theft globally.

About FreightWatch

FreightWatch is the world leader in logistics security services, offering tracking and monitoring solutions that provide organizations with cargo security, transparency, and supply chain integrity from origin to destination. Using real-time visibility technology and layered solutions, organizations can actively monitor their cargo anywhere in the global supply chain, to mitigate the risks associated with theft, spoilage, counterfeiting, and more. With operations across the globe, FreightWatch is uniquely positioned to deliver regionally and globally across diverse supply chains.

The FreightWatch intelligence division collects, analyzes, and reports on cargo theft and supply chain risk across the globe, providing readers, members, and clients with up-to-date, actionable intelligence crucial for making informed supply chain security decisions.

To register for the intelligence center and receive alerts, bulletins and reports, visit FreightWatch at www.freightwatchintl.com.

North America

Cargo theft in North America varies substantially among the three countries. While cargo theft in the United States is predominantly nonconfrontational, with less than 2% of all recorded incidents involving violence, cargo theft in Mexico is almost exclusively violent, with armed gunmen roaming the country, stealing high-value loads seemingly at will.

The differences do not stop there. Cargo theft in Canada is centered in the country's metropolitan areas, with minimal theft occurring in its rural countryside, but Mexico sees thefts occurring throughout the country, with rural locations, particularly

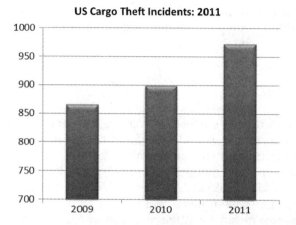

US Cargo Theft Incidents: 2011

those involving traffic bottlenecks, at the same level of risk as large metropolitan areas.

The United States experienced an 8% increase in cargo theft activity in 2011 over the previous year, reaching a record volume. Mexico saw a comparable rise in the rate of cargo theft—up 13% over 2010—although the country continues to face numerous other challenges to its supply chains, including cartel-related violence, natural disasters, and smuggling operations.

Theft data in Canada continued to be sparse in 2011, given the lack of a central recording or information delivery system. Anecdotal data, however, indicate that theft rates in the known high-risk areas of the Greater Toronto Area, Montreal, Vancouver, and Edmonton continued at high rates, requiring shippers to apply additional security measures and protocols to ensure that cargo reaches its destination safely.

United States

FreightWatch recorded 974 cargo theft incidents throughout the United States in 2011—an 8.3% increase over 2010. This represents the highest number of theft incidents per year on record. With an average of 81.2 cargo theft incidents per month, the U.S. supply chain sustained large-scale theft incidents (e.g., full-truckload/container thefts, warehouse burglaries, driver thefts) at a rate of 2.67 incidents per day.

Of the 974 cargo thefts recorded, 853 (87.5%) were full-truckload or container thefts and 34 (3.4%) were facility burglaries. The year 2011 also saw a rash of pickups by deception (fictitious), with 38 recorded for the year. The 38 thefts accounted for 4% of all incidents. Violence remained an insignificant statistical portion of cargo theft incidents in the United States, accounting for only 1% of the total incidents recorded for the year.

Major Trends

One of the most noticeable trends in 2011 was the continued decline in cargo theft incidents targeting the electronics sector. In 2006, this sector comprised 38% of all recorded supply chain theft incidents in the United States, while in 2011 it recorded just 17%. The most commonly targeted product type for the second year in a row was food/drinks at 22%, followed by electronics at 17% and building/industrial products at 14%.

Deceptive pickups continued to rise in 2011, increasing to 38 on the year, up from 29 in 2010. From April 20 through May 5, eight deceptive pickups occurred across Indiana, Ohio, Kentucky, and New York, involving goods across four different product types. This is just one example of organized criminal gangs' effective use of ambiguity in the supply chain process to obtain product—and in this case have the victims literally hand over the cargo to them.

While the rate of cargo theft has continued to climb annually, the average value per incident dropped substantially in 2011, decreasing by 31% for the year. Although numerous factors contribute to the decline in the average loss value, the largest factors include a lack of multiple $1 million-plus incidents, a dramatic decrease in the average value of pharmaceutical thefts and an increase in theft of lower valued product types, specifically from the food/drinks industry.

The rate of incidents grew in the top six states for cargo theft in 2011. California, Florida, New Jersey, Texas, Georgia, and Illinois all saw increases in the total recorded number of incidents for the year. The rate of theft for these six states combined grew by 13.7% in 2011.

The top six states for cargo theft in the United States accounted for 75% of all recorded incidents. California, which recorded 254 cargo thefts in 2011, claimed 26% of the nation's cargo theft incidents.

Illinois, which saw an increase from 33 theft incidents in 2010 to 53 incidents in 2011, overtook Tennessee as the sixth most active state for cargo theft in the country.

The average value per incident in 2011 was $319,000, down 31% from the average 2010 value of $468,500.

The year 2011 also marked the first year on record that the pharmaceutical industry did not have the highest value per theft incident. Instead, the electronics industry averaged just under $1 million per theft for the year, while pharmaceuticals averaged only $585,000.

The substantial decline in the total value of pharmaceuticals stolen for the year is a significant contributing factor to the overall decrease in the loss value per incident. In previous years, the loss per pharmaceutical theft averaged between $3.5 and $4 million, but thefts in 2011 come in at just over a quarter of those figures.

Warehouse and facility burglaries/robberies in 2011 netted criminal gangs an average of $2.92 million per incident. The largest facility robbery occurred in Fremont, California, where armed thieves made off with $37 million in microchips. The largest facility burglary took place in Orlando, Florida, on January 16, 2011, when criminals stole an estimated $10 million in mobile phones.

As cargo continues to be stolen while parked (or otherwise stationary) and unattended, the predominant trend of weekend cargo theft continues. As illustrated in the following chart, cargo theft in the United States is largely centered around weekend periods, with thefts discovered on Sunday evenings and Monday mornings.

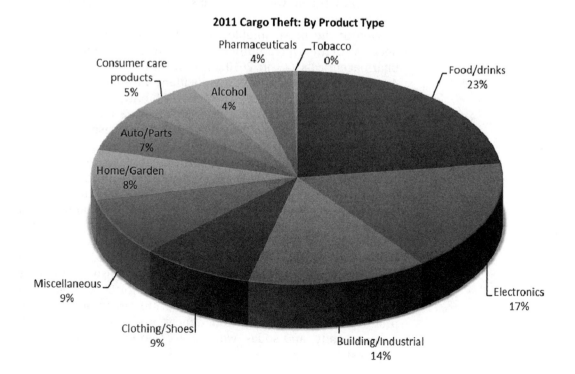

2011 Cargo Theft: By Product Type

- Pharmaceuticals 4%
- Tobacco 0%
- Consumer care products 5%
- Alcohol 4%
- Food/drinks 23%
- Auto/Parts 7%
- Home/Garden 8%
- Miscellaneous 9%
- Clothing/Shoes 9%
- Building/Industrial 14%
- Electronics 17%

The same is true for facility burglaries, as criminals generally take advantage of weekends to have additional time to move the stolen goods before the theft is discovered. In 2011, 24 of the 35 (69%) facility burglaries recorded occurred over a weekend.

Food and drinks were the most sought-after product type for the second year in a row in 2011, accounting for 23%, or 221, of the 974 recorded incidents. Electronics was second at 17%, while building/industrial was third at 14%.

It should be noted that recorded thefts targeting building/industrial products increased from 86 in 2010 to 137 in 2011, a 59% jump. Forty-three of the 137 (31%) thefts recorded in this product type for 2011 occurred in the state of Texas, specifically in the Dallas/Fort Worth metroplex.

As mentioned previously, the rate of theft in the electronics industry has declined as a total percentage of general cargo theft, coming in at 17% in 2011, the lowest rate on record. At the same time, however, the average loss per incident in the electronics sector surged in 2011, increasing 95% from $512,000 per incident in 2010 to $998,000 per incident in 2011.

Of the 166 recorded cargo thefts for the electronics sector in 2011, 63 occurred in the state of California, 22 in Florida, 17 in New Jersey, and 12 in Georgia. The most targeted items in the electronics sector were televisions, consumer electronics, and cellular telephones.

One of the most notable trends for 2011 was not only the decrease in the overall number of cargo theft incidents involving pharmaceuticals (49 in 2010 vs 36 in 2011), but the dramatic decrease in the average value per incident within the sector ($3.78 million in 2010 vs. $585,000 in 2011). With only two thefts valued at more than $1 million, 2011 recorded the lowest overall value of pharmaceutical thefts in the FreightWatch database dating back to 2006.

The food/drinks industry has surged among cargo theft gangs as the most predominantly targeted and stolen product type in the United States. Accounting for just 13% in 2007, food/drinks became the most stolen product type in 2010, at 21%, and grew to 23% in 2011.

Fifty-two thefts occurred in the state of Florida (accounting for 24% of all incidents in the product type), 47 in California, 27 in New Jersey, and 20 in Texas. These four states (also the top four states for cargo theft in general) accounted for 66% of all cargo theft in the food/drinks industry. The most commonly stolen products in this category included meat products, energy drinks, cheese, candy, and sodas, with an average loss per incident of $110,000.

Theft Type and Location

Cargo thieves in the United States continue to predominantly target loaded trailers and containers that are stationary and left unattended. Approximately 85% of all recorded thefts fell into this category in 2011.

Deceptive pickups increased dramatically in 2011. In spring of 2011 more than eight deceptive pickups were recorded in just over a week. While the thefts were related by modus operandi (MO), the locations were spread out across the Midwest and Eastern seaboard, with widely varying types of products targeted.

In 2011, 63% of all cargo theft incidents with a known location occurred in unsecured parking areas. The major locations of this type of theft were truck stops (33%), public parking (18%), drop lots (11.5%), and facility lots (8.6%). Theft from secured lots decreased from 23% of known locations in 2010 to 15% of known locations in 2011.

Canada

Cargo theft in Canada is largely centered in the major cities and hubs of the supply chain industry, most notably the Greater Toronto Area, Montreal, Edmonton, and Vancouver. On a national level, cargo theft reporting comes almost exclusively from the regional police agencies covering the Toronto area. They record theft rates that rival Los Angeles, Dallas/Fort Worth, and the South Florida area of the United States.

The more rural areas of Canada report virtually no cargo theft activity. This is not to say that all shipments are arriving untouched, but rather that reporting in Canada is extremely sparse, precluding a consistent data stream from which to conduct analysis.

In areas of high cargo theft activity, product types targeted by cargo theft gangs in Canada mirror those of the United States. Food/drinks and building/industrial types topped the list of targets in Canada in 2011, although the country experienced a significant number of thefts in the electronics category as well. Cargo theft in the pharmaceutical industry has been increasing steadily since 2009 in Canada, with more incidents involving violence in this sector than any other.

The Greater Toronto Area, including Brampton and Mississauga, is known for having the highest rates of cargo theft in Canada, rivaling the major supply chain crime areas of the United States, including Los Angeles, Dallas/Fort Worth, and Miami. In 2011, Mississauga accounted for the majority of reported cargo theft incidents in the province of Ontario. Theft in Brampton was split evenly among auto/parts, building/industrial, clothing/shoes, electronics, and food/drinks product types.

Also in the Greater Toronto Area, Brampton faces a high risk of cargo theft. In general, trailer thefts in this area are divided evenly between thefts from what are listed as secured lots and thefts from unsecured lots, such as public parking and truck stops. A large number of cargo theft gangs operate in Brampton and hit the city on a weekly basis, causing this area of the Greater Toronto Area to have the highest risk of cargo theft anywhere in Canada.

Montreal, however, is known to Canadian law enforcement and industry personnel as having cargo theft activity comparable to the Greater Toronto Area, although theft data out of the area are very limited. In January 2011, a container of pharmaceuticals destined for Australia was hijacked from the Garfield Transport Yard in Montreal. Montreal also saw full-truckload thefts from secured yards in the pharmaceutical and consumer care product types. This occurs most often as cargo is in transit to and from the port.

Modi Operandi

Organized crime: Cargo theft gangs will travel city to city to follow important loads and even hire licensed commercial drivers to transport lucrative cargo from one end of the country to the other if a buyer can be lined up in advance.

Truck stops: Cargo thefts that occur at truck stops are often carried out by opportunistic criminals. Drivers who leave their cargo unattended and unsecured at these locations often fall victim to cargo criminals.

Warehouse burglary: Criminals target high-value products stored in warehouses. Cargo theft gangs often conspire with employees at the facility or get one of their own gang members hired at the targeted warehouse in order to obtain necessary information on alarms, cameras, and other security measures in place.

Case Studies

In May 2011, approximately five to six suspects forcibly entered a logistics facility in Varennes, Quebec. The employees were locked in a shipping container while the suspects stole almost 4000 metric tons of nickel-molybdenum "nickel-moly" cakes in large sacks. The incident loss was estimated at $1 million.

In July 2011, an unknown number of suspects entered a secured drop lot in New Brunswick and stole a full truckload of power tools and other building products valued at $1.5 million. Police, suspecting the perpetrators were part of an organized cargo theft gang that had been operating in the area for some months, urged industry professionals to take increased security precautions to avoid being victimized by the group.

Mexico

Double-digit increases in the annual rate of cargo theft over the past half dozen years, coupled with the extreme nature of the theft incidents themselves, make cargo theft one of the most serious threats to the supply chain industry in Mexico. Today, more than 10,000 hijackings occur each year on roads and highways across the country, with losses reaching an estimated $9 billion USD.

Steady cargo theft increases of roughly 20 to 40% per year from 2006 to 2010 created serious challenges for companies operating in Mexico, jeopardizing the security of drivers, and increasing transportation and security costs. Despite the annual growth trends through 2010, FreightWatch data for 2011 indicate that total cargo thefts rose *only* 13% for the year.

The top areas for cargo theft in 2011 were the State of Mexico, the Federal District, and the states of Jalisco, Puebla, Veracruz, and Nuevo Leon. The Federal District and the State of Mexico together experienced a 9% decrease in cargo theft activity, while Jalisco saw an 11% decrease. Theft rates increased in all the other statewide hot spots for cargo crime: Puebla's rate soared by 118%, Veracruz's jumped by 38%, while the rate in Nuevo Leon increased by 27%.

With the exception of Puebla and the Federal District, where the total loss value fell by 90 and 63%, respectively,

FreightWatch

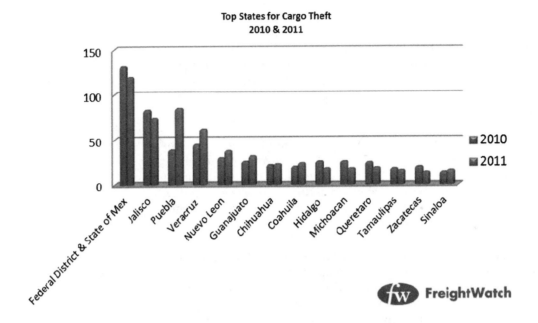

cargo theft losses increased in all the major hot spots. Losses skyrocketed by 569% in Nuevo Leon, jumped by 54% in Veracruz, and rose by 28 and 12%, respectively, in the State of Mexico and Jalisco.

Within the top states for cargo theft, Mexico City and the cities of Guadalajara, Puebla, Monterrey, and Veracruz continued to experience the highest rates of theft in the nation. Since 2006, Mexico City has suffered the highest cargo theft rates in the country. In 2011, almost 50% of thefts recorded in Mexico City occurred in the boroughs of Iztapalapa, at 30%, and Gustavo A. Madero, with 18%. Moreover, the four highway routes reporting the highest number of incidents in 2011 were Mexico–Queretaro, Mexico–Puebla, Guadalajara–Colima, and Puebla–Orizaba.

The food/drinks industry was most targeted by cargo thieves for the second year in a row, claiming 21% of all 2011 theft incidents. Likewise, building/industrial, with 27%, and electronics, with 17%, remained in second and third place. The products most stolen in the three top categories were sugar, meat, milk, grains, steel, copper, cellular phones, televisions, and household appliances.

Overall, the average loss value per theft incident increased by 23% during the reporting period, from $154,000 USD in 2010 to

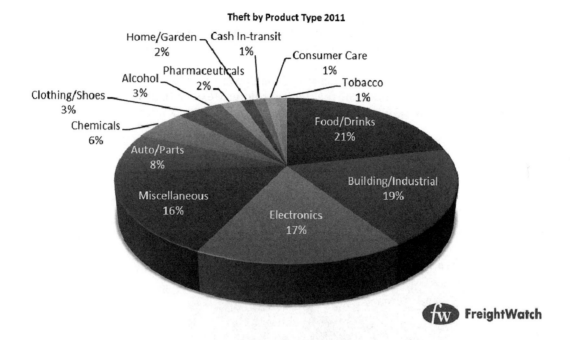

Theft by Product Type 2011

$189,510 USD in 2011. The product types that experienced the largest increases in monetary loss were miscellaneous, which grew by 848%, electronics at 137%, and food/drinks at 97%.

Showing moderate increases in loss value in 2011 were alcohol at 38% growth, building/industrial at 29%, tobacco at 16%, and clothing/shoes at 14%. Losses suffered by the pharmaceutical industry grew by only 4% last year.

Certain product types, however, showed significant decreases in losses in 2011 compared with a year earlier. Home/garden dropped by 98%, cash in transit by 57%, and auto/parts by 46%. Consumer care and chemicals also experienced a decrease in the amount of losses, at 15 and 7%, respectively.

As in previous years, the most common MO employed by cargo thieves in 2011 was interception of the truck followed by the kidnapping of the driver. Although hijackers are always armed, they use the weapons mainly to intimidate drivers. In most hijackings in 2011, however, thieves beat drivers with their fists, but not to the point of causing serious injuries. The big exception, however, involved armored vans transporting cash (cash in-transit thefts) accompanied by security guards. In these cases, the guards often confronted the thieves, resulting in death by gunfire of either the guards or the gang members. The number of cash in-transit thefts nearly tripled year on year, rising from 4 in 2010 to 11 in 2011. The loss value of these thefts, however, dropped by 57%, from $227,360 USD in 2010 to $98,523 USD in 2011.

In 2011, 84% of loads were targeted while in transit. Trucks parked by the roadside along Mexican highways were targeted 6% of the time, while cargo thefts at truck stops comprise 5% of the 2011 total.

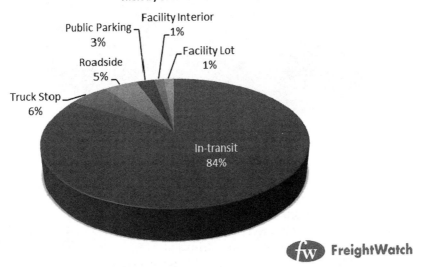

Theft by Location 2011

Facility Interior 1%
Public Parking 3%
Facility Lot 1%
Roadside 5%
Truck Stop 6%
In-transit 84%

FreightWatch

Major Trends in 2011

According to Mexico's National Chamber of Freight and Auto Transport, cargo theft gangs are increasingly targeting loads at the request of clients. These "clients" often include the original, legitimate purchaser of the goods, who makes a deal with the thieves to buy the stolen load at a price lower than he would have paid the company that sold the goods. This type of theft requires planning, as thieves must follow the targeted loads from their point of origin. Most of the time, thieves use GPS jammers or disconnect tracking devices and take the stolen loads to their warehouses before delivery.

Another notable trend for 2011 was the sharp increase in rail thefts over 2010. Containers carrying metals (especially scrap metal), textiles, grains, and electronics were the most targeted in 2011. The preferred MO of thieves targeting rail cars is to jump onto the container in areas where trains are required to travel slowly. The thieves then toss products from the load to the side of the tracks, where other members of the gang load the goods into vans or trucks. The states of Guanajuato, Nuevo Leon, Michoacán, San Luis Potosi, and Sinaloa were the most affected by rail theft.

Finally, Mexico's state-owned petroleum company Petroleos Mexicanos (Pemex) estimates losses resulting from stolen natural gas condensate totaled $300 million USD from 2006 through 2011. Criminal organizations, both cargo theft gangs and drug cartels, have been hijacking tank trucks carrying natural gas condensate and selling it to so-called "ghost" companies, unregistered companies that do not legally exist.

For additional or more specific information about cargo theft in Mexico, please refer to FreightWatch's Mexico annual cargo theft report.

Central and South America

Cargo theft has intensified in most South American countries since 2009, especially in large industrial cities such as Sao Paulo, Rio de Janeiro, Buenos Aires, Bogota, and Caracas. In 2011, Argentina and Brazil were the two top countries for cargo theft on the continent.

Because cargo theft in South America always involves violence or the threat of violence, and the attacks are carried out by well-armed thieves, the majority of incidents are classified as hijackings. Several of the hijackings reported in Peru, Brazil, and Venezuela in 2011 resulted in the death of the drivers and/or the security escorts hired to protect the load. Also, most of the confrontations between police and cargo thieves began with car chases and ended in shootouts that resulted in the injury or death of officers or criminals.

One of the most popular trends among South American cargo thieves in 2011 was the use of the fake police MO. This method was employed principally by large, organized gangs that tend to plan out their hijackings and engage in preattack information gathering—in these cases, collecting information to determine the best locations along highways to place their fake security checkpoints.

Domestic and multinational companies transporting high-value loads (mostly electronics, metals, or pharmaceuticals) are increasingly utilizing state-of-the-art security technology in order to protect their loads and ensure the security of their drivers. For most loads valued in the million-dollar range and above, companies are adding another layer of protection: armed security escorts. This is especially the case in Brazil.

Central America, officially part of the North American continent but often associated more with South America, is the region that pays the least attention to cargo crime. This historically has made it difficult to determine the region's red zones for cargo theft. In 2011, however, authorities and the media in Guatemala provided enough data to make a determination on some of the riskiest highways and states for cargo theft in this country.

Brazil

Although cargo theft is a serious concern in several Brazilian states, nowhere is the situation worse than in Sao Paulo state, the country's primary industrial and economic engine. The Cargo Transporters Union of Sao Paulo State (SETCESP) estimates that more than half of all cargo crime in Brazil takes place in that state.

From January 1 to December 31, 2011, SETCESP recorded 6958 cargo theft incidents in Sao Paulo state alone—a slight 4.6% decrease over the 7294 thefts recorded in 2010. On average, 579 thefts occurred per month in 2011, compared with an average of 607 thefts per month in 2010.

In Brazil, the southeast region presents the highest risk of cargo theft. In 2011, the three states reporting the highest rate of cargo theft were Sao Paulo, Rio de Janeiro, and Minas Gerais. Other states that experienced high cargo theft activities were Bahia, Espirito Santo, Parana, Santa Catarina, and Rio Grande do Sul.

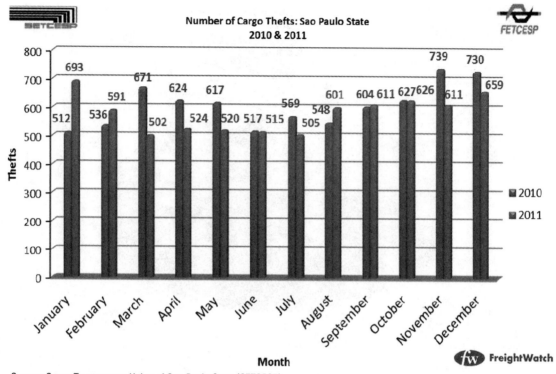

Number of Cargo Thefts: Sao Paulo State
2010 & 2011

Source: Cargo Transporters Union of Sao Paulo State (SETCESP).

Despite a total decrease in the number of thefts in Sao Paulo state during 2011, the amount of cargo theft losses increased by 5.7%, from R$279.7 million ($162.3 million USD) in 2010 to R$295.7 million ($171.6 million USD) in 2011. An average loss value of R$24.6 million ($14.2 million USD) per month was recorded in 2011 and R$23.3 million ($13.4 million USD) in 2010.

The most commonly targeted product type for the sixth year in a row was food/drinks at 30%, followed by electronics at 16% and less than truckloads (various products from two or more shippers) at 14%. Within the food/drinks industry, agricultural products such as grains, soybeans, and sugar were heavily targeted, especially around port areas.

By value, the electronics industry experienced the greatest losses in 2011, at R$85.3 million ($49.3 million USD).

According to SETCESP, 38% of all thefts, or 2673 incidents, were loads valued at less than R$3000 ($1735 USD); 40%, or 2785 incidents, were loads worth R$3001 to R$30,000 ($1736 to $17,356 USD); 14%, or 997 thefts, involved losses of R$30,001 to R$100,000

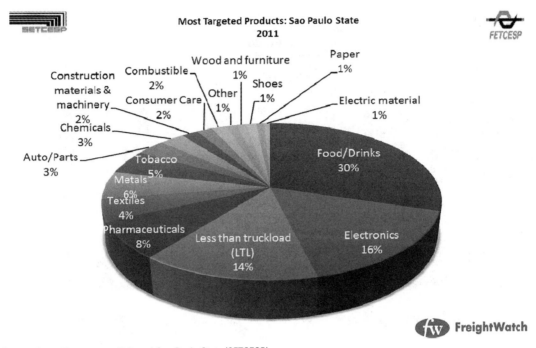

Most Targeted Products: Sao Paulo State 2011

Source: Cargo Transporters Union of Sao Paulo State (SETCESP).

($17,357 to $57,848 USD), and, finally, 7%, or 503 incidents, were loads exceeding R$100,000 ($58,284).

Brazilian cargo theft is highly concentrated in Sao Paulo state, with 52% of all incidents nationwide occurring in this one state. Within the state, 58% of all thefts occur in the city of Sao Paulo, 22% occur on the state's highways, and 12% take place in other cities in the Greater Sao Paulo area. Measuring cargo theft outside of Sao Paulo state is challenging, as law enforcement and other agencies in other states do not keep records on theft incidents.

The three highways within Sao Paulo state reporting the greatest number of thefts in 2011 were Anhanguera with 217 incidents, followed by Dutra with 185, and Regis Bittencourt with 140 thefts.

By day of the week, cargo theft activity intensified on Tuesdays and Wednesdays and started to drop heading into the weekends. The fewest thefts occurred on Sundays but then activity picked up significantly beginning on Mondays. The preferred time range for gangs to steal loads was between 10 a.m. and noon.

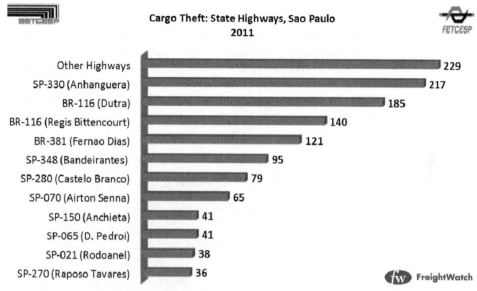

Cargo Theft: State Highways, Sao Paulo 2011

Highway	Thefts
Other Highways	229
SP-330 (Anhanguera)	217
BR-116 (Dutra)	185
BR-116 (Regis Bittencourt)	140
BR-381 (Fernao Dias)	121
SP-348 (Bandeirantes)	95
SP-280 (Castelo Branco)	79
SP-070 (Airton Senna)	65
SP-150 (Anchieta)	41
SP-065 (D. Pedroi)	41
SP-021 (Rodoanel)	38
SP-270 (Raposo Tavares)	36

Source: Cargo Transporters Union of Sao Paulo State (SETCESP).

Major Trends in 2011

Two of the most noticeable trends in 2011 was the high number of cargo theft gangs expanding their operations to other states and the high volume of containers being targeted by cargo theft gangs at Brazilian commercial sea ports.

Moreover, the fake police MO has been one of the most popular methods used by thieves since 2009 in Brazil. Fake cops set up fake police checkpoints and pull drivers over in order to steal the merchandise. The thieves regularly move the fake checkpoints to different highways when they suspect that police have spotted them. Although the thieves' main objective is to steal the load, trucks are also stolen, dismantled, and sold as parts.

Finally, cargo thieves in Brazil have been stealing loads, most often textiles and grains in 2011, from rail cars while the train is moving. Similar to cargo thieves in Mexico, the preferred MO of Brazilian thieves is to jump onto the containers in areas near train stations or small towns where trains are required to reduce speed. The thieves toss the products to the side of the tracks, where other thieves load the merchandise into their vans.

For additional or more specific information about cargo theft in Brazil, please refer to FreightWatch's Brazil annual cargo theft report.

Venezuela

Cargo crime does not receive the level of attention in Venezuela that it gets in other South American countries such as Brazil and Argentina. In Venezuela, high crime rates, corruption, and an unstable political system appear to be higher priorities. As a consequence, law enforcement and security companies rarely provide cargo crime statistics, and even then the information is outdated.

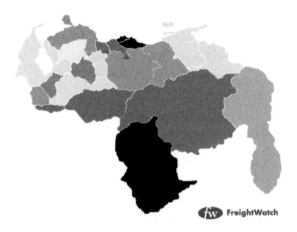

According to local media reports, locales with the highest thefts rates in 2011 were the capital city of Caracas and the Capital District and the states of Amazonas, Bolivar, and Apure. The Central Regional Highway continued to be a red zone for cargo theft, as it connects Caracas with the important cities of Maracay, La Victoria, and Valencia. Most hijackings reported by local newspapers during 2011 involved loads of grains, sugar, and milk in the food/drinks product type; computers, appliances, and cellular phones in the electronics category; and metals in the building/industrial group.

In the southern states, highways close to the borders with Brazil and Colombia were the most targeted by cargo thieves. Another supply chain risk in southern Venezuela is the cross-border, drug-related guerrilla violence between Colombia and Venezuela. Additionally, as Venezuela's borders with Brazil and Colombia are quite porous, drug traffickers and other criminals roam these regions rather freely, hijacking cars or trucks to transport drugs and committing other violent crimes.

The maritime ports that reported high numbers of cargo theft in 2011 were Puerto Cabello in Carabobo state, Puerto Ordaz in Bolivar state, and Puerto Maracaibo in Zulia state. Within these ports, metals such as aluminum and steel were the most stolen products.

Modi Operandi

Venezuela has numerous groups of well-armed thieves targeting trucks whenever an opportunity arises—and the level of violence during these hijackings is very high. Similar to Brazil, several incidents in 2011 ended in the killing of the drivers or security guards. For instance, an incident involving an armored truck carrying $1.7 million VEF ($400,000 USD) in cash occurred early September 21 in Puerto Ordaz. The drivers and escorts were at a restaurant having breakfast when they realized six armed thieves were in the parking lot trying to steal the truck. One of the escorts was killed and the other wounded during the ensuing shootout, and the thieves escaped with the truck and the cash.

As in other Latin American countries, Venezuelan cargo thieves tend to kidnap the drivers and release them later in remote locations after the loads have been secured. Confrontations between police and cargo thieves tend to be very violent, often beginning with long car chases and ending in shootouts, with injury or death on one or both sides.

The fake police MO continues to be one of the most common methods in the country, and some thieves employing this method wear genuine police uniforms provided by corrupt police officers. On June 12, 2011, a gang used this MO to successfully carry out two cargo thefts in one day on the Cantaura–El Tigre highway near the town of Mapiricure, Anzoategui state. The first truck, loaded with cigarettes, was stolen in the morning and the second truck, carrying pharmaceuticals, was stolen in the afternoon.

Case Studies

On February 9, 2011, a group of thieves hijacked a truck loaded with consumer care products, mainly deodorants, body lotions, and diapers, in the city of Barquisimeto, Lara state. The loss value was $400,000 VEF ($93,023 USD). Moreover, the truck driver was never seen again.

On October 7, 2011, five criminals intercepted an armored truck escorted by two security guards near the small town of Mucujepe, Merida state. One guard was shot and wounded during the attack, and the thieves escaped with the truck and $1.8 million VEF ($418,605 USD) in cash. Once they reached the city of El Vigia, also in Merida state, the thieves emptied the load and set the truck on fire.

Later in 2011, two trucks transporting different types of loads were hijacked by the same cargo theft gang within a 24-hour period in the municipality of La Ceiba, Trujillo state. The first truck, loaded with sandals worth $120,000 VEF ($28,000 USD), was stolen on December 21; the second, loaded with 240 boxes of whisky bottles worth $1.5 million VEF ($348,837 USD), was stolen the following morning. A police operation resulted in the recovery of the two stolen loads and the arrests of gang members responsible for the hijackings. Authorities said the gang had been targeting trucks near La Ceiba for several months.

Argentina

Cargo theft in Argentina is centered in major industrial cities with large distribution centers. According to Jose Luis Anselmi,

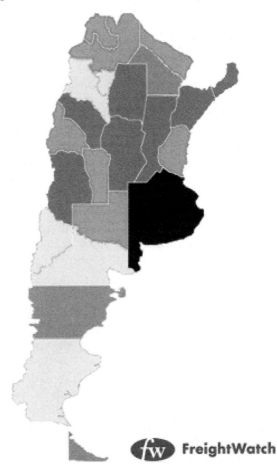

CEO of Assistcargo, an Argentina-based company specializing in cargo theft prevention systems, 70% of all cargo theft activity in Argentina takes place in the federal capital and Greater Buenos Aires. Also reporting high rates of cargo theft in Argentina in recent years are the provinces of Santa Fe, Cordoba, and Mendoza.

Additionally, says Anselmi, 90% of thefts are premeditated—meaning these are rarely crimes of opportunity—and drivers are involved with the gangs in 50 to 60% of all incidents.

Argentina's *La Nacion* newspaper estimates that approximately 4000 cargo thefts take place each year in the country; most of the crimes are never solved and merchandise rarely recovered. Recent industry reports estimate an average loss value of $50,000 per stolen load.

Because the rate of cargo theft is impacted directly by fluctuations in economic activity, local supply and demand strongly influence the rate of cargo theft in Argentina. The most targeted product types tend to be those in highest demand at any given time.

In addition to economic activity, the rate of cargo theft increases over the holidays. According to Anselmi, the risk of cargo theft also increases during election times. In October 2011,

Cargo Theft Incidents
2009 - 2011

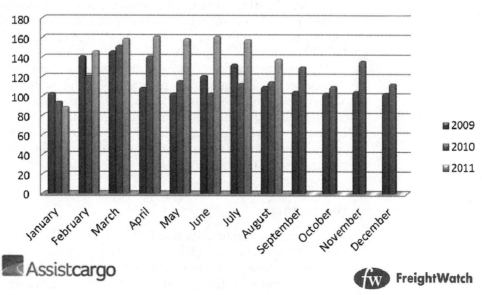

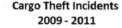

Source: Assistcargo.

cargo theft increased by 20% during the country's presidential election.

Assistcargo reports that cargo theft has been increasing since 2008 in Argentina. In 2011, an average of 146 incidents occurred per month, a 22% increase from the 2010 average of 120 incidents per month. Overall, February and March were the months with highest cargo theft activity since 2008.

Trade barriers in place on imports in Argentina—the result of government attempts to protect local industries—unwittingly led to an increase in cargo theft activity near bonded warehouses in 2011. Thieves apparently were taking advantage of the strict regulations and long inspection periods that cause some loads to sit for weeks or even months in ports and bonded warehouses.

Modi Operandi

As in most of Latin America, the most common MO in Argentina continues to be driver kidnapping. This is when thieves hold the driver captive for up to several hours while they secure the stolen load or, in cases of theft by order, distribute the load to an existing client. In most cases, the driver is released later by the side of a road or highway. According to attorney Gabriel Lezzi, a member of the Inter-Business Cargo Piracy Board, no cargo theft incident has ended in death in Argentina since 2008.

On July 6, 2011, a group of thieves hijacked an in-transit truck loaded with 30 tons of grains in the city of San Andres de Guiles. The driver was set free an hour after the theft in the nearby city of Los Polvorines.

Most gangs operating in Argentina today are sophisticated, experienced, and adept at preattack intelligence gathering. Moreover, criminals' use of GPS jammers is growing into a major problem for companies operating in Argentina, as sophisticated cargo thieves are increasingly making use of these devices. Today it is relatively easy to purchase a GPS jammer online at prices ranging from $175 to $700 USD.

Guatemala

The cities of Guatemala and Palin, in Escuintla Department, reported the highest cargo theft activity in the country in 2011. The Inter-American Highway (CA-9), the Pacific Highway (CA-2), and the Atlantic Highway (CA-9) continued to be hot spots for cargo theft last year.

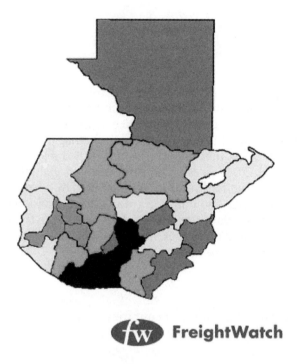

FreightWatch

Industry reports indicate a rise in cargo theft activity during the first 6 months of 2011 compared with the same period in 2010 in western Guatemala and close to El Salvador's border with Guatemala.

Cargo Theft Trends and Techniques

Thieves' most common MO in Guatemala is targeting trucks while in transit; most thieves use weapons as a way to intimidate drivers. Collusion among warehouse employees, drivers, and large organized gangs is very common in Guatemala. Additionally, some large gangs have established relationships with corrupt police, making payoffs to the officers for covering up cargo theft incidents.

In the vast majority of incidents reported in the news and police reports in 2011, stolen trailers were found empty and abandoned in rural areas or small towns. Like the year before, small gangs in Guatemala continued to show interest in stealing trucks both for their cargo and in order to negotiate the sale of truck parts on the black market.

On October 11, 2011, a truck loaded with food products was hijacked at the Port of San Jose, Escuintla Department. Although a witness reported the incident immediately after the theft, the truck was already dismantled when police found it at a facility yard known to house stolen goods. The load of food products was not found at the facility.

Case Studies

On November 11, 2011, two cargo thieves hijacked a truck loaded with paint worth $30,000 USD in the city of Escuintla. On this occasion the National Civil Police of Escuintla were able to find the truck in the municipality of Guanagazapa, Escuintla Department, arrest the suspects, and recover the load.

On May 10, 2011, an escorted truck heading to Puerto Quetzal and loaded with coffee for export was hijacked by a group of cargo thieves in Antigua. The empty rig was found abandoned in the city of Escuintla a day after the incident. Inside the trailer police found weapons and cartridges apparently belonging to the escort guard, who remains missing.

Colombia

As in most Latin American countries, cargo theft in Colombia is concentrated in the major industrial centers. Thus, in 2011 the

cities of Cali, Medellin, and Bogota reported the highest rates of cargo theft. Regions close to the borders with Ecuador and Venezuela and along the Pan-American Highway also continued to be hot spots for cargo theft in Colombia.

On November 18, 2011, police in Bogota captured five members of an organized gang specializing in cargo theft. According to official reports, the thieves were apprehended while attempting to steal a trailer (unknown load). Police confiscated powerful weapons from inside the thieves' van.

Colombian cargo theft gangs are increasingly recruiting preteens and teenagers, some as young as 12 and 13 years old. On November 10, 2011, police captured five suspects ranging in age from 14 to 16 believed to be part of a large, organized cargo theft gang that has been operating for several years in the municipality of Pitalito, Huila Department.

One of the most popular MOs used by Colombian thieves in 2011 was the fake police method. Although pretending to be police officers proved quite successful in many instances, authentic police did make some headway in 2011. On August 18, 2011, following an 18-month investigation, Bogota police dismantled a locally based cargo theft gang whose MO involved establishing fake police checkpoints, mainly along highways in Santander and Tolima departments. Some of the victims reported having been threatened with firearms, kidnapped, tortured for several hours, and later released in remote areas. This same gang also has been linked to warehouse robberies in the same departments, and police have discovered connections between the gang and employees of the warehouses that were hit. Colombian police believe this particular gang was responsible for at least 22 thefts since 2009.

The Port of Buenaventura, Colombia's main port on the Pacific Ocean, continues to be a hot spot for cargo theft. On November 28, 2011, police captured a cargo theft gang believed responsible for at least seven thefts—involving 80 tons of cargo—from trailers and containers at the port. Police recovered powerful weapons from the thieves' vehicles.

On October 27, 2011, 14 suspected members of a cargo theft gang hijacked a truck loaded with 32 tons of coffee worth $430 million COP ($220,796 USD) in the municipality of Caldas, Antioquia Department. The driver was kidnapped and released later in a rural area. A day after the incident, police located the stolen truck traveling along the Medellin–Bogota highway, recovering the load and eventually capturing 11 of the 14 suspected thieves.

Other Supply Chain Risks

Several trucker strikes on the Columbian side of the border with Ecuador in autumn 2011 generated supply chain disruptions and economic losses to the transportation industry in both countries. During the protests, Colombian drivers blocked highways leading into the country, preventing the passage of trucks from Ecuador. In some case, this led to brawls between the drivers, and several Ecuadorian drivers reported having been bitten by their Colombian counterparts. Threatened with further violence by the Colombians, the Ecuadorian drivers returned to their country, failing to deliver loads to their final destination on time. The strikes, launched to protest perceived inequalities such as less expensive diesel prices in Ecuador and lower tariffs on goods coming into Colombia from Ecuador, lasted about 50 days during the months of October and November.

Drivers protesting poor highway conditions in Colombia also caused supply chain disruptions in 2011. For instance, drivers demanding road repairs and maintenance parked trailers across main highways for several hours in the municipality of Villavicencio on October 25.

Also causing major disruptions nationwide was an unusual season of heavy rains beginning in September 2011. Severe flooding throughout the country damaged major transportation routes, especially in central and southwestern Colombia. Heavy rain on November 21 damaged a section of one of the country's most important highways, La Linea, preventing transit between the Port of Buenaventura and the capital and other cities in the interior of the country.

On December 7, 2011, authorities declared a state of emergency in the city of Bogota due to the intensity of the rain and flooding of the Bogota River. Traffic congestion and delays were major problems due to landslides. Thousands of heavy trucks circulating around the country were required to take alternative routes.

Peru

Although there are no official statistics on cargo crime in Peru, news and police reports indicate that the capital city of Lima suffered the highest rate of cargo theft in 2011. Peru's most prolific and powerful cargo theft organizations are extremely violent and often are also involved in drug trafficking.

In a June 11, 2011 incident, five armed thieves shot and seriously wounded the two drivers of a truck transporting soft drinks

near Paijan District in northern Peru—a hot spot for cargo and vehicle theft. The thieves escaped with the truck and the load, leaving the injured drivers by the roadside.

On July 2, 2011, a truck driver was killed in Los Olivos District, Lima Province, after trying to prevent a group of thieves from stealing his load of soccer balls. The driver, shot in the head, died instantly.

Thieves employed the fake police MO in a great number of hijackings reported in Peru during 2011. For instance, at 2:30 p.m. on August 18, a former police officer working as a security escort was shot to death by cargo thieves dressed as police officers in Villa El Salvador, a district on the outskirts of Lima. The former officer had confronted the gang of six thieves as they attempted to steal a load of electronics from the trailer he was escorting.

On June 26, 2011, six members of a cargo theft gang pretending to be police officers intercepted a truck loaded with two tons of activated carbon destined for Lima. The thieves transferred the 44 sacks of carbon into another trailer and abandoned the stolen trailer. The incident occurred along the Southern Pan-American Highway (kilometer 203) close to Chincha Province in the Ica Region.

On February 12, 2011, several armed cargo thieves hijacked a truck in Lima. The incident began when one of the thieves, riding a motorcycle and wearing a police uniform, instructed the driver to pull over and step out of his vehicle to provide documents. According to the driver, once he left his truck, two other armed thieves appeared and the three held the driver captive for about 3 hours. Authorities later located the truck in the district of San Juan de Lurigancho, apparently having been driven there by a fourth thief.

Case Studies

On November 21, 2011, three armed thieves hijacked a truck along the Fernando Belaunde Terry highway (kilometer 392) near the city of Tarapoto, San Martin Province. The criminals intercepted the truck, kidnapped the driver, and held him for several hours. The following morning police found the abandoned truck on the roadside in Soritor District.

On December 3, 2011, a well-organized cargo theft gang stole 30 tons of gold and silver from two trailers. The two drivers disappeared and the load was never recovered. No further details on the theft have been made available.

On February 25, 2011, a truck carrying laptop computers worth $1 million USD was hijacked in the district of Los Olivos, Lima Province. The thieves, who held the two drivers captive for several hours, escaped with the entire load of laptops. No tracking device or security escort had been utilized.

Other Supply Chain Risks

Violent protests by farmers against the $4.8 billion Conga Mining Project in Peru's Cajamarca Region caused major supply chain disruptions in December 2011. Demanding the government cancel the project to avoid potential environmental impacts, such as water shortages and soil/water contamination, farmers established roadblocks and set fires on streets, causing several businesses to close temporarily and some carriers to suspend operations for a time. The protests reportedly led to food shortages in the region. After the protests intensified on December 4, Peruvian President Ollanta Humala declared a state of emergency in Celendin, Cajamarca, Hualgayoc, and Contumaza provinces.

Europe

Cargo theft incidents reported in Europe dropped considerably in 2011, declining by almost two-thirds of those recorded in 2010. This is a direct result of multiple agencies no longer reporting cargo theft incidents due to widespread budget cuts. Thus, statistics indicating drops in theft activity are skewed by the decrease in reporting. The logistics industry is keenly aware of the difficulties faced by law enforcement agencies fighting cargo theft throughout Europe, a task that is increasingly difficult under budgetary constraints.

According to a 2011 study by the European Parliament, however, the cargo theft situation remains serious throughout Europe, with the value of goods stolen by cargo thieves surpassing €8.2 billion ($10.6 billion USD). According to the study, 90,000 attacks on truck drivers and their vehicles occur each year on Europe's highways, and cargo is stolen in nearly 57,000 of the cases. If the numbers are accurate, that is 156 successful cargo thefts *per day* within the European Union (EU).

Over the past few years, cargo criminals in Europe have been notably more skilled, organized, and aggressive in their tactics, targeting loads at secured locations, inside facilities, and even on moving trucks. Theft by fraud is another method by which criminals are effectively stealing cargo and making off with millions of euros in goods—goods the unwitting victims have literally loaded into the cargo criminals' trucks.

The United Kingdom, France, and the Netherlands continue to be the focal point of cargo theft in western Europe, with Germany and Italy also recording high rates of theft.

While data do not exist to show that Spain has a major cargo theft dilemma, information suggests that the risk within the country is growing quickly. Unlike in France and Italy, where violence or the threat of violence during cargo thefts is a growing trend, thieves operating in Spain rarely resort to violence.

With the exception of Italy, the governments and law enforcement agencies in these countries are working to combat cargo crime and prosecute criminals. In some cases they are cooperating with one another and with law enforcement in eastern Europe as well.

The Europe and Africa portions of the Global Threat Assessment are developed by FreightWatch, in partnership with the Transported Asset Protection Association (TAPA) Europe, Middle East, and Africa (EMEA).

About FreightWatch and TAPA EMEA

FreightWatch has collected cargo theft intelligence and produced reports for the region since 2006. In November 2010, the FreightWatch intelligence division was awarded the TAPA EMEA IIS contract, expanding its intelligence function in the region for TAPA members and partner organizations, including law enforcement agencies.

TAPA represents businesses fighting back against cargo crime that want to use real-time intelligence and the latest preventive measures to protect goods in the supply chain.

TAPA is a unique forum that unites global manufacturers, logistics providers, freight carriers, law enforcement agencies, and other stakeholders with the common aim of reducing losses from international supply chains.

The association's mission is to help protect its members' assets by:

- Exchanging information on a global and regional basis
- Cooperating on preventative security
- Increasing support from the logistics and freight industry and from law enforcement agencies and governments
- Promoting and enhancing TAPA's globally recognized and applied security requirements

United Kingdom

Truckpol, the United Kingdom's national freight crime intelligence unit, estimates that cargo theft on the nation's roads costs the U.K. economy up to £250 million ($386 million USD) each year. Not all cargo theft is reported in the United Kingdom, but the reporting is better than in most European countries.

Although 2011 Truckpol reports suggest that cargo crime is on the rise, it is important to mention that in 2010 this unit began recording thefts of fuel from trucks, which influences its overall results greatly. While it is true that fuel theft affects the transportation industry directly, the Global Threat Assessment focuses on the cargo crime phenomenon. Thus, discounting noncargo-related fuel thefts, it appears that the number of cargo theft incidents reported in the United Kingdom decreased in 2011 compared with the year before.

While the number of reported cargo theft incidents decreased in 2011, the average value per theft continued to rise. This trend, first noted in 2010, indicates that thieves are seeking higher and higher returns for their efforts.

FreightWatch

In 2011, the United Kingdom continued its active involvement in national and EU efforts to fight cargo crime. The last phase of an earlier initiative, the North Sea Freight Intelligent Transport Solutions, was tested in late 2011 and further progress is expected this year. The project aims to provide information to drivers about secure parking locations, crime hot spots, and local policing practices.

Another initiative, the "Keep it Locked" campaign, was launched by the U.K. Border Agency and the Serious Organized Crime Agency in summer 2011. Its goals are to increase driver awareness of the cargo crime threat and to encourage drivers to take steps to prevent and reduce thefts of trucks and/or loads.

The scarcity of secured parking areas continues to be a major problem in the United Kingdom. According to a 2011 study by the Department for Transport, the lack of secured parking areas in the United Kingdom causes inefficiencies in the movement of goods, increases the risk of driver involvement in accidents, and puts drivers at risk of crime, as they are forced to park their trailers and their valuable loads on roadsides or other unsecured areas. A 2011 survey by the Logistics Security Network indicates that only 30% of truck drivers park overnight in secure truck stops.

Cargo Theft Trends and Techniques

As in most of Europe, cargo crime in the United Kingdom is most common on the road while loads are in transit. Theft from trailer was the most reported type of incident in 2011, with most thefts taking place in unsecured parking areas such as roadsides and rest areas. Although this mainly occurred while trucks were unattended, some thefts took place while the drivers were asleep in their cabins. Facility burglaries were the second most reported type of incident.

On May 22, 2011, burglars hit a warehouse on London's east side and stole approximately 400 cases of wine. According to reports, the thieves disabled the facility's alarms and security cameras and then apparently used a forklift to load the wine cases. Two men have been arrested in connection with the theft and Scotland Yard authorities continue to investigate. The loss value was estimated at £1 million ($1.6 million USD).

Reported thefts involving weapons and thefts by fraud both increased by 3% in 2011, growing from 2% in 2010 to 5% percent of the total last year. The following are two prime examples of these kinds of thefts:

- Around midnight on October 19, 10 men armed with machetes broke into a Manchester warehouse, tied up the security guards, and then spent about an hour loading three pallets of powerful fireworks into a getaway truck. After the thieves fled the scene, one of the security guards was able to free himself and summon police. The loss value was not disclosed.
- In Felixstowe, east of England, on January 13, thieves posing as legitimate drivers pulled off a multitrailer theft of flat screen TVs after they provided documents and pin numbers required at the transport facility. The loss value was estimated at $493,158 USD.

In the entire United Kingdom, 95% of all reported incidents in 2011 occurred in England, while 5% took place in Ireland, Scotland, and Wales. This does not necessarily mean Ireland, Scotland, and Wales have escaped the cargo theft scourge; rather that thefts are significantly underreported in those countries—and likely in Northern Ireland as well.

Intrusion is by far the MO preferred by cargo thieves in the United Kingdom. Criminals using this method gain access to loads by cutting the curtains of trailers or by breaking the door locks. As in other European countries, trailers in the United Kingdom tend to be soft-sided, making them easier to cut than the more traditional hard-sided trailers. Instead of breaking locks

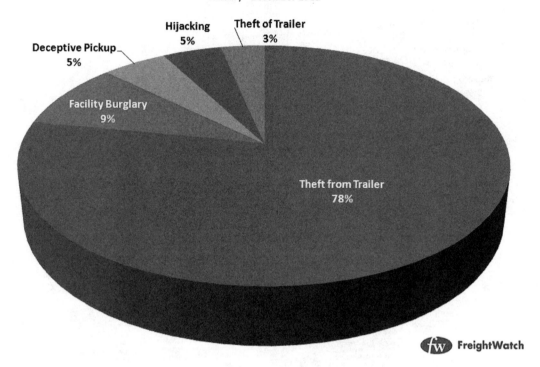

Cargo Theft by Type of Event
January - December 2011

Hijacking
5%

Theft of Trailer
3%

Deceptive Pickup
5%

Facility Burglary
9%

Theft from Trailer
78%

FreightWatch

and seals, the thief simply has to cut through the material to gain access to the load.

As in 2010, electronics was the product type most targeted by thieves last year, with flat screen TVs and DVD players among the items most stolen. The building/industrial category occupied second place, with thieves displaying an overwhelming preference for metals. The clothing/shoes category was in third place, with brand-name clothing as the main target.

In England, the East of England Region—with major highway and rail routes, as well as Harwich International Port and three international airports—reported most of the cargo theft incidents in 2011, at 20%. East Midlands, a bustling business/industrial region crisscrossed by some 140,000 tractor–trailers each day, accounted for 18% of the total thefts last year. Finally, prosperous South East England, which claims the second largest regional economy in the United Kingdom, was third, at 15% of total thefts. Thus, more than half of all incidents reported in 2011 took place in these three regions.

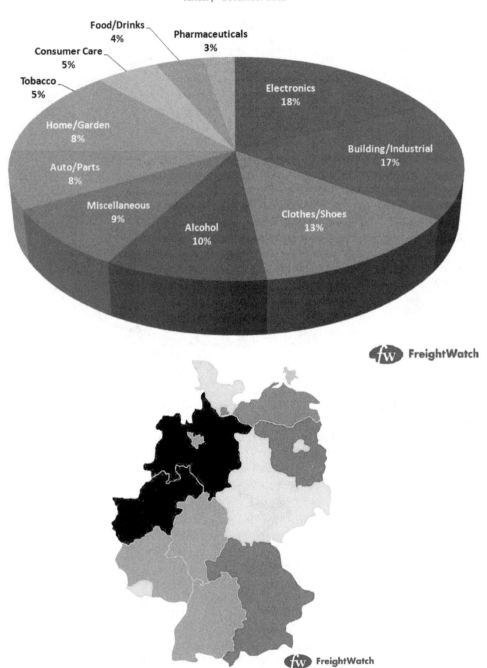

Cargo Theft by Product Type
January - December 2011

Food/Drinks 4%

Consumer Care 5%

Tobacco 5%

Pharmaceuticals 3%

Electronics 18%

Home/Garden 8%

Building/Industrial 17%

Auto/Parts 8%

Miscellaneous 9%

Clothes/Shoes 13%

Alcohol 10%

FreightWatch

FreightWatch

Germany

In addition to having a modern transportation network and one of the most developed economies in the EU, Germany is an important transit hub for goods traveling through Europe and beyond. This last factor, coupled with Germany's sparse and poorly lighted parking areas, however, is what makes it a prime target for cargo thieves.

According to a 2011 study by the European Parliament, cargo thefts in Germany alone add up to annual losses of €1.5 billion ($1.9 billion USD).

"Nowhere in Europe are more trucks on the road than on German highways," Frank Federau, superintendent of the Lower Saxony State Office of Criminal Investigation, was quoted as saying in an article on the German website Autobild.de. This state of affairs, Federau suggested, makes Germany particularly targeted by thieves.

Not surprisingly, Lower Saxony was one of the four German states most affected by cargo crime in 2011. The other states were North Rhine-Westphalia, Brandenburg, and Bavaria.

Like other European countries most targeted by cargo criminals, Germany works actively to combat the problem. Early in 2011 German law enforcement joined with police in France, Hungary, Romania, and Austria on an operation that resulted in the arrest of 22 suspected cargo criminals in France, Hungary, and Romania. The organization is accused of targeting trucks parked along French highways. According to Europol, each country played a specific role in the gang's process:

- France: Location of thefts of high-value products
- Austria: Transit country from France to Hungary
- Germany: Logistics operations and truck exchanges
- Hungary: Storage of stolen goods
- Romania: Country of origin of most members and the place the criminal network likely was established

Another initiative—a joint effort by freight exchanges, a private insurance company, and the state of Lower Saxony—provided brochures and checklists to drivers and dispatchers with the goal of improving their security levels and thus preventing thefts carried out via online freight exchange services.

Early in 2011 the General Association of German Insurers (GDV) said in an article on the verkehrsrundschau.de website that cargo crime executed through freight exchanges has increased dramatically in recent years. Brokers and transport insurers, GDV said, have reported a consistent increase in the number of incidents in which truckloads were stolen by fake transport companies that got the job through freight exchanges.

Cargo Crime Techniques

The types of incidents reported most frequently in Germany were theft from trailers, facility burglaries, and theft of trailers. The majority of thefts from/of trailers occurred in unsecured parking areas along highways.

In these cases the criminals take opportunistic thefts to the next level by lying in wait at highway service stations and other rest areas and then taking a peek at the cargo by cutting into the soft-sided curtain. If the load is something they want, they wait until the truck is left unattended or the driver falls asleep inside the cabin before proceeding with the theft.

On the night of October 11–12, 2011, a truck driver traveling from Poland to Great Britain parked overnight in an unsecured parking area on the A-12 federal highway at Rauen, Brandenburg Region. While the driver apparently was asleep in his cabin, thieves made off with 420 computer monitors, about one-quarter

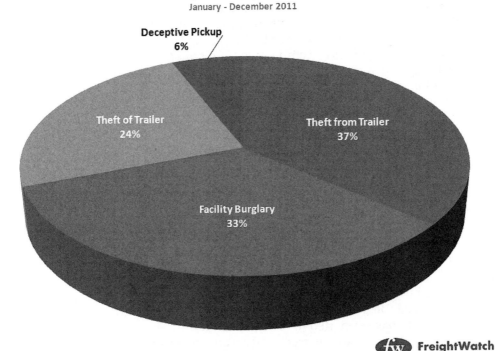

Cargo Theft by Type of Event
January - December 2011

Deceptive Pickup
6%

Theft of Trailer
24%

Theft from Trailer
37%

Facility Burglary
33%

fw FreightWatch

of the load. The loss value was estimated at $204,447 USD (source: TAPA EMEA).

In late April 2011, a trailer loaded with tires headed to Denmark was emptied while the vehicle was parked over the weekend at an unsecured parking area in Langenhagen, Lower Saxony. The loss was valued at $45,722 USD.

Location and Modi Operandi

The majority of cargo theft incidents in Germany occur while cargo is in transit, especially while the truck is stopped for the night or the driver is at rest at unsecured parking areas along highways. The high concentration of trucks along highways, the scarcity of secured parking, and the poorly lighted parking spaces make cargo thieves' jobs easier. Thefts from facilities are not far behind attacks on trucks. Burglaries of warehouses and other facilities in Germany often involve thefts of metals, and thus mostly involve metal processing companies, recycling companies, and metal trade facilities, as well as transportation and storage facilities.

Twenty-nine tons of aluminum banding, stainless steel, and copper were stolen from two motorcycle parts manufacturers in Mylau, Saxony, sometime between 5:30 p.m. Friday and 11:45 p.m. Sunday, November 20, 2011. Authorities believe the thieves used a forklift to load the metals into one or more of their own trailers. The total loss value was estimated at $155,486 USD.

The MO reported most frequently in this region is intrusion into trailers or facilities. However, thieves are increasingly setting up fake transport companies or assuming the name of an existing one in order to swoop in and steal cargo right out from under the noses of shippers.

On May 25, 2011, an iron foundry in the Brandenburg town of Ortrand unwittingly turned over a load of 31 pallets of gray iron casting pipe. Like many similar cases around Europe, the driver provided shipping documents that appeared to be signed and stamped properly. The theft was discovered when the shipment failed to reach its destination in Italy and efforts to locate the truck failed. The loss was estimated at $56,305 USD.

While thefts targeting trucks or warehouse/facilities are the more common types of theft events, from time to time incidents at airports or on railways also are reported. For example, employees of a ground handling agency apparently broke into a container loaded with mobile phones at the Frankfurt-Hahn Airport on August 6, 2011. CCTV showed the suspects placing screens between the camera and the container and then several individuals moving to and from the container behind the screen. It was later discovered that about 900 mobile phones worth $340,488 USD were missing from the container. The thieves had stuffed the container with plastic and netting in an apparent attempt to fill up the empty space (source: TAPA EMEA).

Products in the building/industrial, food/drinks, and electronics categories were the most targeted by cargo criminals in 2011. Although soft drinks, wine, flat screen TVs, mobile phones, and laptop computers were among the items most stolen, copper and other metals in the building/industrial category topped the list. According to industry experts in Germany, at no time has it been easier than the present for thieves to sell stolen metals. This is because of soaring metal prices fueled by elevated demand for metals in emerging markets.

France

The largest country in western Europe, France enjoys a very high level of economic development and a geographic location that makes it a prime crossroads for international trade by land, rail, sea, and air. These factors, however, also make France one of the perennial hot spots for cargo theft in Europe.

FreightWatch

Cargo crime information in France is collected and distributed by the central office for the Fight Against Itinerant Delinquency (OCLDI). Although official numbers for 2011 have not yet been released, informal OCLDI updates provided to the media throughout the year suggest that the number of cargo theft incidents is remaining stable. Underreporting of cargo crime remains a factor in France, but OCLDI updates help provide a fairly clear picture of ongoing cargo theft activity.

If the official numbers, when they are released, do support the theory that cargo crime is leveling off, much of the credit can go to the French government and its law enforcement bodies. France, in fact, is one of the European countries working most actively to reduce crime targeting the transportation and logistics service industry. Efforts to reduce cargo theft and put perpetrators behind bars consistently result in arrests, the disbanding of theft gangs, and the recovery of stolen goods.

In 2011, for example, France played a crucial role in an international operation targeting sophisticated cargo criminals operating on some EU highways. As a result, a total of 22 suspects were arrested on April 5 in France, Hungary, and Romania. The criminal gang is suspected of perpetrating at least 70 thefts involving goods valued at more than €3 million ($4.15 million USD) since 2010 in France alone. The operation was launched in mid-2010 by law enforcement officials in the French city of Tulle, Correze Department, but it soon expanded to national and European levels.

Cargo Crime Trends and Techniques

While cargo crime across the board may have leveled off in France in 2011, a spike in the number of cargo theft incidents in which weapons were involved—especially around the Île-de-France Region (the Paris metropolitan area)—made headlines in the country and elsewhere in Europe. While violence or the threat of violence was occasionally reported in 2010, this tactic was reported in 25% of all reported incidents in 2011. The jump in the number of incidents perpetrated by armed thieves was especially noted during the last two quarters of the year, and into 2012 as well. Although weapons are used to intimidate victims rather than to harm them in most cases, this trend nonetheless has set off alarm bells.

On September 30, 2011, a truck transporting a high-value load of mobile phones was forced off the road by five to six armed thieves traveling in two vehicles on the A-86 highway in Gennevilliers, Île-de-France. The perpetrators, wearing black clothing, gloves, and hooded jackets, forced the driver into the back seat of his truck and drove off in it. They released the driver a short while later in Mitry-Mory and escaped with the truck and its load. The truck was found later in Villiers Adam, but part of its load—eight pallets of phones valued at €1.2 million ($1.63 million USD)—was gone. The thieves had emptied the contents of a fire extinguisher inside the truck's cabin, presumably to destroy evidence.

Sometime after dark in mid-October 2011, several thieves armed with automatic weapons and wearing black clothing and balaclavas broke into a facility owned by a transportation company in Ferriers-en-Brie, Île-de-France. After taking a security guard by surprise, the robbers escaped with a large load of smartphones and tablets valued at approximately €2.3 million ($3.2 million USD)(source: TAPA EMEA).

These are just two examples among many similar heists carried out by a well-organized gang (or gangs) armed with weapons—hammers, handguns, shotguns, tear gas, and even submachine guns have all reportedly been used. Also common among thieves in these incidents was their dress: black clothing, gloves, and the use of hoodies or balaclavas.

While these cargo criminals continue to elude French authorities, there were some notable successes in 2011:

- On October 18, following an OCLDI investigation of several months, 15 suspected members of a cargo theft organization were arrested in at least five different locations in the Île-de-France and Picardy regions. The organization, which used the fake police MO to force drivers to pull over for "routine inspections," is believed responsible for a series of cargo thefts, mainly in the Île-de-France and Centre regions. Targeting high-value loads such as cigarettes, perfumes, and leather products, the gang stole an estimated €2.5 to €3 million ($3.45 to $4.15 million USD) in goods. During searches of the suspects' properties, police recovered about €30,000 ($41,462 USD) in cash, as well as shotguns, cigarettes, and leather goods.
- On July 25 in Autun, Bourgogne Region, gendarmes in Saone-et-Loire foiled a major theft of 24 tons of copper. The incident began after thieves broke into the yard of a transportation company and drove off with a truckload of copper that had been parked at the facility. Alerted to the theft, a gendarme patrol located the stolen truck and began tailing it. However, an accomplice driving another vehicle spotted the tail and rushed in to render assistance. The driver of the stolen truck then jumped into his accomplice's vehicle and the two managed to escape, leaving behind the stolen truck and its load, valued at €200,000 ($287,140 USD).

By far the hottest spot for cargo theft in France from January 1 to December 31, 2011, was the Île-de-France Region, as this area claimed more than half of all reported thefts in the country. Île-de-France is the most populous and wealthiest of France's 22 administrative regions and is home to many of the country's major logistics centers. The Provence-Alpes-Côte d'Azur and Nord-pas-de-Calais regions not only placed a distant second and third in the number of thefts, they did not experience the level of violence seen especially around the Paris area.

Robberies and burglaries targeting warehouses or other facilities, as well as hijackings, were the most common types of incidents reported in France in 2011. In some cases, thieves employed the fake police MO, posing as police or customs officials to get a truck driver to pull over. While incidents of kidnapping during a hijacking were almost nonexistent in 2010, this MO was employed more frequently last year.

Although the vast majority of cargo thefts in France last year targeted trucks and warehouses, French media also reported incidents affecting ports, airports, and railways. On the night of July 7, 2011, for example, France's southern coast was the scene of an unusual, Wild West-style train heist on a Euro Cargo Rail

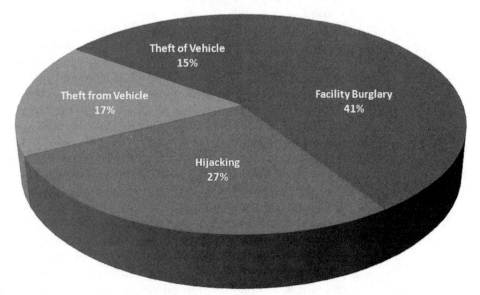

Cargo Theft by Type of Event
January - December 2011

Theft of Vehicle 15%

Theft from Vehicle 17%

Facility Burglary 41%

Hijacking 27%

FreightWatch

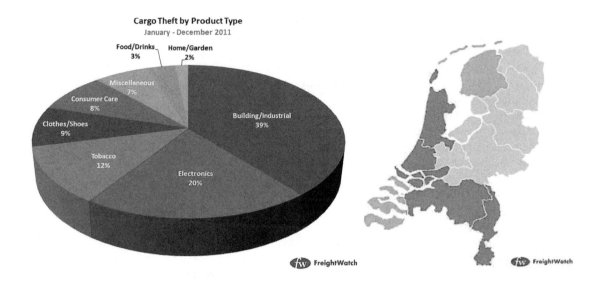

line between Marseille and Miramas. The incident began when a group of about 20 masked thieves blocked the tracks with shopping carts and wooden planks, causing a passenger train to crash into the improvised barrier. Instead of robbing the passengers, however, the gang made off with the cargo on a freight train that was forced to stop because of the collision. Neither the type of products stolen nor the loss value was disclosed.

Building/industrial, electronics, and tobacco were the most targeted product types in 2011, with copper, mobile phones, laptop computers, and cigarettes the preferred products. Gold and even rare metals, however, were also targeted in 2011.

On June 6, 2011, a group of burglars broke into a steel company in Dunkerque, Nord-pas-de-Calais, tampered with the security system, and stole 10 tons of niobium granules. This rare metal is used particularly in the automotive industry, but also in the manufacture of rockets and nuclear power plants. The loss value was estimated at €350,000 ($512,365 USD)(source: TAPA EMEA).

Other Supply Chain Risks

Strikes and demonstrations throughout 2011 caused major transportation disruptions to supply lines in France, as noted in reports from the FreightWatch intelligence center. Because of this ongoing risk, companies transporting goods throughout France should be ready to adjust their logistics operations quickly.

The Netherlands

One of the busiest trade locations in the world and a major European transportation hub, the Netherlands teems with cargo hurtling along its packed roads and railways and through its busy ports. The Port of Rotterdam—the largest port in Europe and the fourth largest port in the world by cargo volume—is a key transit point for goods moving to and from the rest of Europe and other parts of the world.

The vast amount of cargo transiting through the country on a daily basis makes the Netherlands one of Europe's consistent hot spots for cargo theft.

Given the importance of international trade to the Dutch economy, however, the government takes its responsibility to try to protect cargo quite seriously. Dutch authorities, in fact, responded to the ongoing cargo crime problem in 2010 by, among other measures, naming a special prosecutor whose sole job is to fight cargo crime and put perpetrators behind bars. The special prosecutor said in 2011 that he is working to increase cargo crime reporting in his country and to encourage those in the supply chain industry to take preventive measures against theft.

Cargo Theft Trends and Techniques

According to a Netherlands National Police Agency crime report for the first three quarters of 2011, the theft of trailers decreased from 199 incidents in 2010 to 94 in 2011. However, thefts from trailers and deceptive pickups together increased from 539 to 599 incidents over the same time period. Theft incidents involving violence or the threat of violence are rare in the Netherlands.

Electronics were the most commonly stolen product type last year, with computers and audio/visual equipment among the items taken. Food/drinks and clothing/shoes industries placed second and third, respectively, in popularity among thieves in 2011. All of the products in these categories are fairly easy to sell on the black market and, not surprisingly, are often targeted in other regions of the world as well.

Most cargo theft in the Netherlands occurs in the southeast and east, including North and South Holland, North Brabant, and Limburg provinces. North and South Holland, located on the English Channel, are home to some of the busiest ports in the world. North Brabant and Limburg are vital access points to Belgium, Germany, and the rest of Europe.

Cargo theft was at its lowest during July, August, and September and at its highest during February, May, and June.

This trend was also seen in thefts occurring in 2010, except that February's total was significantly higher in 2011. Available reports did not include the October–December quarter, but as trade increased ahead of the holiday season, it is likely that cargo thieves were also quite active during that time.

Theft in the Netherlands is most common in business areas such as warehouses and distribution centers. Although the Netherlands handles enormous amounts of cargo, it does not manufacture many goods, so theft from manufacturing centers is not a major concern. Theft is also common when goods are in transit or parked along public roads.

Unsecured parking is another common theft location. In Gelderland at the end of October a driver who briefly walked away from his truck after stopping at a rest area along the A-50 highway returned to find that thieves had broken the seal and stolen more than 350 pairs of jeans and 3000 pairs of boxer shorts (source: TAPA EMEA).

Other Supply Chain Risks

The Netherlands suffers extensive traffic problems and congestion in major cities. What's more, this fairly small country already has a dense roadway system and little room for expansion. This poses challenges as global trade increases and the Port of Rotterdam remains an essential link in the global supply chain.

The government has taken some steps to try to reduce traffic, such as opening shoulders for traffic during rush hours, but this is only a short-term fix—and traffic is expected to grow even heavier.

Italy

Although cargo theft has been an issue in Italy for quite some time now, efforts by lawmakers and public security forces to combat these crimes are clearly less robust than those seen in the Netherlands, Belgium, and even the United Kingdom. In those countries, and a few others, efforts to fight cargo crime are unceasing and often creative, as lawmakers and law enforcement experiment with new tactics, launch new operations, and implement tougher measures.

Given Italy's lackluster approach to fighting cargo theft and the soft punishments imposed on those who are caught and convicted, this type of crime continues to flourish.

Cargo Theft and Techniques

As in 2010, Italy's northern Lombardy Region claimed the top spot for cargo crime in 2011. With the regional and provincial capital of Milan at its heart, and thriving industrial and services sectors, Lombardy is the richest and most populous of the country's 20 regions. These factors, of course, are the likely reason it attracts thieves. Within the area, most of the cargo theft incidents were reported around Milan province.

Other regions reporting high levels of cargo theft in 2011 were Puglia in the southeast, Veneto in the northeast, and Lazio in the center. Along with Italians, Albanians and Romanians are among those most suspected of involvement in cargo crime activities in Italy.

Hijackings, facility burglaries, and thefts of trailer were the types of incident reported most frequently in 2011. It is worth noting that cargo thefts committed by means of deception or deceptive pickup were also reported during the first trimester of the year, although the year-end tally of incidents carried out by this method was modest.

A case on January 14, 2011, illustrates the theft by deception method seen most often during the first 4 months of the year. In that case, a carrier contracted through a well-known freight exchange website and hired to transport two loads—in the food/drinks and auto/parts product types—turned out to be a fake, even though the documentation appeared to be in order and the loading was carried out normally. The deception was discovered only after the loads failed to reach their destination in Denmark and the hiring company attempted to track the freight. The loss value of both loads was about $120,000 USD.

Even though intrusion is the most common MO employed by cargo thieves in Italy, there nonetheless are a great number of incidents involving violence or the threat of violence. For instance, in the early morning hours of February 10, 2011, a group of 10 armed and masked men attacked an in-transit truck loaded with cigarettes worth $2.7 million USD. The incident took place in Stella di Monsampolo, Marche Region, where the driver was forced to stop at gunpoint. The thieves then attached the trailer to their truck and fled the scene, leaving the driver behind. He immediately reported the incident and police were able to trace the stolen trailer, still bearing the load of cigarettes, to an abandoned warehouse in Corropoli, Abruzzo Region. Although the cargo was recovered, the thieves were able to escape. The driver resumed his journey later that day, this time escorted by police.

In Milan on November 9, 2011, a group of armed criminals posing as police officers forced a truck loaded with cellular phones to stop for a "routine check." The thieves then took control of the truck, forced the truck drivers into another vehicle, and sped away in both vehicles. The drivers were released unharmed about an hour later, but the thieves escaped with the entire load, worth $2.75 million USD (source: TAPA EMEA).

Early on June 29, 2011, in Cerignola, Apuglia Region, a gang of armed criminals forced a truck loaded with sporting goods to stop along the motorway near Foggia. The driver was kidnapped from the scene in another vehicle and later released. The nearly empty truck was located a few hours later in Ordona, about 14 miles north of Cerignola. The thieves had escaped with goods valued at nearly $358,000 USD.

The product categories most coveted by cargo thieves operating in Italy last year were food/drinks, with candies and frozen foods as the most stolen products. This was followed by auto/parts, with tires and engines the most popular. Building/industrial goods, with metals being by far the main targets, rounded out the top three.

According to reported incidents, the vast majority of thefts in 2011 involved organized, frequently armed gangs of thieves targeting trucks in transit. In these cases, thieves forced trucks to stop either by blocking the road or highway with vehicles or by pretending to be police officers engaged in routine inspections. These thefts often appeared to have been planned carefully, the target preselected, and the location and time of the attack determined in advance.

In other words, 2011 saw a significant shift away from the opportunistic thefts from/of trailers discussed in the 2010 global threat assessment. The trend in Italy in 2010 was for thieves to attack trucks parked and left unattended overnight at service areas or unsecured parking areas.

Success Stories

Although cargo crime is not a top priority for Italian law enforcement, authorities nevertheless had some successes in capturing thieves and recovering cargo in 2011. Examples include the following:

- During a routine inspection in the city of Gallo on October 28, police intercepted a truck that turned out to have been stolen the previous night from the premises of a company in Bologna. Inside the truck were copper coils weighing a total of 20 tons and estimated in value at $63,174 USD. As it turned out, the copper had just been stolen from a company in Minerbio, Bologna Province. The thief driving the truck was arrested and the copper was returned to its owner.
- In the city of Salerno, Campania Region, early on November 28, Carabinieri (Italian national police) arrested a 42-year-old man believed to be one of four thieves who had hijacked a truck loaded with toys and video game consoles a few hours earlier. The incident began when thieves fired shots into the air, forcing the targeted truck to exit the A-30 highway (Salerno-Reggio Calabria) and stop in the nearby countryside. The driver was beaten, tied up, and locked in the trunk of the thieves' car. Although he was freed around 4 a.m. in an isolated area of San Marzano sul Sarno, Campania Region, he was rescued promptly by a passing security guard and taken to an area hospital. Notified of the incident, police launched a search for the stolen truck, intercepting it within an hour. Although the suspect was arrested, the truck's contents had already disappeared. The loss was valued at $66,205 USD.

Spain

By all indications, cargo crime continues to increase in Spain, even though underreporting and a lack of official numbers make it difficult to paint a clear picture of the current situation. Most of the information released by Spanish authorities through the media focuses on arrests of cargo criminals and/or recoveries of stolen goods, with little reporting on the thefts when they occur.

FreightWatch

Even so, through reports on successes we learn of the crimes themselves. In addition, anecdotal evidence from supply chain professionals either in the country or doing business with Spain suggests that cargo crime is on the rise.

In July 2011, the Spanish Confederation of Goods Transporters (CETM) reportedly appealed to the country's interior ministry to launch a "special and urgent" effort to address the "enormous increase" in attacks against and robberies of trucks and to bring the perpetrators to justice. Noting "the international nature of the gangs that specialize in this type of crime," CETM also called for coordinated action on the issue at the EU level.

While none of this is positive news, it is important to point out that law enforcement, primarily the national police force Spanish Civil Guard, is working actively to combat cargo crime in the country, with some notable successes.

The regions mostly affected by cargo crime in 2011 were Madrid, Aragon, Castilla and Leon, Andalusia, and Catalonia. While Catalonia, Madrid, and Andalusia were the main regional hot spots in 2010, Aragon and Castilla and Leon are new additions for 2011.

Cargo Theft Targets and Types

Cargo theft gangs in Spain are very well organized and sophisticated, with specific roles or tasks assigned to members. These roles include locating targets; committing the thefts; moving the stolen goods to storage in warehouses, industrial parks, houses, and so on; selling the stolen product; and finally moving the goods out of the country when necessary. Gang members charged with locating targets in some cases will travel miles—visiting service stations, rest areas, and logistics centers—in order to find the products they desire.

The product categories reportedly most targeted in 2011 were building/industrial, food/drinks, and auto/parts. This trend differs from 2010, when electronics and clothing/shoes were among the most coveted by thieves. In the building/industrial category, metals were targeted most often, with copper being especially popular among thieves. Meat products such as salami and ham, as well as olive oil and candies, were among the products most targeted in the food/drinks category.

The types of theft reported most frequently in Spain in 2011 mirror those seen the year before. Hence, theft of/from a trailer remained by far the most popular type of theft in 2011. While placing second, warehouse burglaries were not nearly as common as attacks against trucks.

Case Studies

Although the level of sophistication and versatility displayed by many of these gangs makes the job of catching them quite difficult, operations by the Civil Guard and local police in 2011 and early 2012 led to major arrests and the dismantling of several gangs.

On January 20, 2012, for instance, the Civil Guard and the Catalan police crushed a criminal organization dedicated to the theft and sale of metal products across the country. The lengthy operation, launched in July 2011, culminated in the apprehension of 27 suspects and the recovery of 20 tons of nickel, 35 tons of copper, and three trucks, among other things. The investigation was started after a Cadiz company reported the theft from its facility of 24 tons of nickel worth approximately €400,000 ($575,640 USD).

In March 2011, the Civil Guard broke up a band of cargo thieves operating throughout Catalonia that was believed responsible for more than 30 robberies and estimated losses of more than €1.2 million ($1.69 million USD). In that operation, launched in November 2010, 35 people were arrested and at least 6 people imprisoned, among them the leaders of the gang and the major recipient of the gang's stolen goods. The arrests took place in Barcelona, Tarragona, Cubelles, Sant Feliu de Llobregat, Ripon, Sant Cugat del Valles, Badalona, and Sabadell. Twenty-one searches in all, 13 at the detainees' homes and 8 at industrial parks, led to the recovery of 24 tons of copper valued at €200,000 ($281,958 USD), 22 tons of steel, approximately 200 appliances, 950 car batteries, 18 trailers, and a tractor.

In the municipality of Navatalgordo, Castilla and Leon Region, local authorities arrested a thief and recovered a truck loaded with sausages, hams, and other meats within days of the September 27, 2011 theft. Notified shortly after the incident occurred, police were able to locate the vehicle traveling on the M-501 highway. The getaway driver, however, spotted the police cruiser and managed to escape on a side road. A subsequent investigation shortly thereafter, however, led police to the suspected thief and the load (source: TAPA EMEA).

In early November 2011, police arrested 17 people on charges of stealing cargo from service areas and transport logistics centers throughout Madrid, especially near the national highways A-4 and A-42. Stolen goods worth more than €1 million ($1.3 million) were recovered. As with most well-organized gangs, members of this group had assigned tasks, ranging from locating targets to selling the goods. This gang, however, took the rather unusual precaution of using escort vehicles—one in front and one behind a stolen truck—to protect the cargo from rival groups as it was moved to a secure location.

In another successful ending to a case, the Civil Guard in Maracena on November 15, 2011, intercepted a truck carrying 54 cartons of toys that had been stolen earlier that day in Bailen. Officers arrested the thief driving the truck and recovered its load. Further investigation and interrogation of the apprehended thief led to the arrest of six more suspects 2 weeks later. All seven suspects had criminal records stemming from thefts of cargo from trucks parked at service areas in Granada, Cordoba, and Jaen in the Andalusia Region.

Modi Operandi

Cargo theft gangs in Spain are considered among the most versatile in Europe in that they are constantly evolving, trying out new MOs and adapting to changing circumstances. Employing escort vehicles to protect stolen cargo, for example, is not a common tactic. However, unlike in France and Italy, where violence or the threat of violence during cargo thefts is a growing trend, thieves operating in Spain rarely resort to violence.

The fact that intrusion is the most popular MO in the country suggests that thieves go out of their way to avoid confrontation. In the intrusion method, thieves break into a trailer or cut its curtain or they break into a warehouse in order to gain access to the cargo. Thefts involving the intrusion MO most often take place at night when loaded trucks are parked and unattended at service areas or industrial parks. In warehouse burglaries, intruding thieves also wait until a facility is closed before breaking into its gated yard and stealing loaded and parked trailers, as well as any metal products found in the yard. Thieves also will break into the building itself in order to steal cargo and other goods.

Thefts from vehicles in motion, first reported in the GTA for 2009, continued into 2011. Again, however, the Spanish Civil Guard made some headway on this front. In February 2011, an investigation by the Civil Guard resulted in the arrest of 10 people of Romanian nationality. The operation was launched after several transportation companies complained that cargo was disappearing from their trucks, usually at night, while they traveled along major roads.

To carry out a theft from a vehicle in motion, one of the thieves' vehicles moves in front of the target truck and then slows down so that the truck also is forced to slow. Then, thieves traveling closely behind the target truck in a pickup or similar vehicle jump from the hood of their vehicle to the back door of the target truck, where they saw or force open the lock. In some reported cases in 2010, the thieves actually harnessed themselves to the target truck.

The thieves then pass boxes from the target truck to their accomplices in the cargo bed of the pickup, repeating this action until several pickup trucks are loaded with the goods. These thefts often are discovered only after the trucker arrives at his destination.

Russia

Although the true depth and complexity of Russia's severe cargo theft situation remained as murky as ever in 2011—the result, as always, of extremely limited official incident reporting—thefts appear to have increased once again, based on anecdotal evidence and available reports from police and insurance companies.

A January 2012 report by the Moscow Police Criminal Investigations Department said police registered 373 more vehicle thefts in 2011 than in the previous year. In addition, 304 trucks (heavy vehicles) and 209 vehicles with special equipment were stolen. These last two categories of vehicles are increasingly gaining the attention of thieves, according to the report.

An insurance company report issued in July 2011 indicated cargo theft increased by 30% in Russia during the first semester of the year, although the report did not provide numbers of incidents. The report did suggest, however, that thieves are broadening their theft techniques. In 2011, for example, an increase in the number of thefts from vehicles in motion was registered. It is still too early to say whether this MO is an emerging trend, however.

Supply Chain Challenges

Nearly 70% of all cargo is moved by road and 15% by railway in Russia. Although the country's aging and overcrowded road network continues to pose a serious threat to transporters and logistics providers, a government plan to invest 1.3 trillion rubles ($41 billion USD) on the country's road system by 2019 is a hopeful sign. Some of the heavily used "M" highways (national roads leading to and from Moscow) affected by this initiative are the M-1 to Belarus, the M-3 to Ukraine, the M-4 to southern Russia, and the M-11, a 400-mile toll road from Moscow to St. Petersburg intended as an alternative route to the heavily transited M-10. The first stage of the tollway is expected to open in 2013.

In addition to cargo crime and infrastructure deficiencies, endemic corruption and the blurry lines between Russian organized crime and government remain as serious issues for companies needing to ensure that supply lines run smoothly. This remains the case even though 2011 saw some much-publicized movement regarding Russia's stance on bribery.

In May 2011, President Dmitry Medvedev signed legislation that imposed higher monetary fines for bribery, including both commercial bribery and bribery of foreign public officials to gain business advantages. Importantly, this step by Medvedev resulted in an invitation for Russia to join the Organization for Economic Cooperation and Development (OECD) Anti-Bribery Convention. (In February 2012, Medvedev signed into law Russia's accession to the convention).

The OECD invitation is likely one of the reasons Russia moved up a few notches in Transparency International's 2011 Corruption Perceptions Index. While Russia was ranked 154th out of 182 countries, with an abysmal score of 2.1 out of 10, in the 2010 index, it inched into 143rd place with a score of 2.4 last year. Countries that score below 3 points, however, are considered "highly corrupt" and, despite last year's improvement, Russia's public sector is still considered the most corrupt of the world's major economies.

Cargo Theft Trends and Techniques

Cargo thieves in most European countries tend to employ classic, nonconfrontational methods, such as theft of or from trailers left attended at service stations, rest areas, or unsecured parking areas, and warehouse burglaries achieved through intrusion. Violence is rare in most of Europe, and there continues to be a degree of opportunistic theft.

While Russian cargo thieves also target in-transit trucks and warehouses, they most often are heavily armed and focused on loads they have targeted in advance. The most common types of incidents in Russia are armed hijackings—with driver kidnapping often involved—and armed robberies. The fake police MO (deceptive stop), in which criminals dress in police or customs uniforms to get truck drivers to pull over on highways and roads, is also very common. While Russian thieves will hit parked trucks, they prefer to force drivers to stop.

Thefts from trailers in motion increased in Russia in 2011, although this MO is not employed as frequently as others in Russia. This method reportedly occurs along stretches of road where one of the thieves can force a truck to slow to about 30 mph by driving slowly in front of it. Then, other members of the cargo theft gang commence their maneuvers at the rear of the trailer. As in other countries where this MO is seen, the victimized drivers discover the theft only after they arrive to deliver the cargo.

Even though cargo theft occurs throughout Russia, the areas around Saint Petersburg and Moscow continue to be at highest risk, following the 2010 trend.

Among the product types preferred by cargo thieves in Russia are alcohol, electronics, and food/drinks. However, the pharmaceutical and the building/industrial categories also saw thefts in 2011, as the following two examples demonstrate:

- On March 13, thieves posing as police officers hijacked two trucks after forcing the drivers to stop near the city of Veliky Novgorod, which sits on the M-10 highway connecting Moscow and St. Petersburg. The thieves kidnapped the drivers and made off with an estimated $6 million USD in pharmaceuticals, later releasing the drivers unharmed. Authorities eventually located the trucks, missing their loads and their license plates, near St. Petersburg.
- On Sunday morning, December 25, a gang of armed cargo thieves wearing balaclavas broke into a Russian factory in the southwestern city of Astrakhan. Once inside, they tied up and gagged the security guards and made off with 42 sheets of platinum worth approximately $5.7 million USD (source: TAPA EMEA).

Africa

The African continent continues to pose major challenges to the supply chain industry. Cargo theft, high rates of violence,

infrastructure deficiencies, corruption, poor service delivery, and weak governance are among the problems faced regularly by companies doing business in or with Africa.

The security situation on the continent differs from country to country, and even from region to region within each country. According to media reports and warnings issued by outside governments, the most dangerous countries on the continent are Libya, Kenya, Chad, Somalia, Niger, Nigeria, Democratic Republic of the Congo, Cote d'Ivoire, Burundi, Eritrea, and Republic of South Sudan, among others.

These countries are considered among the least safe places in Africa for various reasons, including high crime rates, political instability, banditry, and the risk of terrorist attacks or sudden outbreaks of armed violence.

Recent reports suggest that security has improved to a certain degree in some African countries, including Angola and South Africa. In Angola, for instance, the overall security situation has improved since the country's 27-year civil war ended in 2002. However, crime remains a serious problem, especially in North and South Lunda provinces, Cabinda Province, and Luanda Province, home of the nation's capital city of Luanda. Meanwhile, in South Africa, although police report a drop in crime levels, crime rates remain high and violent incidents are still frequent in townships and isolated areas.

South Africa, economically the most important country in Africa and one of the major ports of entry onto the continent, remains one of the continent's principal hot spots for cargo theft.

In 2011, piracy around Africa reached its highest levels in history. It was estimated that piracy costs the world's economies $7 to $12 billion USD annually, and the enormous amount of piracy occurring off of Africa's coasts contributes greatly to the high losses globally. Because of the growing problem, this year's Africa GTA includes an overview of the piracy situation.

Cargo Crime and Truck Theft

As in previous years, cargo crime data collection and incident reporting remained extremely poor throughout Africa in 2011. Although media report on the cargo crime situation from time to time, most of the news releases issued by law enforcement tend to highlight successful arrests or recoveries of stolen goods, with little or no mention of incidents in which thieves escaped with the goods.

According to an October 2011 news report out of Kenya, for example, at least two cargo theft incidents involving trucks occur nightly along the Mombasa–Malaba highway, especially in the areas of Naivasha and Eldoret. The head of the Kenya Transport Association was quoted as saying authorities have not addressed the lack of security adequately, while transportation companies continue to suffer great losses and drivers' lives are at constant risk.

Slightly better than in most other countries is reporting from South Africa, where statistics are occasionally released by the South African Police Service (SAPS).

According to SAPS, 999 trucks were hijacked in South Africa for the year running April 1, 2010, to March 31, 2011. That number was considerably down from the 1492 reported hijackings for the same period the previous year, according to SAPS figures. Historically, Gauteng Province is by far the most affected by truck hijackings and cargo theft. In fact, in the latest SAPS report, 600 of the 999 incidents reported took place in this province. Mpumalanga, Kwazulu-Natal, and North West provinces are also areas with high theft rates.

Overall serious crime in South Africa fell by 2.4% year on year, according to the SAPS report for the year ending March 31, 2011. The report says homicides and other serious crimes dropped from just over 2.1 to 2.07 million in the reporting period. SAPS claims that improvements in police intelligence, investigations, and rapid response to crime have resulted in better arrest and conviction rates.

Modi Operandi and Product Types

Violence or the threat of violence is present in most cargo theft incidents in Africa. As in previous years, the most common MOs in 2011 were armed robberies and truck hijackings. Road blockages and theft by deception, in which thieves pose as police officers, were other methods used by thieves, although to a lesser extent than hijackings and armed robberies. The constant involvement of violence and the crude theft methods common in Africa stand in stark contrast to cargo theft operations seen in other parts of the globe, particularly Europe and the United States, where violence is rare and thieves are constantly inventing new ways to carry out their crimes.

The variety of products stolen is wide in Africa, although the product categories most targeted were food/drinks, electronics and building/industrial. This is quite similar to the trends seen in some European countries.

Case Studies

On February 7, 2011, six thieves, all residents of Johannesburg, were apprehended while trying to steal a load of mobile phones at O.R. Tambo International Airport. Apparently one of the thieves worked in the cargo section at the airport. The arrests took place while the suspects were loading a truck with the stolen merchandise. The value of the load was estimated at €162,173 ($220,122 USD).

On March 9, 2011, In Nairobi, Kenya, a container loaded with coffee was stolen by thieves who apparently managed to disable the truck's tracking system. The driver was suspected of involvement in the incident. The empty truck was found later in Naivasha. The loss value was not disclosed.

In South Africa, three men hijacked a truck loaded with refrigerators in Dobsonville, Gauteng Province, on August 23, 2011. Thanks to a tip provided to law enforcement, however, the offenders were arrested and the truck and its cargo were recovered the following day.

On October 17, 2011, three cargo thieves were arrested in the city of Germiston near Johannesburg, South Africa, for possession of stolen copper cable worth $95,160 USD. According to SAPS, once authorities spotted the stolen truck and closed in on it, the thieves fled, leaving the stolen cargo behind. All three suspects were apprehended a short time later. The truck had been hijacked in the nearby township of Daveyton (source: TAPA EMEA).

The driver of a petroleum transport truck was hijacked and his cargo stolen on South Africa's South Coast Road in Durban,

KwaZulu-Natal Province, in October 2011. The empty truck was recovered a few days later on the N2 highway. The amount of the loss was not released.

Also in October on the South Coast Road, the driver of a truck transporting sugar valued at about €183,945 ($258,235 USD) was kidnapped and his load stolen. Freed the day after the kidnapping, the driver and his assistant reported the incident to authorities, whose investigation led to the arrest of some members of the gang. Further investigation led police to the recovery of 31 tons of sugar in Clairwood, about 3 miles from the theft site.

Piracy in Africa

International governments are putting more pressure on their African counterparts to enforce the punishment of pirates as a method of deterring their activities. Although maritime security in African waters is improving, and thus piracy success rates are dropping, pirates are fighting back by increasing the frequency of attacks and by showing an increasing willingness to use force. Armed confrontations at sea are more common nowadays because pirates do not appear to be backing down when faced with increasing and well-armed security patrols.

High-Risk Regions

Piracy off the coasts of Africa is at its highest rate in recorded history. Attacks are most common off the continent's eastern coast, especially between the Gulf of Aden and the Indian Ocean. Other high-risk areas are the Arabian Sea and the Red Sea, although pirate attacks have decreased slightly in the Red Sea area. With improved transportation technology allowing Somali pirates to expand their range, incidents of piracy are expected to increase near Tanzania and Kenya in the coming years.

Although pirate attacks along Africa's western coast, particularly in the Gulf of Guinea, are notoriously underreported, significant attacks in this region are increasing, based on the reports that do come in. As many of the countries in the Gulf of Guinea are oil producers, the rising trend is likely to continue in this region.

Piracy is particularly significant off of the coasts of Nigeria and Benin. The nations, however, have begun to patrol their waters more heavily and have created a joint effort to target criminals.

Products Targeted and Means of Piracy

Ships operating along Africa's western coast often are carrying cargo the pirates covet, especially oil. Thus, oil tankers in particular are heavily targeted for their cargo. However, because the pirates' goal is not ransom, they are more likely to harm the crew. East coast pirates, however, are more likely to hijack a ship for ransom. In many cases, pirates working these waters are not even interested in a vessel's cargo, but rather in the crew on board.

Historically, piracy off of Africa's eastern seaboard has been the most prevalent following the monsoon season, which typically runs from June to September. This is because the criminals typically operated from small skiffs that moved fast but could not hold up in a heavy storm. However, pirates are shifting from lightweight skiffs to larger and more powerful fishing boats, making seasonal storms less of a deterrent to determined pirates.

Case Studies

In early October 2011, pirates hijacked a chemical tanker in the Gulf of Guinea and held the 20-member crew hostage for 5 days. It is believed the pirates' target was the load, not the crew, as they left the tanker after apparently transferring all of the cargo and equipment that their own vessel could carry.

On October 31, 2011, Somali pirates in the Gulf of Aden hijacked a Greek chemical tanker bound for India with a crew of 22 on board. As late as January 9, 2012, reports surfaced that the pirates remained in control of the tanker and were likely planning to use it as a base of operations to attack other vessels.

Ransom was believed to be the motive behind a December 27, 2011, attack by Somali pirates against an Italian tanker transporting nearly 16,000 tons of caustic soda from the United Arab Emirates to the Mediterranean. It was speculated that the pirates intended to ransom the 18-member crew composed of six Italians, seven Indians, and five Ukrainians.

As of January 2012, it was believed that Somali pirates were holding 13 different ships hostage—with a total of more than 200 people on board.

Asia

When examining large-scale cargo theft on a global level, the Asian continent is the safest of the seven, presenting moderate levels of risk overall to supply chain operations. However, cargo theft is prevalent, and difficult to control, in some Asian countries and regions. Malaysia and the Philippines both report frequent incidents of in-transit cargo hijackings, with violence or the threat of violence involved in the commission of crimes. In China, however, small-scale pilferage of cargo is considered rampant and intellectual property rights are at the core of multinational business concerns. India is becoming increasingly noted for large-scale theft incidents, including truck hijackings and warehouse robberies.

As manufacturing and logistics functions continue to flourish in many areas of the continent—increasing the appetite for less-costly products—there is little doubt that cargo theft and supply chain risk have increased throughout Asia. While this trend is clearly of concern, it is important to note that the rate of theft experienced throughout Asia is significantly lower than the rates seen in countries such as Mexico, Brazil, and South Africa.

The powerful earthquake and tsunami that struck Japan in March 2011 is a prime example of factors other than cargo crime that can seriously impact supply chain operations and security. In addition to natural disasters, these other factors can include infrastructure weaknesses, regulatory problems, worker strikes/ demonstrations, and government readiness and response issues. While the FreightWatch intelligence division is focused primarily on cargo theft, it is increasingly looking at these and other issues that can lead to supply chain disruptions in order to provide readers with a broader spectrum of information they can use to help keep their cargo secure throughout the global supply chain.

China

China is the second-largest economy and the most-populated country in the world, making it tremendously important for

business and trade. From January through November 2011, China handled 50.3 billion tons of cargo by air, 25.5 billion tons of cargo by highway, and 3.6 billion tons of cargo by rail. Despite the obvious opportunities for thieves, China historically has been a low-risk country for cargo theft. Companies doing business in and with China, however, have seen an increase in cargo theft in recent years. Furthermore, as domestic consumption among China's growing middle class increases demand for all kinds of consumer goods in the coming years, cargo thieves can be expected to fully exploit the opportunities.

Unprecedented urbanization has put enormous pressure on China's infrastructure, including roads and highways in and around its major cities. Beijing and Shenzhen tied for second place (behind Mexico City) on IBM's 2011 global Commuter Pain Index, which lists cities with the world's worst traffic. When scores of Chinese cities have populations greater than 1 million (and a good number over 10 million), however, the pressure on infrastructure is enormous. Heavy traffic not only takes an emotional and economic toll on Chinese commuters, it forces cargo to sit idle for long periods of time, making it an easy target for thieves. Although China is developing its highway system, American-style multilane highways are still uncommon outside of the major urban areas. Many roads connecting the major cities are not well-paved and are riddled with potholes.

Cargo Theft Trends and Techniques

Most cargo theft in China is of a nonviolent, nonconfrontational nature, as it does not involve interaction with drivers or employees. Facility burglaries from warehouses or ports/terminals are the most commonly reported types of cargo theft. This means it is vital that companies closely monitor cargo as it is transported from manufacturing facilities and loaded into containers for transport via ship, plane, rail, or truck. Theft of trailers with full truckloads of goods also occurs, usually when vehicles are left unattended. In one instance in December, a driver parked his truck in an unsecured parking lot and fell asleep in the cab. When he awoke, his trailer, filled with a load of frozen chicken, was missing.

An MO seen in 2010 was also quite common last year. This is thefts of loads while trucks are in motion. This type of theft is frustrating for drivers because they rarely know the theft occurred until they arrive to deliver their load.

As is the norm in China, employee pilferage continued in 2011 at ports, terminals, and other areas where workers have easy access to cargo. Designer goods and other originals are especially susceptible to pilferage, as they often are used to create the counterfeit products that abound in China and many other global markets.

Most of the theft in China takes place in coastal provinces in China's eastern and southern regions, including Guangdong, Fujian, Shanghai, and Hong Kong. The food/drinks industry was among those most targeted by thieves in 2011, as stolen consumable products can be sold easily to stores. Consumer electronics produced in China for export and domestic consumption are also popular among thieves. Clothing/shoes are another commonly targeted product type because of the popularity of these goods on the black market.

China's rapid growth and industrialization has put metals of all kinds in extremely high demand. As a result, cargo thieves in China are increasingly targeting shipments of metals as well as the rail lines themselves for the metals that can be removed. Chinese railway police, while not always successful at stopping thefts of this nature, scored a major success in early 2012, apprehending a total of 343 suspects in various locations around the country in connection with a series of thefts of track components and other items from active rail lines. The thefts had incapacitated some lines, forcing trains to stop for track repairs, thus delaying the delivery of cargo. The suspects are believed to be members of criminal gangs.

Interestingly, the extreme demand for metals in China has led to a good number of thefts of copper and iron from railways in Europe—for export to China.

Other Supply Chain Risks

Travel along the Lancang-Mekong River proved dangerous in 2011 as hundreds of ships were hijacked. This waterway passes through China, Myanmar, Thailand, Laos, Cambodia, and Vietnam, making it a vital trade route for those countries. The river, however, is increasingly rife with criminals, drug traffickers, and rebel groups that attack cargo and fishing vessels. The killing of 13 Chinese sailors in an October 5, 2011, attack against two Chinese cargo ships on the Mekong prompted China to suspend navigation until early December. At that time, Chinese police launched joint patrols with police from Laos, Myanmar, and Thailand with the goal of reducing cross-border crime and thus restoring security along the river.

Malaysia

A middle-income country today, Malaysia is emerging as a major trading partner in the global market. This is due in part to Malaysia's growing export sector as well as the country's unique geographical position on the Malay Peninsula and the Strait of Malacca. Surging trade in the Asia-Pacific region, particularly in neighboring Singapore, greatly enhances Malaysia's importance as a trade route.

International trade increased by 29%, to $363.5 billion USD, in 2011, Malaysia's deputy finance minister was quoted as saying in January 2012. He further said Malaysia's cross-border trade is expected to increase 88% over the next 15 years. As trade soars, however, so does international attention—and with that will come pressure on the government to address the severe problem of cargo theft on roads and rails and at ports and airports.

The Malaysian government has taken some steps in recent years to strengthen cargo security. For instance, it has ordered police departments and customs officials to work in closer cooperation, requiring that they share information on potential theft cases and suspicious individuals. Malaysia is also participating in and dedicating resources to a trial program with the International Air Transport Association to improve airport security and avoid bottlenecks. The goal is to help reduce the large amount of thefts that occur in the air cargo sector.

Despite efforts to date to improve cargo security, law enforcement rarely recovers loads or captures suspects, a fact that has only served to embolden thieves to go after cargo of higher and higher value.

In the Asia-Pacific, only Hong Kong has had a higher rate of cargo theft. What's more, truck hijackings involving threats against drivers are the most common form of cargo theft in the country. Employee involvement in thefts, either directly in the act

FreightWatch

or indirectly as a source of insider information for thieves, is another major challenge to the supply chain industry.

Cargo Theft

Reports of cargo theft have decreased over the last couple years in Malaysia, although theft remains a common and severe problem. Making it more difficult to pinpoint the degree of cargo theft today is the trend among companies against reporting cargo thefts. This apparently stems from the desire to avoid increases in insurance premiums or the desire to protect a victimized company's reputation. In some cases, it might also to be embarrassing for a company to acknowledge the thief or thieves were on the payroll.

Workers within the supply chain are thought to pose a significant challenge to cargo security throughout the country. Cargo handlers, truck drivers, security guards, and other lower level employees at ports, warehouses, and other facilities are believed to be behind a good portion of the incidents that take place. Furthermore, employee collusion with corrupt law enforcement in some cases makes solving cases much more difficult.

Cargo Theft Trends and Techniques

Malaysia's supply chain suffers under the enormous burden of corruption, crime, and violence. This situation is reflected in the most popular MOs and the incidents of cargo theft in 2011. Armed hijackings accounted for the majority of cargo theft during the year. As in most other countries where hijackings occur regularly, thieves in Malaysia usually block roads and highways with vehicles, forcing trucks to a halt. Once at rest, the truck and its driver become easy pickings for thieves.

Another MO used on roadways in 2011 was the fake police method, in which thieves wearing police uniforms set up fake checkpoints to force truck drivers to pull over and stop.

Weapons most often were used in hijackings just to threaten drivers, so physical attacks were rare and no driver was reported killed during a hijacking in 2011. Cargo thieves did act aggressively toward drivers by tying them up and at times gagging them.

After hijacking, facility/warehouse burglaries were the second most common form of cargo theft in 2011. As with many of the hijackings, thieves committing burglaries of warehouses or other facilities either worked at the facility or had access to inside information. By staging "inside jobs" or using insider information, the thieves were able to target the products they desired. Furthermore, knowledge of the security measures in place at a specific location allowed many of these thieves to avoid detection.

Product Type and Location

Thieves most often targeted the food/drinks product type in 2011, perhaps because these products are quite easy to sell to vendors. Even though this category topped the list, it is likely that many more thefts of foods and beverages went unreported because these loads generally are lower in value than others. The electronics industry, especially cell phones, microchips, and computers, was the second most targeted sector in Malaysia in 2011. Because Malaysia's economy is highly dependent on exports of electronics, these goods are transported regularly throughout the country, making them frequent targets for theft. The building/industrial product type, especially copper, cement, and steel, was a popular target for cargo thieves as well.

Rubber and palm oil, consistently valuable export products for Malaysia, experienced soaring price increases of 72 and 71%, respectively, from June 2010 to June 2011. As a result, these two products, which fall under the miscellaneous product type, were targeted increasingly by cargo thieves.

Most reported cargo thefts in 2011 occurred in the states of Selangor, with 43% of all incidents, Penang with 21%, and Malacca and Johor, both with 14%. Not surprisingly, these states are located along the Strait of Malacca on the Malay Peninsula, two of the world's most important trade routes. Trucks heading south from Ipoh on the North–South Highway were often targeted by cargo theft gangs based in Penang or Kuala Lumpur. This highway, which runs from northern Malaysia to Singapore, is used quite extensively by thieves transporting stolen goods.

Case Studies

In March 2011, Malaysian police reported the arrest of six suspects and the recovery of more than 700,000 condoms from a warehouse and a private home in northern Perak state. The load, worth an estimated $1.5 million USD, had gone missing while being shipped to Japan from Malaysia's Port Klang 2 months earlier. Some of the suspects reportedly worked for the company that transported the condoms from the factory to the port, located in Selangor state.

A truck driver was arrested in Juru, Penang state, after falsely claiming in April that his truck had been hijacked on the North-South Expressway. The driver was accused of involvement in the

FreightWatch

theft of his load, 300 laptops bound for a school. Police recovered the laptops, valued at more than $100,000 USD.

A truck transporting a load of mobile phones valued at nearly $500,000 USD was hijacked in August 2011 in Glenmarie, Selangor state. The hijackers, who threatened the driver with hammers, staged the attack around midnight while the driver was parked at a convenience store. They escaped with the load.

Philippines

The Philippines, a traditionally agricultural society with a growing industrial sector, is expected to emerge as a trade and economic power in the coming decades. Although the industrial sector is still in its infancy, cargo thieves already have discovered the opportunities that present themselves when trade—and thus the transportation of goods—increases.

Transparency International's Corruption Perceptions Index ranks the Philippines as one of the most corrupt countries in the Asia-Pacific region. This state of affairs affects the supply chain industry on several fronts: First, direct or indirect involvement by police or other authorities in any given cargo theft incident is a strong possibility. Second, rampant graft and bribery within the public sector often create the need for shippers, manufacturers, and transportation companies to "grease the wheels" to ensure that cargo is kept moving. Finally, reporting of cargo theft incidents is affected because victims don't trust the system.

Serious infrastructure inadequacies in the Philippines also affect the supply chain greatly. Not only do congested and clogged roads, railroads, and ports cost the industry a fortune in delays and other inefficiencies, major bottlenecks in the flow of goods make cargo easier to steal. In an effort to address infrastructure deficiencies, the Philippine government announced in 2011 a plan to promote private investment in road and port improvements. Additionally, $1.4 billion USD of the Department of Public Works and Highways (DPWH) budget was dedicated to building and expanding roads, highways, and bridges. Other projects planned to begin in 2012 include building regional airports, improving railways, and upgrading the Manila International Trading Terminal, which handles 90% of the country's imports. DPWH did complete many road projects in 2011, but the major projects involving airports and the trading terminal have yet to begin.

With systemic corruption, poor infrastructure, and the increasing movement of goods, the Philippines is a high-risk area for cargo theft.

Cargo Theft Trends and Techniques

The northernmost and largest Island, Luzon, experiences almost all of the reported cargo thefts in the Philippines. Luzon is the Philippines' gateway to many of its major trading partners, including Japan, Hong Kong, and Taiwan. The major regions where theft occurs on the island of Luzon are Calabarzon, Central Luzon, and the National Capital Region of Manila. All of these regions have major ports, providing thieves plenty of opportunity to steal imports and exports either in transit or at the cargo terminals.

Philippine National Police reported a 26% decrease in hijackings in 2011 compared with 2010. According to official statistics, 34 hijackings occurred in 2011, down from the 46 cases reported a year earlier. It is likely, however, that a good number of hijackings go unreported. Regardless, hijacking was by far the most common form of cargo theft reported in the Philippines. In most cases the thieves forced drivers to stop by using vehicles to block roads and highways. Thieves also have been known to use the fake police MO, dressing in police uniforms to get drivers to pull over and stop.

Thus, cargo moving by road in the Philippines is at a steady risk of hijacking. Most often the theft gangs are armed with guns or knives, although in large part the weapons are there to intimidate truckers. This is not always the case, however. During a hijacking in Manila in September, the perpetrators stabbed both the truck driver and his partner, killing the driver and seriously wounding the other. They then transferred the cargo, $20,000 USD worth of soap, shampoo, and detergent, to their own truck and disappeared.

Violence also erupted in October after thieves hijacked a truck transporting $57,000 USD in baking products in Calabarzon. In that incident, a shootout ensued when pursuing police cornered the armed suspects, and three of the suspects were killed.

While hijacking is the most commonly reported form of cargo theft, other types of theft seen regularly in the Philippines in 2011 were warehouse/facility burglaries, thefts by driver, and thefts of trailers. Employee theft, particularly by warehouse workers, is another serious concern in the Philippines. Employees have been implicated not only in the "theft by driver" category but in hijackings, facility burglaries, and thefts of trailers as well.

After a truck loaded with $113,000 USD in pharmaceuticals went missing in November 2011, police said they believed the driver was responsible, since he disappeared along with the truck. Another theft in Quezon on April 15 has been attributed to a warehouse security guard who had recently been fired. The suspect, who is in police custody, is accused of stealing more than $45,000 USD in car parts during the month he frequently returned to the warehouse to visit his former co-workers. Authorities suspect other employees were complicit in the thefts.

Philippines authorities did have some success capturing thieves and recovering vehicles in 2011. In fact, the Philippine National Police have said they intensified operations to counter hijackings and intend to continue those efforts in 2012. In Laguna in early November the Criminal Investigation and Detection Group cornered and killed four members of the Ferrer hijacking gang. The Ferrer gang was active in hijacking cargo trucks throughout Cavite, Batangas, and Laguna.

The same month, authorities broke up the Sociro-Manlapaz gang, arresting the gang's leader and four other members, in Cavite Province. Police captured the gang after its members hijacked a truck filled with $45,000 USD in grocery items in the Bulacan Province. Following the arrests, police recovered more than $160,000 USD in goods stolen previously by the gang.

The product types stolen most often in the Philippines in 2011 were food/drinks, building/industrial, and electronics. These just happen to be product types the country either exports or imports to a large extent. Thus, food/drinks accounted for 42% of reported stolen cargo, building/industrial products, including cement and steel, accounted for 16%, while electronics accounted for 11%.

India

As India's economy, population, and middle class continue to grow, so too does international trade—and with increasing trade comes increasing demand on the country's fragile transport infrastructure and associated services. According to the Indian Ports Association, cargo tonnage at the country's major ports alone increased by 7.69% during the April–December period of 2011 compared with the same period in 2010.

In an effort to reduce congestion at the ports, India's government has announced a 10-year, $110 billion USD program to build new ports and upgrade others. The project isn't scheduled for completion until 2020, meaning improvements will not be seen for some time.

With more and more goods moving into, through, and out of India, the risk of cargo theft is growing. India is vulnerable to cargo criminals on virtually all transport fronts: roads and highways, railroads, ports, and airports. Cargo traveling on the county's roadways is most at risk, however, particularly to theft involving violence or the threat of violence. Given that 65% of freight is moved via road in India, truckers and their cargo face heightened risks. As in previous years, warehouses were also frequent targets of cargo crime in 2011, especially during the overnight hours.

The threat of cargo theft is fairly high throughout the country, while recovery of stolen loads—with a notable exception at midyear—remains very low.

Punjab, Madhya Pradesh, Uttar Pradesh, and Karnataka are the states at highest risk of cargo theft, based on 2011 reporting. Of those, Punjab state saw the highest increase in theft incidents for the year. Rajasthan and Maharashtra states also reported increases in cargo crime last year. Tamil Nadu on the southern tip of India, home to the major Chennai Port, is another state at significant risk of cargo theft.

Not only did Punjab state experience an increase in cargo theft in 2011, it saw the highest number of reported warehouse thefts as well. Although Punjab took the No. 1 spot for thefts of this nature, warehouse thefts continued to occur throughout the country, particularly after dark when facilities are vacant.

Cargo Theft Trends and Techniques

Truck hijacking, at times combined with the fake police MO, was the most commonly reported method of theft employed by Indian cargo criminals in 2011. In some cases, thieves donned police uniforms as a way of forcing unwitting drivers to pull over and open their trailers. In nearly all kidnapping incidents last year, the thieves came armed with guns or knives, and often with rope for tying up the drivers. Hijackings often were carried out by three or more members of the theft gang, while their partners in crime waited at a designated location to unload the cargo and dispose of the truck.

On National Highway 2 in Maharashtra state, a slew of hijackings occurred during April, May, and June 2011. Authorities eventually captured the gang responsible for many of the incidents, but not before the highway earned a reputation as a "kidnapping zone." Many violent thefts and hijackings also occurred in 2011 on India's western coast in Goa and Karnataka states.

Imports to India are frequently targeted for theft and pilferage by contract employees at cargo handling agencies. Although the likelihood of theft by these laborers is well known, they continue to have easy access to cargo, providing them the opportunity to pass stolen goods to third parties with little threat of exposure. Unscrupulous employees working cargo bays have even more chance of success when they steal from damaged crates, as they can always claim a loss occurred by cargo falling out of the crate during shipment.

Sitting railcars were another common target throughout India last year, although these thefts tend to be crimes of opportunity and the work of the country's dire poor, as often in these cases the culprits simply jump into the stopped railcars and make off with as many items as they can carry.

While cargo theft in this country has long been primarily the domain of opportunistic criminals who take advantage of isolated trucks or loads left unattended, sophisticated gangs and members of the Indian mafia operate in an organized manner. These gangs, known to collude with corrupt police and/or employees of warehouses or freight forwarding yards, were suspected in several large-scale cargo thefts in 2011.

When pursued by authorities, Indian cargo theft gangs are known to resort to violence, often with guns or machetes, and this knowledge has served to make a good number of police officers think twice before attempting pursuit.

A notable exception occurred March 29, 2011, near Bangalore in the town of Devanahalli shortly after a gang of seven cargo thieves hijacked a truck carrying raw tobacco. Alerted to the theft, police located the stolen truck, which was parked by the side of the road, and moved in to apprehend the suspects. The thieves, however, spotted the approaching officers and sped off in the truck, launching a 30-minute chase that ended when police overtook the stolen truck. The thieves responded by attacking the officers with machetes, injuring two of them. The confrontation ended when police fired their weapons, wounding one of the suspects.

The food/drinks industry was the most targeted by thieves in 2011, with products such as sugar, tea, and wheat among those most stolen. Following closely behind food/drinks in popularity were tobacco products, including cigarettes, and goods in the building/industrial category, especially metals such as copper, aluminum, and iron. Other product types favored by thieves in 2011 include auto/parts, clothing/shoes, pharmaceuticals, and electronics.

Update on Iron Thefts

The 2010 Global Threat Assessment addressed the outbreak of thefts of iron, principally in the central Indian state of Uttar Pradesh but on a national level as well. With the price of iron still high in 2011, thefts of the product continued to be a problem throughout the year. Although theft and pilferage of iron by individuals are common, police focused their efforts on the gang and mafia members believed to be responsible for large-scale thefts of iron ore.

Indeed, on June 20, 2011, authorities arrested 23 suspected mafia members accused of involvement in a series of iron ore thefts over several years. The operation also resulted in the seizure of more than 100 tons of iron ore from the forests of Sundargarh District in the eastern state of Orissa. This major win for law enforcement likely led to a reduction in iron ore thefts in Orissa state and in neighboring West Bengal and Jharkhand states.

Other Supply Chain Risks

India's rapid growth has put extreme pressure on the country's already fragile infrastructure. As such, the narrow roadways and low traffic capacity cause extreme congestion in cities, while roads in rural areas are rarely paved and are not designed to withstand the elements.

Trucker strikes at the Port of Chennai in June and July 2011 caused serious congestion, making sitting cargo an easy target for thieves.

Contact
Dan Burges
Senior Director, Intelligence
512.532.0159
dan.burges@freightwatchintl.com

REFERENCES

Adams, D., 2011. 4 men get probation in theft of cargo in Botetourt County. Retrieved July 14, 2011. www.roanoke.com. http://www.roanoke.com/news/roanoke/wb/292856.

Aleccia, J., 2011. Half of hospitals buy back door drugs, new survey shows. MSNBC. Retrieved September 8, 2011. http://www.msnbc.msn.com/id/44280296/ns/health-health_care/t/half-hospitals-buy-back-door-drugs-new-survey-shows/#.TmjVEexvAZN.

Amerman, K., 2009. Upper Macungie warehouse supervisor gets probation for formula theft conspiracy. Of the Morning Call July 2, 2009.

ASIS, 2004. Protection of Assets Manual.

Badolato, E., 1999. Cargo Security: Avoiding Theft & Loss in the New Millennium. NCSC Presentation to Supply Chain Solutions '99.

Blanchard, D., 2006. Protecting the global supply chain. Industry Week December 2006.

Burges, D., 2006. Cargo Theft: From Silent Crime to Violent Crime? Strategic Forecasting Inc. September 25, 2006.

Burges, D., 2009a. Intercontinental risk. Cargo Security International 7 (3), 47–48.

Burges, D., 2009b. Global risk. Cargo Security International 7 (1), 46–47.

Burges, D., 2011. FreightWatch Annual US Cargo Theft Report. FreightWatch International. January 2011.

Chavez, S., Tello, G., 2009. Mexico highway robberies boost costs. Retrieved June 4, 2009. The Latin Business Chronicle. http://www.latinbusinesschronicle.com.

Cheah, E.T., Chan, W.L., Chieng, C.L., 2007. The corporate social responsibility of pharmaceutical product recalls: An empirical examination of US and UK markets. Journal of Business Ehtics vol. 76, 427–449.

Court, D., Elzinga, D., Mulder, S., Ole, J.V., 2009. The consumer decision journey. McKinsely Quarterly. Retrieved July 1, 2009. http://www.mckinseyquarterly.com/Marketing/Strategy/The_consumer_decision_journey_2373#.

Davidson, W., Worrell, D., 1992. Research notes and communications: The effect of product recall announcements and shareholder wealth. Strategic Management Journal vol. 3, 467–473.

Dean, D., 2004. Consumer reaction to negative publicity: Effects of corporate reputation, response, and responsibility for a crisis event. Journal of Business Communications 41 (2), 192–211.

DeBenedetti, C., 2011. The largest high-tech heist in Bay Area history was an inside job. MercurityNews.com. Retrieved July 25, 2011. http://www.mercurynews.com/ci_18537890?IADID=Search-www.mercurynews.com-www.mercurynews.com.

Dertouzos, J., Larson, E., Ebener, P., 1999. The Economic Costs and Implications of High-Technology Hardware Theft. RAND Corporation.

Eiserer, T., 2008. Stolen cargo can be quite profitable for all involved. The Dallas Morning News. Retrieved June 23, 2009. http://www.swtsc.org/page14.

Evans, K., 2011. Intel needs an App for revenue growth. The Wall Street Journal July 20, 2011.

Falkner, J., 2009. FTA angry over lack of truck stops. International Freight Weekly. http://www.ifw-net.com Accessed July 21, 2009.

Federal Bureau of Investigation, 2008. Bank Crime Statistics. Retrieved June 4, 2009. http://www.fbi.gov/publications/bcs/bcs2008/bank_crime_2008q1 .htm. http://www.fbi.gov/publications/bcs/bcs2008/bank_crime_2008q2 .htm. http://www.fbi.gov/publications/bcs/bcs2008/bank_crime_2008q3 .htm. http://www.fbi.gov/publications/bcs/bcs2008/bank_crime_2008q4 .htm.

Fennelly, L., 2004. Handbook of Loss Prevention and Crime Prevention. Elsevier.

Gale Group, 2005. Cargo theft on the rise despite increase in enforcement. http://www.thefreelibrary.com/Cargo+theft+on+rise+despite+increase+in+enforcement-a0133642961 Accessed July 27, 2009.

Gonzalez, R., 2009. Thieves have target set on big-rig cargos. San Gabriel Valley News Group. Retrieved June 24, 2009. http://www.transportsecurity.com/blog/index.php/2009/03/14/thieves-have-target-set-on-big-rig-cargos/.

Greene, R., Garcia, V., 2010. Smart Cargo. FreightWatch International.

Gu, T., 2007. Cargo theft: Easy come, easy go. Northeast-Export. http://www.northeast-export.com/newsletter01/feature2.php Accessed June 8, 2009.

Hudson Reporter. Former leader of famed "Conrail Boyz" gang arrested in North Bergen. June 03, 2010.

Hyslop, J. (2003) Sugarman, Marine. Master Minds: Conrail Boyz–TRU TV Documentary, 2003.

Identity theft.com. http://www.identitytheft.com/identity-theft-punishment.

Kavilanz, P., 2011. Prescription drugs worth millions to dealers. CNN Money. http://money.cnn.com/2011/06/01/news/economy/prescription_drug_abuse/index.htm?hpt=hp_t2 Accessed June 1, 2011.

Klara, R., 2009. Copying machines: Counterfeiting used to be called a nuisance. Now, there's a new word for it: epidemic. Brandweek. http://business.highbeam.com/137330/article-1G1-203281123/copying-machines-counterfeiting-used-called-nuisance Accessed March 9, 2011.

Lacey, D., Cuganesan, S., 2004. The role of organizations in identity theft response: The organization-individual victim dynamic. Journal of Consumer Affairs 38 (2), 244–261. Academic Search Premier, Harvard University Library, Boston, MA.

Mento, P., 2004. C-TPAT and ISA, understanding the effectiveness of trade partnerships for customs enforcement. lulu.com.

Morasch, C., 2008. Grand theft cargo. Land Line Magazine. http://www.landlinemag.com/Archives/2008/Nov08/Cover/grand_theft.htm Accessed June 8, 2009.

Palmer, J., 2009. The effects of cargo theft in a down global economy. International In-house Counsel Journal 2 (8), 1169–1174.

Peral, M., 2003. It's not always about the money. Journal of Criminal Law & Criminology 94 (1) 40p Academic Search Premier, Harvard University Library, Boston, MA. 26 May 2011 94 (1), 169–208.

Schmallyer, F., 2009. Criminal Justice Today. Pearson Prentice Hall.

Serafine, D., Henderson, S., Serafine, M., 2005. Cargo crime: The silent killer. Security World International January–February.

Smothers, R. (2003) 24 are indicted in ring that looted cargo trains. New York Times. Section B; Column 4; Metropolitan Desk; p. 5.

Swartz, N., 2005. ID thief gets 14 years. Information Management Journal Vol. 39 (Issue 2) Academic Search Premier, Harvard University Library, Boston, MA. 23 May 2011 39 (2), 16.

Sweet, K.M., 2006. Transportation and Cargo Security: Threats and Solutions. Prentice Hall. Upper Saddle River, NJ. 70–71.

Thomas, A., 2010. Supply Chain Security: International Practices and Innovations in Moving Goods Safely and Efficiently, vol. 1, Praeger Security International, Santa Barbara, CA. 21–24.

Tirschwell, P., 2003. The Bottom Line on Security. Journal of Commerce, 6. January 27 – February 2.

Transportation Security Administration, 2011. Air cargo. Retrieved August 1, 2011. http://www.tsa.gov/what_we_do/tsnm/air_cargo/index.shtm.

U.S. Department of Transportation, 2010. U.S. International Merchandize Trade by Transporation Mode: 2009. Accessed July 29, 2011. http://www.ops.fhwa.dot.gov/freight/freightanalysis/nat_freight_stats/docs/10factsfigures/figure2_2.htm.

Van Zandt, C., 2009. Do crime rates soar in recession and how can we save our youth from self-destruction? MSNBC.

Voss, M., Whipple, J., Closs, D., 2008. The role of strategic security: Internal and external security measures with security performance implications. Transportation Journal, 5–23. Spring 2008.

Zambito, T., 2009. Jersey gang busted in freight-train jobs. Daily News (New York), 30 July 11.

INDEX

Page numbers with "f" denote figures; "t" tables; "b" boxes.